Queer Theory: Law, Culture

Queer Theory: Law, Culture, Empire uses queer theory to examine the complex interactions of law, culture and empire. Building on recent work on empire, and taking contextual, socio-legal, comparative, and interdisciplinary approaches, it studies how activists and scholars engaged in queer theory projects can unwittingly advance imperial projects and how queer theory can itself show imperial ambitions. The authors – from five continents – delve into examples drawn from Bollywood cinema to California's 2008 marriage referendum. The chapters view a wide range of texts – from cultural productions to laws and judgments – as regulatory forces requiring scrutiny from outside Western, heterosexual privilege. This innovative collection goes beyond earlier queer legal work, engaging with recent developments, featuring case studies from India, South Africa, the United States, Australasia, Eastern Europe, and embracing the frames offered by different disciplinary lenses.

Queer Theory: Law, Culture, Empire will be of particular interest to students and researchers in the fields of socio-legal studies, comparative law, law and gender/sexuality, and law and culture.

Robert Leckey is assistant professor in the Faculty of Law at McGill University, where he teaches and researches in constitutional law, family law, and comparative law. He is the author of *Contextual Subjects: Family, State, and Relational Theory* (2008).

Kim Brooks is associate professor and the H. Heward Stikeman Chair in the Law of Taxation in the Faculty of Law at McGill University. She is the editor of *Justice Bertha Wilson: One Woman's Difference* (2009).

Queer Theory: Law, Culture, Empire

Edited by Robert Leckey
and Kim Brooks

Routledge
Taylor & Francis Group
a GlassHouse book

First published 2010
by Routledge
2 Park Square, Milton Park, Abingdon, Oxfordshire OX14 4RN

Simultaneously published in the USA and Canada
by Routledge
711 Third Avenue, New York, NY 10017

A GlassHouse book

*Routledge is an imprint of the Taylor & Francis Group,
an informa business*

First published in paperback 2011

Typeset in Times and Gill Sans by
RefineCatch Limited, Bungay, Suffolk

British Library Cataloguing in Publication Data
A catalogue record for this book is available
from the British Library

Library of Congress Cataloging-in-Publication Data
Queer theory : law, culture empire / edited by Robert Leckey and
Kim Brooks
    p. cm.
  Includes bibliographical references
  1. Homosexuality—Law and legislation.   2. Gay culture.
  3. Queer theory.   I. Leckey, Robert.   II. Brooks, Kim.
  K3242.3.Q44 2010
  342.08′7—dc22   2010012665

ISBN13: 978-0-415-57228-6 (hbk)
ISBN13: 978-0-415-69773-6 (pbk)
ISBN13: 978-0-203-85611-6 (ebk)

For Eve Kosofsky Sedgwick
In memoriam

Contents

Notes on contributors   ix
Acknowledgements   xi
Tables of cases   xiii
Tables of statutes   xv
Tables of statutory instruments   xvii

1 **Introduction**   1
ROBERT LECKEY AND KIM BROOKS

PART I
Constitution   19

2 **Queer theory, neoliberalism and urban governance**   21
JON BINNIE

3 **De-radicalising the rights claims of sexual**
  subalterns through 'tolerance'   37
RATNA KAPUR

PART 2
Representation   53

4 **Bollywood cinema and queer sexualities**   55
SHOHINI GHOSH

5 **Post-apartheid fraternity, post-apartheid**
  democracy, post-apartheid sexuality: queer
  reflections on Jane Alexander's *Butcher Boys*   69
JACO BARNARD-NAUDÉ

6   **The judicial virtue of sexuality**   86
    LESLIE J. MORAN

PART 3
Regulation   103

7   **Reproductive outsiders – the perils and**
    disruptive potential of reproductive coalitions   105
    JENNI MILLBANK

8   **Queer–religious potentials in US same-sex**
    marriage debates   122
    JEFFREY A. REDDING

9   **What's queer about polygamy?**   137
    MARGARET DENIKE

PART 4
Exclusion   155

10 **An 'imperial' strategy? The use of comparative**
    and international law in arguments about
    LGBT rights   157
    NICHOLAS BAMFORTH

11 **Reproducing empire in same-sex relationship**
    recognition and immigration law reform   173
    NAN SEUFFERT

12 **UnSettled**   191
    RUTHANN ROBSON

Index   209

Contributors

Nicholas Bamforth is fellow in law at Queen's College, Oxford, and a member of the Law Faculty of Oxford University.

Jaco Barnard-Naudé lectures in the Faculty of Law at the University of Cape Town.

Jon Binnie is reader in human geography at Manchester Metropolitan University.

Kim Brooks is associate professor and the H. Heward Stikeman Chair in Tax Law in the Faculty of Law at McGill University.

Margaret Denike is associate professor of human rights and the coordinator of the Human Rights (BA) Program at Carleton University.

Shohini Ghosh is Sajjad Zaheer Professor at the AJK Mass Communication Research Centre, Jamia Millia Islamia, New Delhi.

Ratna Kapur is director of the Centre for Feminist Legal Research, New Delhi, India, and also teaches at the Geneva School of Diplomacy and International Relations, Geneva.

Robert Leckey is assistant professor in the Faculty of Law at McGill University.

Jenni Millbank is professor of law, University of Technology, Sydney.

Leslie Moran is professor of law at Birkbeck College, University of London.

Jeffrey Redding is assistant professor at the Saint Louis University School of Law.

Ruthann Robson is professor of law and University Distinguished Professor at the City University of New York School of Law.

Nan Seuffert is professor of law and Director of International Relations at the University of Waikato in Hamilton, New Zealand.

Acknowledgements

This collection is the outcome of a workshop called *Queer/Empire: Exploring the Reach of Queer Theory and Its Relationship to Law*, which we hosted at the Faculty of Law, McGill University, on 17–18 April 2009. The enterprise originated over an Indian buffet lunch in autumn 2007. We thought it would be fun to collaborate and bring to McGill some people we admired to talk with us about things we found interesting. It was and it has been. We owe thanks to a number of individuals and organizations.

The Social Sciences and Humanities Research Council of Canada (SSHRC; file no. 646–2008–0027) provided the lion's share of funding for the workshop and preparation of the collection. The Faculty of Law, McGill University, provided additional funding, and we acknowledge the enthusiastic support of its then dean, Nicholas Kasirer. Margaret Denike helped in creative and practical ways throughout the process, from pointing us to the idea of empire at the outset to brainstorming book covers. For their contributions to our development of the workshop themes and comments on presentations now reflected in this collection, we thank those other participants in the workshop whose papers do not appear in this collection: Brenda Cossman, David Eng, Chantal Nadeau, Becki Ross, Kendall Thomas, and Kenji Yoshino. Several administrative colleagues at McGill – Thomas Chalmers, Linda Coughlin, Maria Marcheschi, and Gina Sebastiao – helped with the workshop in various ways. Three collaborators call for special mention. Derrick McIntosh provided valuable research and administrative assistance in preparation of the grant application, the book proposal, and the workshop; he also commented on an earlier version of the introduction. Naomi Greckol-Herlich copy-edited the revised chapters in preparation of the book manuscript. Julie Fontaine efficiently managed various administrative elements of the workshop and manuscript preparation, including the processing of travel expenses. We thank Colin Perrin and Holly Davis at Routledge for their enthusiasm and help throughout the process. We gratefully acknowledge the permission granted by sculptor Jane Alexander to use images of her work on the cover and in Chapter 5, and we thank Jaco Barnard-Naudé for his efforts in working with her.

The book's dedication to Eve Sedgwick reflects the sorrow, gratitude, and indebtedness felt by many of us at the workshop less than a week after her death on 12 April 2009.

Robert Leckey and Kim Brooks
Montreal, October 2009

Table of cases

Ali *v.* Canada (Minister of Citizenship & Immigration) (1998), 154 FTR 285 150

Baker *v.* Vermont, 744 A.2d 864 (Vt. 1999) 142
Bowers *v.* Hardwick (1986) 478 US 186 158–9

Davis *v.* Beason (1890) 133 US 333, 341, 10 S.Ct. 299, 33 L.Ed. 637 151
Du Toit and Another *v.* Minister for Welfare and Population Development
   and Others (2002) (10) BCLR 1006 79
Dudgeon *v.* United Kingdom [1981] 4 EHRR 149 .... 158, 159

Foster *v.* Florida (2002) 537 US 990 159

Goodridge *v.* Massachusetts Department of Public Health 798 NE2d 941
   (2003) 115, 143

Hassan and Hassan, Re (1976), 12 OR (2d) 432 (HC) 150
Hernandez *v.* Robles (2006) 7 N.Y.3d 338 130
Hyde *v.* Hyde (1866), LR. 1 P & D 130 .... 139, 150

Indian Hotel & Restaurants Ass'n (AHAR) *v.* State of Maharashtra
   (Bombay High Court, 2006) 50
Ismail Faruqui *v.* Union of India (1994) 6 Supreme Court Cases 360 50

Kerrigan *v.* Commissioner of Public Health (2008) 289 Conn. 135 .... 126, 130, 134

Lawrence *v.* Texas 123 S.Ct. 2472 (2003) 6, 143, 157–61, 164
Lee Cheong (1923), Re, 33 BCR 109 150
Lim *v.* Lim [1948] 2 DLR 353 (BCSC) 140

M. Ismail Faruqui *v.* Union of India (1994) 6 Supreme Court Cases 360 50
M. *v.* H. [1999] 2 S.C.R. 3 133
Marriage Cases, In re (2008) 43 Cal.4th 757, 76 Cal.Rptr.3d 683,
   183 P. 3d 384 .... 125, 133, 147
Minister of Home Affairs *v.* Fourie and Others (2006) (1) SA 524 (CC) 79

National Coalition for Gay and Lesbian Equality and Another *v.* Minister of
Home Affairs (2000) (2) SA 1 (CC) 77–8
National Coalition for Gay and Lesbian Equality and Another *v.* Minister
of Justice and others (1999) (1) SA 6 (CC) 75–7, 79–80
Naz Foundation *v.* Government of National Capital Territory of Delhi and
Others, Delhi High Court, 2 July 2009 (MANU/DE/0869/2009) 50, 163, 164

Ohio *v.* Freeman (2003) 155 Ohio App. 3d 492, 801 N.E.2d 906, 909 151

People *v.* Scott (2007) 157 Cal.App. 4th 189, 68 Cal.Rptr.3d 592 151
Potter *v.* Murray City (C.D.Utah 1984) 585 F.Supp. 1126, 1137–40, affd.
(10th Cir.1985) 760 F.2d 1065, 1068–71, cert. den. (1985) 474 U.S. 849,
106 S.Ct. 145, 88 L.Ed.2d 120 151

R. *v.* Bear's Shin Bone (1899), 4 Terr. LR 173 (NWT SC) 139, 150
R. *v.* Harris (1906), 11 CCC 254 (Qc. Sup. Ct.) 150
R. *v.* Human Fertilisation and Embryology Agency, ex parte Blood [1997]
2 All ER 687 118
Reynolds *v.* United States (1878) 98 US 145 .... 146, 151
Romer *v.* Evans 517 U.S. 620 (1996) 142, 150

S. *v.* K. 1997 (4) SA 469 (C) 83
S. *v.* Makwanyane and Another (CCT3/94) [1995] ZACC 3;
1995 (6) BCLR 665; 1995 (3) SA 391; [1996] 2 CHRLD 164;
1995 (2) SACR 1 (6 June 1995) 80
Sara *v.* Sara (1962), 31 DLR (2d) 566 150
Smith *v.* State (Tenn.Crim.App. 1999) 6 S.W.3d 512, 518–20 151
State *v.* Freeman (2003) 155 Ohio App. 3d 492, 801 N.E.2d 906, 909 151
Swami Ramdev *v.* Naz Foundation and Others, Special Leave Petition,
Supreme Court of India, 8 July 2009 .... 45, 50

Varnum *v.* Brien (2009) 763 N.W.2d 862 (Iowa) 133
Volks NO *v.* Robinson and Others (2005) (5) BCLR 671 .... 78, 79

Yew *v.* Attorney-General of British Columbia (1924), 33 BCR 109 (BCCA) 150

Table of statutes

Australia

Assisted Reproductive Technology Act 2007
s. 19(b) 107
Assisted Reproductive Treatment Act 2008 (Vic)
Part 4
s. 14 118
s. 42 118
Cloning for Reproduction and other Prohibited Practices Act 2003 (NSW)
s. 16 113–14
Prohibition of Human Cloning Act 2002 (Cth)
s. 21 113
Status of Children Act 1996 (NSW)
s. 14 118

Canada

Civil Marriage Act 2005 173
Criminal Code
s. 278(a) 139

India

Dissolution of Muslim Marriages Act 1939 129
Hindu Marriage Act 1955 129
Indian Christian Marriage Act 1872 129
Indian Divorce Act 1869 129
Penal Code 1860 .... 41, 164
Protection of Women from Domestic Violence Act 2005 134

New Zealand

Civil Union Act 2004 .... 173, 182
Immigration Act 1987 183
Relationships (Statutory References) Act 2005 182
s. 7 187
s. 12 187
Sch. 1 187
Sch. 4 187
Settlements Act 1863 202

South Africa

Aliens Control Act 1991
s. 25 83
Bantu Homeland Citizens Act 1970 196
Civil Union Act 2006 .... 79, 82, 173
Group Areas Act 1950 196
Immorality Act 74
Maintenance of Surviving Spouses Act 1990 78
Marriage Act 1961 .... 78–80, 82
Natives Act 1952 196
Prohibition of Mixed Marriages Act 1947 .... 74, 196
Reservation of Separate Amenities Act 1953 196
Terrorism Act 1967 196

United Kingdom

Civil Partnership Act 2004 173

United States

California Family Code 204

California Marriage Protection Act
 2010 132

Defense of Marriage Act
 1996 .... 142, 143–4
 s. 1740 150

Table of statutory instruments

New Zealand

Immigration Amendment Regulations
    (No. 3) 2003 187
Immigration Regulations 1999
    r. 20 187
Immigration Regulations 2009
    f. 2.10.1 187
    f. 2.15 187

f. 2.20.15a 187
f. 2.20.15c 187
f. 2.20b 187
r. 2.1.10 187
r. 2.1.15 187
r. 2.1.20 187
r. 2.10.1 187
r. 2.15.1.5 187

Chapter 1

Introduction

Robert Leckey and Kim Brooks

The cover of this book shows a close-up of what appears to be the sculpture of a man, sitting. He seems to be naked (how quickly the personification of that which is perceived as human: he, not it). Fabricated from bone and plaster, he is unquestionably white. It might be more usual, for a male nude sculpture, for him to be standing. But he looks normal. And yet, something might be slightly off. He looks relaxed, almost languid. The legs crossed at the knee, the arms so loosely crossed at the wrist are unmanly, somewhat effeminate. He sits like a gay man gossiping on a bar stool, in a way that many men may have been instructed – perhaps by their fathers – not to sit.

If one's perspective shifts, if one sees more of the figure, the oddness intensifies. Despite the first impression in the close-up, the larger figure is not normal, at all. He is not human, or not fully. Part of what disturbs about the larger sculpture he forms part of – he and the other two of Jane Alexander's *Butcher Boys* – is how human he remains nevertheless. He is too human to be rejected entirely as animal or other. The bestiality of the head and the intimations of violence notwithstanding, the part in the close-up remains beautiful. Indeed, as men who desire other men know, to call a grown man a 'boy' is to eroticize him, to make him 'something you play with' (Mendelsohn 1999: 101). Their hybridity makes these figures far more perturbing than a representation of things wholly bestial or monster. *The Butcher Boys* are categorical abominations, beings that disrupt by eluding categorization. By their calling established categories into question, and standing outside the normal, they are decidedly queer. As elaborated by Jaco Barnard-Naudé in Chapter 5 in this collection, that queerness is specifically located. *The Butcher Boys* dwell in the South African National Gallery in Cape Town, a location that evokes histories of colonialism, institutionalized racism, and the deployment of law for repressive and emancipatory ends. The need to view or read carefully in order to appreciate the close-up's queerness makes it an apt portal into this collection.

The attraction of queer theory is its resistance to definition. It has little claim to be a unified theory of any sort. If it has a core, queer theory is about resisting categorization, for itself and for its subjects. It has been described as 'a zone of possibilities in which the embodiment of the subject might be experienced otherwise' (Edelman 1994: 114). 'Queer' can refer to 'the open mesh of possibilities, gaps, overlaps, dissonances and resonances, lapses and excesses of meaning when the constituent elements of anyone's gender, of anyone's sexuality aren't made (or *can't be* made) to signify monolithically' (Sedgwick 1993: 8). This collection celebrates such a refusal of definitions – as well as the insistence that definitional closure is impossible or undesirable. It also exemplifies two distinct but related approaches to queer.

First, as a noun or adjective, queer can denote particular subjects. As such, queer theory can reflect on what it means to be queer (Colebrook 2009: 11). Thus, some contributors use queer to refer to subjects, identities, or other things, in line with early queer theorists who devoted energy to disarticulating what it means to be 'normal', to creating non-normativities, and to embracing anti-assimilationism (Warner 1999). Here, queer risks stabilizing into an identity rather than remaining a radical critique of identity (Halberstam 1997: 260). Yet the identities signified and produced as queer have remained contested and in flux, with new identities insisting on their queerness too (for example, transgender, two-spirited, intersex, and questioning).

Second, in resistance to reification, many queer theorists focus on queer as a verb. As a verb, queer can better perform 'its outlaw work' (Freccero 2006: 5), including that of disorientation (Ahmed 2006: 4). Thus, other contributors to this collection use queer more as a lens for viewing the world askant. Deployed this way, queer changes the way in which we theorize. Queer can signify not specific subjects, but 'a political and existential stance, an ideological commitment, a *decision* to live outside some social norm or other' (Ford 2007: 479).

The collection embraces the definitional instability of queer. At the same time, its contributors ask what queer theory might bring to an exploration of the confines and openings sustained by law, culture, and empire. The three terms of the subtitle appear advisedly without linking words so as to leave their relations unarticulated. Our aim is not to shut down their possible modes of interaction. Earlier collections have explored law in the domains of culture, such as cultural property, copyright, and popular culture (Sarat and Kearns 1998), and law *as* culture (Sarat and Simon 2003). In the present collection, by contrast, it would be a mistake to posit at the outset the relation in which law, culture, and empire connect one to another. Before sketching ways in which this collection's chapters align those key terms, it is worth situating this enterprise, however provisionally, in relation to recent work holding itself under the (anti)label queer.

Queer disciplines

Some have suggested that queer theory is already somehow over, or 'rapidly approaching its expiration date' (Halley and Parker 2007: 421). Undeniably, some deployments of queer have had a flattening, if not deadening, effect. At times, queer has been conscripted into service as a sexier, more marketable label for lesbian and gay identities. Such a transformation may reflect 'the inevitable absorption of political dissent within late capitalism into consumer culture' (Halberstam 1997: 256). Queer theory's postmortem has been attempted (Nunokawa 2007), and interveners have asked whether queer theory remains queer and, if so, in what ways (Eng with Halberstam and Muñoz 2005). It has been noted, too, that many of the leading pioneers of queer theory have moved on, nowadays writing on other matters, from other perspectives (Halley and Parker 2007: 421–2). One might, however, regard with suspicion any announcements, from sites of privilege, that the queer party is over. The timing of such proclamations warrants their scrutiny. They come at a moment when the interlocutors in the queer conversations are increasingly varied and less localized in élite educational institutions of the United States. Readers in law may recall the objections to the critical legal scholars' discrediting of rights, precisely when historically marginalized groups were mobilizing rights discourse for political purposes (Williams 1987).

Foucault's work would insist that whatever queer theory heralds, it cannot be unalloyed emancipation. It appears, nevertheless, that a number of contemporary scholars find in queer theory a source of pleasure and analytic and political energy. On one recent view, queer has 'maintained an acute and enabling sense of the discomforts and incoherencies around speaking of the livability of previously marginalized identities, identities which furthermore have been the objects of fantasies or practices of annihilation' (Flannery 2007: 3). The chapters in this collection, drawing on that sense of discursive discomforts and incoherencies, speak against the claims that queer theory is over. Taking queer as 'a continuing moment, movement, motive' (Sedgwick 1993: xii), they show that queer theory and its intersection with law, culture, and empire yield rich analytical and conceptual stories about the world around us, fractured and contested as it remains.

In disciplinary terms, queer remains a rich resource in a number of areas. It retains prominence in literary and film studies. Making an affective turn, recent queer scholarship has scrutinized particular affects, such as loss (Love 2007), love (Restuccia 2006), optimism (Snediker 2009), and shame (Halperin and Traub 2009). Theorists have resisted the teleology of temporality, specifically – and with furious brio – denouncing futurity (Edelman 2004). Another queer intervention on temporality has challenged the homophobic valorization of the history of difference between past and present (Menon 2008). Space and place remain matters of keen interest to queer theorists, or queer theory continues to be a valuable resource to those interested in space and place. Queer interventions persist in areas concerned with space, movement, and belonging: geography and urban studies (Browne et al. 2007; Bell and Binnie 2004; Binnie 2004; Oswin 2008), citizenship studies (Stychin 2003; Bell and Binnie 2000); and migration studies (Luibhéid 2008). If its incursion there was slower than that into, say, literary or cultural studies, queer has finally insinuated itself into theology and religious studies (Bohache 2008; Loughlin 2007; Wilcox 2007; Jordan 2006). While it has been put forward that 'the queer is not radically outside or beyond recognition and selfhood; it is that which makes a claim to be heard as human' (Colebrook 2009: 15), recent interventions nevertheless challenge the construction of the normatively able human body (McRuer 2006). Indeed, they reach beyond the human as a site for queer investigations (Giffney and Hird 2008).

By contrast, it has been suggested that the queer theory performed in law schools is comparatively uninteresting (Halley and Parker 2007: 422–3). One of the few collections dedicated to queer theory and law is now relatively dated (Moran et al. 1998). A recent compendium has brought together queer and feminist legal scholarship (Fineman et al. 2009). Certainly jurists and political scientists have written about the law and sex. Recent years have witnessed sustained work on the legal developments in terms of civil rights and relationship recognition for same-sex couples. But such work is usually taken up through a presumptively unqueer lens of liberal legalism, including the courts' responses to activists' deployment of liberal rights instruments. Much of this research connects itself explicitly to a gay rather than a queer politics (e.g. Pierceson 2005; Smith 2008), although some critical work with a queer edge embeds legal changes in relation to same-sex couples in larger movements of neoliberal governance (Osterlund 2009). It is against that backdrop that this collection brings queer theory to bear on law, culture, and empire.

Law/culture/empire

One premise of the collection is the intricate, indeed often inextricable, relation of law and culture. Many of the chapters follow this premise, placing one foot in law and the other in another discipline or other disciplines.

From the outset, queer theory has entangled itself with the touchstones of the Western canon (Sedgwick 1990: 48–59). The queer theory industry, it has been said, 'has been mobilised around a re-reading of the canon's images of heterosexual desire to show moments of instability, deviation and mobility' (Colebrook 2009: 21). Indeed, figures such as Shakespeare remain subjects for contemporary queer analysis (Menon 2008). But queer legal theorists, drawing on Foucauldian insights about the multiple locations and sources of regulation, have also turned their gaze to the productive and regulatory effects of a wide variety of cultural texts that are indisputably non-canonical. Popular television shows and films thus come under the microscope of queer legal or regulatory theory (Cossman 2007).

The contributors to this collection whose training or institutional location marks as lawyers adopt a capacious definition of legally relevant texts. Indeed, at the workshop leading to this collection, it was the non-lawyers who expressed occasional bashfulness about the relevance of their texts of study, such as popular film, to the lawyers, while the lawyers unhesitatingly grasped those texts' salience as regulatory instruments. The Bollywood films studied by Shohini Ghosh, the sculpture treated by Jaco Barnard-Naudé, the judicial swearing-in speeches parsed by Leslie Moran, and the New Zealand parliamentary debates analyzed by Nan Seuffert – to give an incomplete list – are all appropriately scrutinized as potentially regulatory and productive texts. The chapters show those sources, in their gaps, insinuations, and excesses of meaning, to partake in queer theory's 'certain unsettling in relation to heternormativity' (Freccero 2007: 485). And all the chapters are carefully alert to their studied texts' implications for subjects positioned outside the privileged sites of heterosexuality and heternormativity. The treatments of cultural texts provoke reflection on the extent to which cultural or artistic representations, if not themselves sources of law (Kasirer 1995), are nevertheless potentially normative and regulatory.

The disputed terrain of empire and empire studies furnishes ground on which the complex relations between queer theory, law, and culture intensify. The collection's invocation of empire inscribes itself against the recent flourishing of related scholarship, including a resurgence of interest in the concept of empire as a political analytic. Some scholars have focused directly on empire, defining it as an 'open tendency', denoting among other things 'an attempt at a sovereign ordering of economic globalization' (Negri 2008a: 3, 2008b; Hardt and Negri 2000). On some understandings, empire is 'a process of constitution of sovereignty – a new sovereignty – over the global market' (Negri 2008a: 8; compare Douzinas 2007). Other scholars advance the related notion of 'imperial formation' as analytically fruitful, positing that it underscores 'not the inevitable rise and fall of empires, but .the active and contingent process of their making and unmaking' (Stoler and McGranahan 2007: 8; see also Stoler 2006, 2002). For Stoler and McGranahan (2007: 8), imperial formations are 'politics of dislocation, processes of dispersion, appropriation, and displacement', depending simultaneously on 'moving categories and populations'. The analytic of imperial formation connects directly to culture, along the lines of this collection's inquiry: 'imperial formation' includes cultural practice among a 'broader set of practices structured in dominance' (ibid.). Processes associated with empire propel a number of imperatives. Agathangelou et al. (2008: 123) write: 'To (re)consolidate itself, empire requires and solicits the production of certain ways of being, desiring, and knowing (while destroying others) that are appropriately malleable for what comes to be constituted as the so-called new world order.'

Commentators have used notions of empire, traced out in contemporary conditions, to read and lament the catastrophes of recent Western foreign policy. It has been argued that abuses by the American military enact a preconstructed heterosexed, racialized, and gendered script firmly grounded in the colonial desires and practices of the larger social order (Richter-Montpetit 2007). Such arguments vociferously resist the individualizing, exonerating trope of the few bad apples. For this collection's purposes, empire's connections with sexuality and queer theory are at least twofold.

The first is that, as some chapters show, the project of empire can recruit into a productive role subjects identifying as sexually non-normative and, indeed, as queer. The assumption of such a role may be witting or unwitting. Negri (2008a: 35) writes: 'In order to produce, global capitalism and imperial sovereignty need to control our entire existence. What is in play is entirely biopolitical, and has to do with desires and ways of life.' These desires and ways of life are precisely the subject of law reform efforts towards recognition of historically non-normative forms of kinship and alliance, which can marry themselves with imperial agendas in relation to domesticity and orderly consumption. More specifically, the institution of marriage functions as a site of citizenship production, critical to the formation of a properly gendered, properly racialized, properly heterosexual nation (Brandzel 2005). Law reform efforts towards recognition of historically non-normative kinship thus inscribe themselves specifically in relation to marriage's intimate ties to citizenship as states continue to maintain and police the racial, gender, and sexual configuration of their citizenries. 'Queer' does not per se 'necessarily disrupt national modes of belonging' (Hong 2006: 98), and queer theory has often left intact dominant liberal notions of the US citizen-subject (Freccero 2007: 490).

The 2003 anti-sodomy judgment of *Lawrence v. Texas* marked a watershed in the United States. That judgment situated itself on a terrain on which scholars and in many cases political activists (particularly those who have engaged in recent years with legal regimes) had spent countless hours laboring in an effort to reconstitute queerness as normal, acceptable, or at least as requiring tolerance. Indeed, some scholars now write of 'queer liberalism' (e.g. Eng 2007), 'queer citizenship' (Trevenen 2009; Johnston 2008), 'homonormativity' (Duggan 2003), and 'homonationalism' (Puar 2007), notions once viewed as oxymoronic. Does not celebrating *Lawrence* entail a celebration of the highest court's valorization of private property, domesticity, and monogamy, all decidedly not queer, at least by the usual metrics (Ball 2008; Eng 2007; Rollins 2005; Franke 2004).

In the US, queer theorists have expressed alarm at a toxic conjunction that they perceive to be no coincidence: an intensification of the project of militarized empire and the gay victory of *Lawrence*. Agathangelou et al. (2008: 130) have expressed alarm at the prospect that the 'privatization of the freedom of the queer subject enshrines a culture of loss of rights for non-US citizens while naturalizing the backdrop of (specifically black) (non) subjects within the United States whose civically dead or dying status has rarely been assigned rights to lose'. In other words, the partial validation, for some purposes, in some places, of some queer subjects can conscript queers into 'empire's incessant production of internal and external enemies' (ibid.: 138). Margaret Denike's and Nan Seuffert's chapters draw on such concerns. They explore the ways in which the state's recognition of some historically non-normative sexualities presses still further outside those relationship forms not recognized, in the process fortifying traditional notions of monogamous domesticity that advance imperial projects.

Queer theory's second connection with empire concerns the potential for queer theory itself to be imperial. Ratna Kapur speaks (in this volume, Chapter 3) of queer theory as the 'new imperium in legal scholarship'. Queer theory's imperial ambitions have been discernable from the outset. This imperialism is partly intellectual, in the thrust of ideas associated with queer theory. Queer can be viewed as imperial for its impulse towards 'the transformation of everything' (Hoad 2007: 516), and for its 'insatiable appetites and marvelous elasticity' (Freccero 2007: 490). The sense that its anti-identitarianism makes queer theory applicable to identity politics generally (Ford 2007: 479) may presumptively override or invalidate queer's inflection by local politics and conditions.

Queer theory's other imperial aspect is empirical, emerging from its Western origin and provenance in the United States. Queer theorists have criticized 'the provinciality of American-based queer criticism', and scrutinized the relation between the United States' neocolonialist, capitalist presence and the proliferation of 'queer subjects', produced and encouraged through the dissemination of queer theory (Arondekar 2005: 246). Hoad (2000) critiques the title of the queer theory classic *Fear of a Queer Planet* (Warner 1993a), arguing that it links queer theory to queer subjectivity's site in the United States and its own colonizing fantasies.

The prevalence of white gay men, situated in Western societies, within queer theory – at least during its early years – poses complex puzzles when queer theory travels. Is it a politically salient resource, or itself a technology of neocolonialism, captured by the interests of those most or earliest represented by it? The specifically national character of US queer theory generates concern on the part of diasporic queer theorists that much queer theory in America is based on white male experience and privilege, excluding people of color and limiting its relevance to third world activism (Baruddoja 2008). This privileged location may severely constrain its meaning and usefulness for those outside those zones of privilege, a possibility explored by Ratna Kapur (Chapter 3) and Jon Binnie (Chapter 2), in this volume. Queer theory's ostensible definitional openness, capaciousness, and indeterminacy can stand in tension with the impulses to anchor queer theory in the experiences of privileged, Western gay men.

Yet despite this Western, and indeed national, specificity, queer theory has enjoyed enormous success as an export. The global propagation of Western gay culture has been perceived in some quarters as a progressive development of liberating sexual minorities in third world countries – a global queering (Yeoh 2006). On this narrative, an emancipating and glamorized Western gay culture transforms the rest of the world. But such narratives require contestation, including rejection of the 'dominant tendency to use singular binaries or reductive trajectories (e.g., West to East, first world to third world) to map out global queer lives in the so-called non-Western world' (Lim 2005: 384). Subtler accounts recognize that while, to some extent, a globalization of gay identity has occurred, giving rise to the figure of the global gay, that figure is a hegemonic yet unstable point of self-identification. Subjects who so identify may be simultaneously privileged and marginalized, local and global, indigenous and cosmopolitan (Benedicto 2008).

Scholars attaching themselves to queer theory but writing from outside Western privilege have increasingly labored in recent years to queer the diaspora, in the process aiming to 'disrupt a singular and normalized queer subject and constituency' (Arora 2007: 31). Ideally, such disruption might serve 'to dismantle mainstream hegemonic understandings of queer as white, male', making space instead for the 'contextual multiplicity of queer subjects' (ibid.). Such efforts have proliferated, bringing queer theory into contact with race, post-colonialism, globalization (Riggs 2006), insistently locating queer theory outside the global north (Gopinath 2005; Rodríguez 2003), and especially outside the US (Martin et al. 2008). Taking queer theory elsewhere can reveal that the ostensibly queer analysis of same-sex marriage – that is, the fierce opposition to it (Warner 1999) – may be parochially American rather than universal. Debates on relationship recognition might be inflected differently in other locales, and their relation with queer theory may be more fluid than some US critics, writing in universalizing language, have assumed (Boellstorff 2007).

Unsurprisingly, this project of diasporic queer analysis itself calls for care. Wesling (2008) has argued for careful examination of the recent emergent articulations of normative and queer as theoretical twins: one subverting gender normativity, the other troubling geographic and national stability. It has been argued that 'queer racialized and queer diasporic subjects are the most telling register of the contradictions of nationalism under contemporary global capital' (Hong 2006: 98), although the dynamics of transnationalism operate unpredictably (Boellstorff 2008: 116). Taking particular locations into account, seeing queer theory as contingent and specific, can aid in disrupting the universalizing tendencies of queer academic and activist discourses (Blackwood 2005; Shiu-Ki 2004). Consistent with these calls, a number of the chapters in the collection locate their exploration of queer outside the global North, and indeed a number of them cross political boundaries.

The collection's four parts

Each of the following chapters explores in some detail the intersections of queer theory and law, culture, and empire. Many of them do so, not through universalizing theory, but through alertness, in a rooted, local way, to the contingency of the materiality of sex lives and regulatory forces. The contributors to this collection remain attentive to the material social conditions of their subjects. Remaining true to the possibilities of queerness and queer theory more generally, none of the authors explores only one of these themes independently, and in many cases the boundaries between law, culture, and empire are blurred. Furthermore, a number of the chapters, when addressing legal matters, do so comparatively, to some extent calling into question the impermeability of the jurisdictional borders ostensibly established by states and empires. While the chapters' affiliations and alliances are multiple, the collection organizes them in four parts.

The chapters in Part 1, 'Constitution', explore the tensions that become evident in any reading of queer theory and queer politics, in relation to the forces that produce and modulate the subjectivities and identities associated with non-normative sexualities. Drawing on the insight that imperial projects are predicated on and produce politically powerful epistemological claims (Stoler and McGranahan 2007: 11), they contrast the constitutive effects of discourses of neoliberalism, rights, and liberal tolerance.

Part 2, 'Representation', illuminates the collection's principal themes in several ways. Interrogating the relationships between performativity, performance, and queerness has been a longstanding preoccupation of queer scholars (e.g. Butler 1999 [1990]). Chapters in this part investigate some of the complicated ways that queerness is represented, performed, seen, and rendered intelligible. Attentiveness to empire and its function in the process of commodification and unification assists the authors in this collection to resist the draw to tell simple, universal stories. Instead, each undertakes a carefully situated reading of one or more 'texts', defining the term largely.

The chapters in Part 3, 'Regulation', deepen the examination of law's regulatory and repressive effects in relation to non-normative sexualities and subjectivities. These authors find queer theory useful for throwing into relief the potential alliances between unlikely groups for political mobility. They take queer not only as denoting those who identify as sexually non-normative (lesbian, gay, bisexual, transgender, and so on), but also as encompassing those who fail to fit within other historically organized and valorized categories. These chapters take three settings regulated by law – assisted reproduction, polygamy, and same-sex marriage – and identify ways in which queer claims (perhaps rooted in legal argument) align in surprising ways with claims made by those commonly cast as decidedly not-queer. The authors argue for building alliances by noting the 'queerness' of the claims of the identified allies – heterosexuals who also experience fertility challenges, polygamists, and religious heterosexuals.

Finally, Part 4, 'Exclusion', focuses on the broad theme of exclusion and foreignness, a long-standing preoccupation of queer theorists. This part returns to key themes identified in the first part of the collection, focusing on the need to resist hegemonic presumptions of normalcy as well as to call into question the signification of being foreign. These chapters disconcert comfortable definitions of the domestic or national and the foreign, setting such demarcations against backdrops of power relations. Exclusionary definitions of foreignness emerge as unstable, contingent, and contestable.

If some of the chapters stand in continuity with the queer agenda presaged by Michael Warner nearly twenty years ago – queer struggles aiming 'not just at toleration or equal status but at challenging' homophobic and heterosexist social institutions and standard accounts of the world (1993b, xiii), others unquestionably reflect successive waves of queer struggle by engaging with questions that could not have been posed then, such as recent legal developments' unintended material and discursive consequences. While bringing a variety of richly complementary – and at times contradictory – approaches to their subjects, the chapters attest that queer remains 'a volatile, contentious, and enabling term' (Flannery 2007: 3). And they bring it to bear on contemporary examples that were not available in the earlier years of queer theory, such as the aftermath of Proposition 8, (the anti-gay marriage plebiscite in California), the rise of the gay rights movement in Eastern Europe, the same-sex couple's respectable entry into migration law, and the recent gay rights litigation in post-apartheid South Africa. The chapters embody various affects, some of them delineating, for instance, hostile forces of racism, heterosexism, and homophobia. Yet they also hint at queer theory's hope that 'even the most pernicious and powerful modes of control have within them contradictions from which new modes of living and knowing emerge to contest, explain, and unsettle' (Hong 2006: 98).

Constitution

Jon Binnie's chapter advances the important task of connecting class relations, neoliberalism, and the politics of non-normative sexualities. Seeing the relation between neoliberalism and queer sexualities as ambivalent, he argues that we must attend to the material circumstances in which queer subjectivities are produced and contested. His focus on the politics of LGBTQ organizing in Poland and Central and Eastern Europe generally provides a reminder of the parochialism with which much Anglo-American theory constitutes queer. If its pejorative connotations make queer edgier in Anglo-American discourses than the language of gay or lesbian identities, queer's utter unintelligibility equips it to operate more successfully in Poland than the more disruptive terms gay and lesbian. Binnie calls us to challenge discourses that produce queer subjects as materially and geographically privileged. At the same time, he suggests that relations ordinarily figured as commercial and consumerist may constructively enter the field of politics: he thus identifies a blurring of tourism and activism on the part of Western European queer subjects in Eastern Europe.

Ratna Kapur, writing her chapter from posts in New Delhi and Geneva, deliberately decenters queer theory. Like Binnie, she illuminates the limits of Western queer theory. Drawing on post-colonial theory, she challenges the binary matrices against which queer discourse operates: the West–the Rest, the colonizer–the colonies, the powerful–the impoverished, the here–the there. In the arena of sexuality, specifically, such binary thinking associates pleasure, desire and agency with the West while constituting third world sexual subjects through lenses of violence, victimization, impoverishment, and cultural barbarism. Kapur argues that queer as prevalently constituted fails to capture the multiple positions of sexual subalterns. She traces an explosion of public representations of non-normative sexualities, while expressing caution that the call for tolerance associated with them proves cause for concern. In a context shaped by colonial encounter, tolerance – inflected as a notion for religious minorities – operates as a technology for social and political control, rather than empowering the groups being tolerated. It is not only queer, then, but also strategies sought to improve the lives of sexual subalterns that must be scrutinized for their signification in given contexts.

Representation

Shohini Ghosh's chapter takes us to Bollywood Cinema, reading cinematic texts not as an authoritative archive of contemporary cultural sensibilities, but as specifically sexual representations. Ghosh offers a textured reading of classic cinematic texts, arguing that the layers of reading, rereading, and misreading that they induce reveal the complicated positions of non-normative desires. Male and female protagonists, unmoored from the structures of predictable moral choices, confront a queer world of moral flux and ambiguity. Ghosh argues that films in the late 1990s did more than present new queer stories to the cinematic spectators. Rather, by erotically charging ordinary interactions, they mainstreamed an interpretative strategy commonly used by queer subcultures, thereby opening older texts to retrospective queering. Her chapter traces a perceptual process through which spectators of Bollywood Cinema not only learned to see the queer, but learned to see queerly, reading queerly the ambiguities and gaps. Ghosh's interpretative performance in her context of Bollywood Cinema models a hermeneutics for queer reading of texts of many kinds in many locations.

Jaco Barnard-Naudé's chapter explicitly connects a cultural representational text with the constitutional law and politics of South Africa to involve the question of the sexual within democracy. He takes Jane Alexander's sculpture, *The Butcher Boys*, resident in the South African National Gallery in Cape Town, as point of departure for an analysis of Derrida's critique of a political founded in fraternity. The chapter locates the sculpture in its patriarchal setting and translates what it represents into reflections on the trajectory of the same-sex marriage debates in South Africa, including judgments by the Constitutional Court. Consistent with queer theory's impulse to destabilize fixed boundaries, the chapter challenges the inclinations – both, as experience shows, violent and indeed murderous – to found the nation on

fraternal sameness and to anchor marriage in a sexed, fundamental opposition. He traces the influence of a patriarchal configuration of the political
discernable in the same-sex marriage debate and eventual legalization of
same-sex marriage in post-apartheid South Africa. He suggests, in a way more
widely applicable, that South Africa's litigation on sexual emancipation
illustrates how easily even a well-meaning, self-conscious, pro-queer discourse
can lapse back into patriarchal and fraternal language and institutions.

Leslie Moran's chapter moves the reader from cinema and sculpture to
another kind of performance, those texts performed when judges are sworn
into office. Swearing-in speeches have not been the subject of any sustained
comparative analysis, and Leslie Moran's piece – analyzing speeches from
New South Wales – is a welcome addition to the queer theory literature as
well as the literature on judges and judging. His starting point is the official
determination that, unlike gender, race, and religion, sexuality is irrelevant to
efforts to ensure a diverse judiciary. Queer theory's insights about the public
character of sex as well as the unmarked prevalence of heteronormativity set
the stage. He examines the relation of sexuality to these texts, including its
absence as well as its traces or echoes. Sexual norms are reproduced obliquely
but persistently through the trope of family, although some representations
hint at the fragility of the heterosexual family's position. Drawing on queer
critiques of kinship and family, Moran traces how his studied texts also figure
the legal profession as a family or kinship network. Despite glimmers of
non-normative sexuality in the representations of a handful of judges, Moran
concludes that heterosexuality remains a key dimension of the judiciary's
project of individual and institutional formation.

Regulation

Jenni Millbank's chapter makes an important contribution by arguing that it
is unduly narrow to suppose that it is only same-sex couples who are 'queering reproduction' (Mamo 2007). She identifies a gap between literature and
political activism addressing the experiences and claims of heterosexual parents undergoing fertility difficulties and literature and political activism
aimed more directly at gays' and lesbians' desire to become parents. Millbank
deploys the the language of 'reproductive outsiders' to denote individuals
and couples who are pursuing a desire to parent outside the confines of the
hetero-nuclear, sexually reproductive family. She connects the two solitudes
of heterosexual and same-sex couples. Indeed, she contrasts the self-
perception on the part of heterosexual couples of infertility as a private,
shameful condition with the rejection by gay men and lesbians of their sexuality as precisely that. Millbank cautiously presents case studies illustrating
the room for alliances in law reform efforts in this area. She is nevertheless
conscious of the potential clashes or conflicts of interest and of the fractures
cutting across the alliances she calls for. Given the openness of regulatory

regimes in the United States, her arguments apply most directly to the contexts of countries such as Australia, Canada, New Zealand, and the United Kingdom.

Like Millbank's, Jeffrey Redding's chapter also urges queers to consider the potential for alliances, focusing on the opposition between religious people and queers in the United States. He argues that the protests and animosity fueling the opposition around same-sex marriage debates have been counterproductive. Redding sees potential for some religious people and queers to consider how their experiences of family law might be similarly ostracized by the mainstream secular and religiously informed state. Failing such consideration, potential is lost in a largely silent queer retreat into a strictly secular sexuality politics. He argues that the historic animosity between some religious activists and queer populations have undermined the social and legal developments that might enhance their positioning. Drawing on a notion of queer agency, Redding suggests that queer advocates should seek dignity in places other than majoritarian marriage. To the extent that the creation and elaboration of 'queer legal spaces', such as non-marital, domestic partnership relationship–recognition regimes, facilitate such agency, such alternatives might be developed with the participation and assistance of groups and organizations, often religiously affiliated, that have experience in developing and occupying alternatives to majoritarian marriage.

Margaret Denike turns to a more philosophical exploration of the relationship between queer lives and the practice of polygamy. Her chapter explores the deeply colonial, racialized, and orientalist slippery slopes evident in the language of policy makers and scholars who oppose and prosecute polygamy. She analogizes those arguments with the arguments that are often used to resist same-sex marriage claims by queers. Denike is critical of those who argue for recognition of same-sex relationships precisely by contending that they are so distinct from polygamy. Such discourses cast polygamy as hyper-patriarchal, perverse, and inherently inequitable, while upholding monogamous same-sex unions as normal, democratic, and exemplary of gender equality. At the same time, her exploration is thoroughly empirical and historical in the sense that the prohibition of polygamy can never escape its past deployments as an instrument of racially specific nation building. Those who occupy non-normative sexual subjectivities should be alert to the possibility that the simultaneous crackdown on polygamy and valorization of same-sex relationships serve a consolidation of a relatively narrow, traditionally Christian form of monogamous conjugality in the service of Canadian and US national identities.

Exclusion

In his chapter, Nicholas Bamforth interrogates the process of othering that purports to exclude legal interpretations and ideas from other states when laws applying to queer lives are at issue in the United States. Specifically, he challenges the contention, presented after *Lawrence v. Texas* by conservative, nationalist interlocutors in US debates, that an international pro-gay legal discourse threatens the integrity of domestic constitutional law and democratic processes. Bamforth is alert to the risk that human rights discourse can be imperial and colonizing, but he argues that use of comparative legal materials is not per se imperialistic. What is necessary is context-specific evaluation of the relative power positions of the parties and the normative sources at issue. From that perspective, it was Justice Scalia's outright rejection of the value of the foreign that is rightly seen as imperialist. Bamforth argues that absolute universalism and pure moral relativism are both undesirable and inadequate. He sketches an intermediate position for framing human rights claims, one that retains space for belief that one conception is better than any alternative, while acknowledging that, to avoid imperialism, it is necessary to persuade members of other societies of this point.

Nan Seuffert's chapter turns a queer, post-colonial lens on a different law reform setting – relationship recognition and immigration law reform in New Zealand. Media and parliamentary debates about proposed reforms show that, while the content of debates changes, discourse remains in continuity with long-standing tropes of empire, nation building, domesticity, and exclusion. Debates cast the recognition of same-sex relationships as a sign of modernity, evolution, and progress, one differentiating the nation from other, more benighted regulatory approaches. Moreover, such recognition valorizes domestic, monogamous same-sex relationships, while further othering those least like marriages. Immigration rules recognizing committed same-sex couples have in turn produced new categories of unwelcome foreigners. Instead of seeking to transform the area of relationship recognition, Seuffert concludes that recent reforms have simply reproduced and re-embedded historic relationships of domination, including ones through which imperial subjects subjugated and domesticated those whom they colonized.

The collection concludes with a chapter by Ruthann Robson. Robson's experimental, performative essay draws together the themes of all four parts of the collection. This chapter performs the experiences of being constituted as queer, being seen, allying with unlikely allies, and being foreign. It grapples with the implications of empire, law, and culture on being and being queerly. Its rhetorical performance connects with examples explored in earlier chapters. Robson's journey thus touches on the South African history of apartheid that frames Barnard-Naudé's chapter, the projects of empire and colonialism against which the chapters by Kapur and Seuffert position themselves, and Proposition 8's struggles over same-sex marriage in California, addressed by Redding.

The contributors' journeys – from the complexities of queer activism in

Eastern Europe, in Jon Binnie's chapter in this volume (Chapter 2), to the unsettling effects of colonialism and settlement in Ruthann Robson's (Chapter 12) – show the need to read texts carefully, with an eye on the weight of the past and alertness to the assumed and the implicit. At a moment when law reform efforts for recognition of same-sex relationships have, in many places, enjoyed success, these chapters call for alertness to the unintended consequences of such achievements, including their potential shoring up of nationalist agendas and othering of non-normative sexualities unsuited to domestication. They remind us that legal interventions by subjects positioned as queer unfold against a complex backdrop of cultural representations and imperial inclinations. These chapters show that, in the legal arena as in others, queer theory remains a valuable lens for viewing the world askant, for advancing thought and the analysis of modes of political intervention. On a further look at the cover's close-up, it appears different, standing in for this volume's rich, at times disorienting, accounts.

References

Agathangelou, A. M., Bassichis, M. D. and Spira, T. L. (2008) 'Intimate Investments: Homonormativity, Global Lockdown, and the Seductions of Empire', *Radical History Review*, 100: 120–43.

Ahmed, S. (2006) *Queer Phenomenology: Orientations, Objects, Others*, Durham, NC: Duke University Press.

Arondekar, A. (2005) 'Border/Line Sex: Queer Postcolonialities, or How Race Matters outside the United States', *interventions*, 7(2): 236–50.

Arora, A. (2007) 'Rituals of Queer Diaspora in Nisha Ganatra's *Chutney Popcorn*', *South Asian Popular Culture*, 5(1): 31–43.

Ball, C. A. (2008) 'Privacy, Property, and Public Sex', *Columbia Journal of Gender and Law*, 18(1): 1–60.

Baruddoja, R. (2008) 'Queer Spaces, Places, and Gender: The Tropologies of Rupa and Ronica', *NWSA Journal*, 20(2): 156–88.

Bell, D. and Binnie, J. (2000) *The Sexual Citizen: Queer Politics and Beyond*, Cambridge: Polity.

—— (2004) 'Authenticating Queer Space: Citizenship, Urbanism and Governance', *Urban Studies*, 41(9): 1807–20.

Benedicto, B. (2008) 'Desiring Sameness: Globalization, Agency, and the Filipino Gay Imaginary', *Journal of Homosexuality*, 55(2): 274–311.

Binnie, J. (2004) *The Globalization of Sexuality*, London: Sage.

Blackwood, E. (2005) 'Transnational Sexualities in One Place: Indonesian Readings', *Gender and Society*, 19(2): 221–42.

Boellstorff, T. (2007) 'When Marriage Falls: Queer Coincidences in Straight Time', *GLQ: A Journal of Lesbian and Gay Studies*, 13(2 & 3): 227–48.

—— (2008) 'Queer Trajectories of the Postcolonial', *Postcolonial Studies*, 11(1): 113–7.

Bohache, T. (2008) *Christology from the Margins*, London: SCM Press.

Brandzel, A. L. (2005) 'Queering Citizenship? Same-Sex Marriage and the State', *GLQ: A Journal of Lesbian and Gay Studies*, 11(2): 171–204.

Browne, K., Lim, J. and Brown, G. (eds.) (2007) *Geographies of Sexualities: Theory, Practices and Politics*, Aldershot: Ashgate.

Butler, J. (1999 [1990]). *Gender Trouble: Feminism and the Subversion of Identity*, New York, NY: Routledge.

Colebrook, C. (2009) 'On the Very Possibility of Queer Theory', in C. Nigianni and M. Storr (eds.) *Deleuze and Queer Theory*, Edinburgh: Edinburgh University Press.

Cossman, B. (2007) *Sexual Citizens: The Legal and Cultural Regulation of Sex and Belonging*, Stanford, CA: Stanford University Press.

Douzinas, C. (2007) *Human Rights and Empire: The Political Philosophy of Cosmopolitanism*, London: Routledge-Cavendish.

Duggan, L. (2003) *The Twilight of Equality? Neoliberalism, Cultural Politics, and the Attack on Democracy*, Boston, MA: Beacon.

Edelman, L. (1994) *Homographesis: Essays in Gay Literary and Cultural Theory*, New York, NY: Routledge.

—— (2004) *No Future: Queer Theory and the Death Drive*, Durham, NC: Duke University Press.

Eng, D. L. (2007). 'Freedom and the Racialization of Intimacy: *Lawrence v. Texas* and the Emergence of Queer Liberalism', in G. E. Haggerty and M. McGarry (eds.) *A Companion to Lesbian, Gay, Bisexual, Transgender, and Queer Studies*, Blackwell Publishing, Blackwell Reference Online: </www.blackwellreference.com/ subscriber/tocnode?id=g9781405113298_chunk_g97814051132983> (accessed 12 October 2009).

Eng, D. L. with Halberstam, J. and Muñoz, J. E. (2005) 'What's Queer about Queer Studies Now?', *Social Text*, 23(3 & 4): 1–17.

Fineman, M. A., Jackson, J. E. and Romero, A. P. (eds.) (2009) *Feminist and Queer Legal Theory: Intimate Encounters, Uncomfortable Conversations*, Aldershot: Ashgate.

Flannery, D. (2007) *On Sibling Love, Queer Attachment and American Writing*, Aldershot: Ashgate.

Ford, R. T. (2007) 'What's Queer about Race?', *South Atlantic Quarterly*, 106(3): 477–84.

Franke, K. M. (2004) 'The Domesticated Liberty of *Lawrence v. Texas*', *Columbia Law Review*, 104(5): 1339–426.

Freccero, C. (2006) *Queer/Early/Modern*, Durham, NC: Duke University Press.

—— (2007) 'Queer Times', *South Atlantic Quarterly*, 106(3): 485–94.

Giffney, N., and Hird, M. J. (eds.) (2008) *Queering the Non/Human*, Aldershot: Ashgate.

Gopinath, G. (2005) *Impossible Desires: Queer Diasporas and South Asian Public Cultures*, Durham, NC: Duke University Press.

Halberstam, J. (1997) 'Who's Afraid of Queer Theory?', in A. Kumar (ed.) *Class Issues: Pedagogy, Cultural Studies, and the Public Sphere*, New York, NY: New York University Press.

Halley, J., and Parker, A. (2007) 'Introduction', *South Atlantic Quarterly*, 106(3): 421–32.

Halperin, D. M., and Traub, V. (eds.) (2009) *Gay Shame*, Chicago: University of Chicago Press.

Hardt, M., and Negri, A. (2000) *Empire*, Cambridge, MA: Harvard University Press.

Hoad, N. (2000) 'Arrested Development or the Queerness of Savages: The Imperial and Neo-Imperial Uses of Male Homosexuality', *Postcolonial Studies*, 3(2): 133–58.

—— (2007) 'Queer Theory Addiction', *South Atlantic Quarterly*, 106(3): 511–22.

Hong, G. K. (2006) '"A Shared Queerness": Colonialism, Transnationalism, and Sexuality in Shani Mootoo's *Cereus Blooms at Night*', *Meridians: feminism, race, transnationalism*, 7(1): 73–103.

Johnston, C. (2008) 'The PACS and (Post-)Queer Citizenship in Contemporary Republican France', *Sexualities*, 11(6): 688–705.

Jordan, M. D. (2006) *Authorizing Marriage? Canon, Tradition, and Critique in the Blessing of Same-Sex Unions*, Princeton, NJ: Princeton University Press.

Kasirer, N. (1995) 'Larger than Life: A Review Essay of *Broken Tablets: The Cult of Law in French Art from David to Delacroix* by Jonathan Ribner', *Canadian Journal of Law and Society*, 10(2): 185–200.

Lim, E.-B. (2005) 'Glocalqueering in New Asia: The Politics of Performing Gay in Singapore', *Theatre Journal*, 57(3): 383–405.

Loughlin, G. (ed.) (2007) *Queer Theology: Rethinking the Western Body*, Oxford: Blackwell Publishing.

Love, H. (2007) *Feeling Backward: Loss and the Politics of Queer History*, Cambridge, MA: Harvard University Press.

Luibhéid, E. (2008) 'Queer/Migration: An Unruly Body of Scholarship', *GLQ: A Journal of Lesbian and Gay Studies*, 14(2 & 3): 169–90.

Mamo, L. (2007) *Queering Reproduction: Achieving Pregnancy in the Age of Technoscience*, Durham, NC: Duke University Press.

Martin, F., Jackson, P. A., McLelland, M. and Yue, A. (eds.) (2008) *AsiaPacifiQueer: Rethinking Genders and Sexualities*, Urbana, IL: University of Illinois Press.

McRuer, R. (2006) *Crip Theory: Cultural Signs of Queerness and Disability*, New York, NY: New York University Press.

Mendelsohn, D. (1999) *The Elusive Embrace: Desire and the Riddle of Identity*, New York, NY: Vintage Books.

Menon, M. (2008) *Unhistorical Shakespeare: Queer Theory in Shakespearean Literature and Film*, New York, NY: Palgrave Macmillan.

Moran, L. J., Monk, D. and Beresford, S. (eds.) (1998) *Legal Queeries: Lesbian, Gay, and Transgender Legal Studies*, London: Cassell.

Negri, A. (2008a) *Empire and Beyond* (trans.) E. Emery, Cambridge: Polity Press.

—— (2008b) *Reflections on Empire* (trans.) E. Emery, Cambridge: Polity Press.

Nunokawa, J. (2007) 'Queer Theory: Postmortem', *South Atlantic Quarterly*, 106(3): 553–63.

Osterlund, K. (2009) 'Love, Freedom and Governance: Same-Sex Marriage in Canada', *Social and Legal Studies*, 18(1): 93–109.

Oswin, N. (2008) 'Critical Geographies and the Uses of Sexuality', *Progress in Human Geography*, 32(1): 89–103.

Pierceson, J. (2005) *Courts, Liberalism, and Rights: Gay Law and Politics in the United States and Canada*, Philadelphia, PA: Temple University Press.

Puar, J. K. (2007) *Terrorist Assemblages: Homonationalism in Queer Times*, Durham, NC: Duke University Press.

Restuccia, F. L. (2006) *Amorous Acts: Lacanian Ethics in Modernism, Film, and Queer Theory*, Stanford, CA: Stanford University Press.

Richter-Montpetit, M. (2007) 'Empire, Desire and Violence: A Queer Transnational Feminist Reading of the Prisoner "Abuse" in Abu Ghraib and the Question of "Gender Equality"', *International Feminist Journal of Politics*, 9(1): 38–59.

Riggs, D. W. (2006) *Priscilla (White) Queen of the Desert: Queer Rights/Race Privilege*, New York, NY: Peter Lang.

Rodríguez, J. M. (2003) *Queer Latinidad: Identity Practices, Discursive Spaces*, New York, NY: New York University Press.

Rollins, J. (2005) '*Lawrence*, Privacy, and the Marital Bedroom: A Few Telltale Signs of Ironic Worry', in H. N. Hirsch (ed.) *The Future of Gay Rights in America*, New York, NY: Routledge.

Sarat, A. and Kearns, T. R. (eds.) 1998. *Law in the Domains of Culture*, Ann Arbor, MI: University of Michigan Press.

Sarat, A. and Simon, J. (eds.) (2003) *Cultural Analysis, Cultural Studies, and the Law: Moving beyond Legal Realism*, Durham, NC: Duke University Press.

Sedgwick, E. K. (1990) *Epistemology of the Closet*, New York, NY: Penguin Books.

—— (1993) *Tendencies*, Durham, NC: Duke University Press.

Shiu-Ki, T. K. (2004) 'Queer at Your Own Risk: Marginality, Community and Hong Kong Gay Male Bodies', *Sexualities*, 7(1): 5–30.

Smith, M. (2008) *Political Institutions and Lesbian and Gay Rights in the United States and Canada*, New York, NY: Routledge.

Snediker, M. D. (2009) *Queer Optimism: Lyric Personhood and Other Felicitous Persuasions*, Minneapolis, MN: University of Minnesota Press.

Stoler, A. L. (2002) *Carnal Knowledge and Imperial Power: Race and the Intimate in Colonial Rule*, Berkeley, CA: University of California Press.

—— (2006) 'Intimidations of Empire: Predicaments of the Tactile and Unseen', in A. L. Stoler (ed.) *Haunted by Empire: Geographies of Intimacy in North American History*, Durham, NC: Duke University Press.

Stoler, A. L. and McGranahan, C. (2007) 'Introduction: Refiguring Imperial Terrains', in A. L. Stoler, C. McGranahan and P. C. Perdue (eds.) *Imperial Formations*, Santa Fe, NM and Oxford: School for Advanced Research Press and James Currey.

Stychin, C. F. (2003) *Governing Sexuality: The Changing Politics of Citizenship and Law Reform*, Oxford: Hart Publishing.

Trevenen, K. 'Queer Citizenship: The Politics and Language of LGBT Human Rights', Paper presented at the annual meeting of the American Political Science Association, Marriott, Loews Philadelphia, and the Pennsylvania Convention Center, Philadelphia, PA, 2009-05-24: <www.allacademic.com/meta/p150604_index.html>.

Warner, M. (ed.) (1993a) *Fear of a Queer Planet: Queer Politics and Social Theory*, Minneapolis, MN: University of Minnesota Press.

—— (1993b) 'Introduction' in M. Warner (ed.) *Fear of a Queer Planet: Queer Politics and Social Theory*, Minneapolis, MN: University of Minnesota Press.

—— (1999) *The Trouble with Normal: Sex, Politics, and the Ethics of Queer Life*, New York, NY: Free Press.

Wesling, M. (2008) 'Why Queer Diaspora?', *Feminist Review*, 90: 30–47.

Wilcox, M. (2007) 'Outlaws or In-Laws? Queer Theory, LGBT Studies, and Religious Studies', *Journal of Homosexuality*, 52(1): 73–100.

Williams, P. J. (1987) 'Alchemical Notes: Reconstructing Ideals from Deconstructed Rights', *Harvard Civil Rights–Civil Liberties Law Review*, 22(2): 401–34.

Yeoh, P. (2006) 'Writing Singapore Gay Identities: Queering the Nation in Johann S. Lee's *Peculiar Chris* and Andrew Koh's *Glass Cathedral*', *Journal of Commonwealth Literature*, 41(3): 121–35.

Part I

Constitution

Chapter 2

Queer theory, neoliberalism and urban governance

Jon Binnie

Contested histories and geographies of queer theory

This collection is timely in questioning the institutionalization of queer theory and studies. The impact of queer theory has been highly uneven geographically, and the history of queer theory is also contested. I am currently engaged, with my colleague Christian Klesse, in a project on transnational activism around LGBTQ (lesbian, gay, bisexual, transgender, queer) politics in Poland, and I have found specific concern over the parochialism of British and North American debates on queer theory. Our project has focused on notions of transnational solidarity around LGBTQ politics in Poland, and has involved interviews with activists and other actors in Poland, Germany, Belgium, the Netherlands and the UK about their experiences of transnational solidarity work. Discussing 'queer' in a European context, Nico Beger argues:

> The term carries with it an excess of meanings, which it can never fully recognise or fulfil. Alongside this abundance of meaning, it is also a profoundly Anglo-American term that has become common currency in many international l/g/b/t cultures without ever taking on board all its Anglo-American contents, while at the same time being enriched by new meanings in different language contexts.
>
> (2004: 40–1)

Beger draws attention to the different contexts for thinking about queer in Europe, compared to the US. He argues that in Europe lesbian and gay politics has been more closely allied to left politics and there has been a different history of AIDS politics and activism. In Europe the Christian right has been much less powerful than in North America. While not wishing to generalise about queer theory and politics in a European context it is important that we recognise the differences in the way it has been mobilised and (re)produced.

For instance, in Polish activist and academic environments, there are significant differences in the way queer has been deployed as compared to

British and North American contexts. Because there is no equivalent term in the Polish language, the term has not had the same pejorative resonances as it does in the English language. It can therefore pass under the radar of homophobic inscription, as Joanna Mizielinska (2009: 3) argues: 'one must notice that the very unreadability of the word was used by Polish queer scholars on purpose to introduce queer theory into Polish academia'.[1] In the Anglo-American academy and activist circles, queer has commonly (and sometimes problematically) been seen as somehow 'more progressive', more radical and more challenging than, say, lesbian and gay, or LGBT politics. However, in a Polish context, queer has often been deployed because the terms gay and lesbian have sometimes been seen as too challenging and confrontational. To some extent, then, it is the unintelligibility of queer that has given activists and academics some protection to create space to debate non-normative sexual politics. Likewise, it is important to recognise the specific conditions of doing queer work in what Sikora et al. (2008: 1) term: 'the predominantly conservative Polish cultural and academic landscape'.[2]

In a similar vein, activists have termed marches for lesbian and gay rights in Polish cities as equality marches (Warsaw), or marches for tolerance (Krakow). To some extent this has been a conscious tactic to court diversity in order to build coalitions with other outsider and minority groups in the country. For instance, the most recent Poznan equality event in 2008 embraced issues such as ageism and fat activism. On the other hand, the use of the terms 'tolerance' or 'equality' is strategic and pragmatic in trying to articulate a less confrontational, less provocative approach to homophobic mainstream society. Writing about the first 'March for Tolerance' in Krakow in 2004, which was attacked by far-right protestors, Tornquist-Plewa and Malmgren (2007: 25) argue that 'it was striking that it was the concept of tolerance, i.e. the respect for the (different) view or behaviour of others even if one does not like it and not the concept of acceptance, which permeated the defence of the march'. The violence on successive annual marches for tolerance in Krakow (where far-right counter-demonstrators have thrown acid, hammers, stones and eggs as well as insults) ensured that the Krakow March for Tolerance has become the focus of considerable national (and international) media attention and much greater visibility of LGBT politics in the public sphere. This has in turn helped to change the very meaning of the word tolerance, which has now become synonymous with homosexuality (Tornquist-Plewa and Malmgren 2007 provide a detailed discussion of the events around the Krakow March for Tolerance). We therefore need to recognise geographical context when discussing queer politics and theory, and be attuned to the ways queer can be bent and moulded to suit local purposes – but also how local contexts can shift understandings of the term.

In this chapter I wish to explore what I see as one of the most significant contemporary challenges to queer politics and theory, which is the question of economics and the relationship between material inequalities and the production of sexualities. In so doing, I wish to evaluate an emerging body of theoretical work on the sexual and queer politics of neoliberalism. Having done this, I wish to examine how the sexual politics of neoliberalism are configured in Central and Eastern Europe, focusing on Poland. By focusing on this geographical context I wish to see how insights from this location can inform work on the sexual and queer politics of neoliberalism and economics more widely.

Sexual politics and economics

Questions of material inequality have generally been marginalized within queer politics and theory. As Diane Richardson (2005: 517) argues: 'there has been relatively little written on how sexual politics, communities and identities are shaped by economic processes'. However, there is a growing body of work that is examining the relationship between economics and sexualities in a range of contexts including development studies (Cornwall et al. 2008; Lind and Bergeron forthcoming), the European Union (Beger 2004; Stychin 2003) and urban studies (Bell and Binnie 2004; Binnie 2004; Hubbard 2004a, 2004b). There have also been a number of vigorous critiques of the mainstreaming and professionalization of the gay and lesbian movement (Richardson 2005), and its neglect of material inequalities (Chasin 2000), as well as its conservatism more generally (Robinson 2005).

However, when articulating a queer perspective on social and economic inequalities, we need to recognise the potential for harm in the reproduction of stereotypes about gay affluence that have been thoroughly debunked by writers such as Lee Badgett (2001). In some accounts of the market, however, it is hard to escape from the assumption that both lesbians, and particularly gay men, are a uniformly privileged section of society. As Badgett stresses, there are costs associated with coming out in the workplace. It is these social and economic costs that are sometimes overlooked in a narrow focus on the politics of redistribution:

> Whether it is queer youth who are kicked out of their homes, transpeople who face limited employment prospects, gays and lesbians who are fired, or single mothers who have little support in raising their children, living outside accepted gender and sexual norms puts people at risk in ways that directly implicate both sexual and economic justice.
>
> (Bedford and Jakobsen 2009: 18)

Despite the ways in which homophobic and transphobic discrimination impacts on social and economic inequalities, the myth of gay affluence persists, and serves to mask inequalities between LGBT people. The harmful stereotype of gay affluence is an enduring one that still underpins much discussion of sexuality both in popular culture and academia. We have also seen that the stereotype of gay affluence can play into the interests of the right. For instance Badgett (2001: 259) argues: 'During the recession in the early 1990s, the myth of affluence helped to fuel anti-gay rhetoric and referenda in Oregon and Colorado'. Furthermore Hardisty and Gluckman (1997: 218) argue that 'recently, a new stereotype has crept into the antihomosexual literature of the right. In addition to being portrayed as immoral, disease-ridden child molestors, gay men and lesbians are now described as superwealthy, highly-educated free spenders'. Despite long-standing critiques of the pink economy discourse and the way it can feed into Christian right and other homophobic discourses, the myth of gay affluence persists.

Bedford and Jakobsen (2009) argue that it is difficult to reconcile thinking about sexual and economic justice because of the way in which both have been framed. They argue that theorists of sexual justice tend to overlook questions of social and economic inequalities, while thinking on social or economic justice tends to ignore sexual politics. Discussing and critiquing recent trends in work on sexual citizenship, Angelia Wilson is critical of both approaches that stress LGBT rights in terms of liberal individualism, *and* materialist approaches that are reductionist in framing the economic basis of sexual citizenship primarily in terms of gay consumption to the neglect of broader relationships between capitalism and sexual citizens. Wilson argues: 'Rights claims embedded in liberal individualism run . . . a risk of constructing debates in isolation of broader concerns' (2009: 77).

When writers on sexual politics do engage with questions of material inequalities there can be problems. For instance, consider the pioneering work of David Evans on the materiality of sexual citizenship. While Wilson finds great merit in this work, she finds his focus on gay consumption limiting, arguing that his work 'highlights the importance of capitalism in the dynamic of citizenship, but the reduction to consumerism ignores a larger field of enquiry regarding the power interplay between capital, the state, welfare and other intervening agendas' (2009: 80). This tendency to focus on gay consumption to the neglect of broader questions about the relationship of LGBT people to capitalism is unfortunate. Moreover, it is frustrating that work purporting to offer a critical take on gay consumption can sometimes end up reproducing a discourse by which gay male consumption practices are seen as false consciousness. For instance consider Matthew Tinkcom's discussion of gay consumption in which he bemoans the banalisation and erosion of gay male politics arguing that 'the relatively affluent gay male (and lesbian) urban sector goes about their business of making or acquiring children, becoming fascinated with the gyrations of the property value, and consuming the most sentimental proclamations of celebrity culture' (2002: 190). While it is necessary to challenge conservatism with gay politics and the movement, I do find the equation of gay men with sentimentality and obsession with celebrity culture a bit disturbing. However, others have challenged queer theory's clichéd distinction between the politics of assimilation and transgression. For instance, Carl Stychin argues that 'I have yet to meet anyone who is a politically "pure" form of either, and I am increasingly aware that *things are not always as they seem* when it comes to how people construct their ways of living' (2003: 140). Stychin's assertion demonstrates a more nuanced and less judgemental perspective on gay consumption and the relationship of LGBT people to the market. While economic conditions do shape sexual identities, politics and culture, we should be careful to avoid deterministic statements about the relationship between economics and sexuality. One of the most productive ways in which the relationship between queer, sexuality and economics have been theorised is the area of neoliberalism and this is the focus of the next section.

Queer theory and neoliberalism

> Within academia, conversations about poverty, structural adjustment, and neoliberalism have occurred largely apart from research on sexual rights, the emergence of 'global gay' identity, sex tourism, trafficking, and sex work.
>
> (Bedford and Jakobsen 2009: 3)

As Kate Bedford and Janet Jakobsen remind us, academic debates on neoliberalism have tended to ignore issues around sexual politics. Diane Richardson argues that 'there has been relatively little explicit discussion in the literature on the relationship between neoliberal governance and the politics of sexuality' (2005: 517). A body of work has recently emerged, however, that has examined the relationship between sexuality and economics under neoliberalism, primarily in North American contexts (Duggan 2002, 2003; Osterlund 2009), but also in the UK (Bell and Binnie 2004; Hubbard 2004a,2004b; Richardson 2005) and Latin America (Bedford 2009). Lisa Duggan's work has been particularly influential in queer studies in stating that 'neoliberalism in fact *has* a sexual politics' (2002: 177). Duggan's discussion of neoliberalism focuses on the public–private divide, and the way in which the private sphere has been configured within struggles for sexual citizenship, both historically and in the contemporary period. She suggests there has been a parallel between the right-wing ideological promotion of individual autonomy confronted with the overbearing power of the state and campaigns for sexual dissidents to protect the private sphere from invasive state interference and control of same-sex intimacies: 'progressives ambivalently and unevenly, but increasingly, defended a right to sexual and domestic privacy for all, defined as autonomy or liberty from state interference' (180). Yet these attempts to defend the right to privacy have not been uniformly successful. In the UK, for instance, arguments for the right to privacy failed in the Spanner case in which 16 gay men were prosecuted for consensual sadomasochistic (SM) sex in 1990 (see Bell 1995; Moran 1995). It is instructive to contrast the SM activists' campaign against the interference of the state in the Spanner case, and Duggan's statement above, with Stephen Tomsen's (2006) more recent work on homophobic hate crimes and policing in New South Wales. He argues that campaigners against homophobic violence have tended to invoke the state's punishment of perpetrators of homophobic violence, which often reflects a specific class-based hierarchy whereby the victims are constructed as gay consumers of gentrified urban lesbian and gay space.

The legal recognition of same-sex relationships and the politics of normalization has been a key focus of work on the self-governing subject in neoliberalism. For instance Diane Richardson argues that 'in the context of neoliberalism's policy agenda for "rolling back" the state it is possible to see how governments are motivated to introduce civil recognition of lesbian and gay relationships insofar as these are seen as a form of private welfare, providing economic interdependency and support' (2005: 522). She is critical of the way in which debates on same sex marriage under neoliberalism have promoted the politics of normalization. Richardson's call for us to challenge normalization is echoed in Katherine Osterlund's insightful essay on legal debates on same-sex marriage in Canada in which she critiques the deployment of what she terms a 'normalizing love discourse' in which marriage is reconfigured from a legal relationship primarily based on reproduction to one of love. She argues that this 'normalizing love discourse' has been ideological in reinforcing neoliberal notions of the privatization of care and responsibility: 'implicitly monogamous, responsibilized, and explicitly devoted and caring love has been established as *the* legally recognizable love, marking acceptable love from the unacceptably and unspeakably queer' (2009: 94). The 'unspeakably queer' may be more likely to suffer economic hardship on grounds of discrimination, compared to those who conform to the normalizing love discourse outlined by Osterlund. Volker Woltersdorff has argued that 'gay men and lesbians have been depicted as [the] vanguard of neoliberal transformation' (2007: 6). He argues that while many gay men and lesbians have found neoliberal conditions preferable to traditional conditions, others have been less able to benefit from neoliberalism because of their queerness.

A number of writers, including Brenda Cossman, Diane Richardson and Angelia Wilson, have argued that the state's limited granting of rights to sexual citizens feeds into neoliberal political agendas such as the privatization of welfare and care. Cossman has sought to shift debates on sexual citizenship away from a narrow focus on the politics of assimilation versus transgression in LGBT rights claims to the privatization and self-governance in neoliberalism:

> as neo-liberal citizenship has become more about self-governance, this responsibilitized citizenship includes an explicitly sexual dimension; individuals are called upon to make the right choices about sex, managing

sexual risks through self-discipline. Like freedom more generally, sexual freedom has become a terrain to be managed.

(2007: 196)

Cossman seeks to broaden debates on sexual citizenship, from a narrow focus on same-sex marriage, to encompass questions such as the racialised and gendered politics of welfare reform in the US. In so doing she highlights the ways in which certain gay and lesbian subjects are celebrated in some popular cultural formations as model neoliberal citizens:

> Not unlike the Fab Five of *Queer Eye for the Straight Guy*, gay and lesbian subjects are the new model citizens, the heroic citizens, standing for all that is valued in American citizenship. In an extraordinary reversal of the more traditional terms of heterosexual sexual citizenship, gay men and lesbians are here becoming the most becoming of citizens.
>
> (ibid. 177)

This discourse of the savvy, self-disciplined, urbane, knowing, fabulous citizen described by Cossman, and the power of hegemonic representations of gay men as affluent, mean that it becomes increasingly difficult to think of gay men or lesbians in the same breath as poverty or economic disadvantage. As Volker Woltersdorff argues:

> growing queer visibility in advertising continues to be mistaken as a realistic picture of society. As a consequence, political discourse draws the image of people getting the straighter the poorer they are. According to that, homosexuality seems to be a kind of luxury that only wealthy people can afford.
>
> (2007: 5)

Woltersdorff argues that while there may be a distinctive relationship between queerness and neoliberalism, it is one characterised by precariousness.

I have argued that work on the sexual politics of neoliberalism has tended to concentrate on how discourses of 'normalization', privatization and responsibilisation have shaped debates on same-sex marriage. Moreover, the media visibility and academic scrutiny of queer conspicuous consumption in shows such as *Queer Eye for the Straight Guy* has reinforced the notion that some gay men and lesbians have, to some extent, become model neoliberal citizens. However, it is important to remember that there is not a single logic that defines the relationship between neoliberalism and sexuality. We need to recognise that neoliberalism can also be associated with the promotion of homophobic politics. In Lesley Hoggart's essay on the sexual politics of neoliberalism in the UK in the 1980s she stresses the *ambivalence* of the relationship between neoliberalism and queer subjects: 'There is an obvious contradiction between on the one hand, the individualism and libertarianism fundamental to neoliberalism and on the other, the call for state intervention to regulate sexuality within private lives' (2005: 154). We need to retain an awareness of this ambivalence when we consider the distinctive geographies of neoliberalism and their sexual politics.

Having traced the trajectory of some of the main debates on the sexual politics of neoliberalism, I now wish to focus on the difference that space makes to these discussions by considering the ways in which these debates can be grounded in specific urban locations, and the ways in which sexual politics are implicated in the transformation of cities through neoliberal regimes of governance.

The sexual politics of neoliberal urban governance

In this section of the chapter, I examine the ways in which the sexual politics of neoliberalism have been configured in work on urban entrepreneurialism and contemporary transformations in urban governance. Phil Hubbard argues that the gendered and sexual politics of neoliberal urban policy have been ignored in the vast literature that has emerged recently on the politics of neoliberal urban space. For instance, Hubbard argues that sex workers have become the target of aggressive interventionist neoliberal urban policy that has sought to transform the place imagery of marginal urban areas that up to now had been areas of street prostitution. Echoing the calls from Brenda Cossman for work on sexual citizenship to go beyond a narrow LGBT focus, Hubbard (2004b) argues that sex workers have been the targets of neoliberal urban governance. In contrast, some dimensions of gay and lesbian commodity culture have in fact been embraced within policy making that has, for instance, sought to promote the development of gay villages in a number of UK cities.

In a key essay on the neoliberalisation of urban space, Jamie Peck and Adam Tickell describe neoliberal intra-urban competition as a self-fulfilling prophecy in neoliberal conditions, as cities feel propelled to follow an urban entrepreneurial agenda and seek to attract hallmark cultural events and investment. This in turn creates the conditions for capital and labour to become more ever more mobile: 'in selling themselves, cities are therefore actively facilitating and subsidizing the very geographic mobility that first rendered them vulnerable, while also validating and reproducing the extra-local rule systems to which they are (increasingly) subjected' (2002: 393). Public investment therefore fuels the mobility of capital in a zero-sum game. In this context we see the competition for global events such as the gay games and the promotion of pride events and other high-profile queer cultural festivals such as film and arts festivals. Often underlying this competition to attract such events are assumptions about gay affluence that I critiqued earlier. Reflecting a similar logic to the neoliberal intra-urban competition, the gay affluence discourse is self-perpetuating. As Abraham (2009: 294–5) argues: 'What has developed from the conflation of homosexuality, consumption, and cities is ... a self-perpetuating system ensuring that the gays who are taken to represent modern urbanity in Chicago, Madrid, and Sydney remain a familiar moneyed, white, and male group'. This is dangerous because it produces a homogenous gay subject and renders invisible racialised, classed and gendered differences.

Peck and Tickell (2002: 393–4) argue that 'neoliberalism is associated with an extremely narrow urban-policy repertoire based on capital subsidies, place promotion, supply-side intervention, central-city makeovers, and local boosterism'. This focus on transforming the fabric of central areas and place promotion has had direct consequences for urban territories where there is a spatial concentration of venues aimed at the LGBT market. In some instances in the UK such spaces have been seen as prized assets in the promotion of international tourism and the transformation of the dominant place image from de-industrialised wasteland to desirable hub of post-industrial creativity. While the local state did play a significant role in the development of Manchester's gay village in the 1990s (see Bell and Binnie 2004; Quilley 1997), what was new in recent years has been the conscious attempt by urban policy makers to create or designate gay villages in cities such as Liverpool in a classic me-too-ism strategy which is commonplace in contemporary urban regeneration strategies where cities look to copy what are seen as successful regeneration strategies from elsewhere.

The queer politics of neoliberalism in Central and Eastern Europe

> The extent to which economics is in large measure *constitutive* of sexual identities deserves consideration, for it suggests that East/West, North/ South divisions may well be central – for economic reasons – to the way in which sexuality is constructed within Europe, especially given the historical focus of sexual citizenship on consumer consumption.
>
> (Stychin 2003: 20)

In Central and Eastern European contexts contemporary discussions of neoliberalism are inseparable from discussions of the European Union (EU) as an economic and political actor. Discussing neoliberalism and the politics of the EU, John Milios (2005) claims that the EU acts to serve the interests of capital and against labour describing neoliberalism as a class policy aimed at weakening labour in the struggle against capital. In sharp contrast, Jan Toporowski (2005: 219) argues that Western European states, including those such as the UK that have been most neoliberal in their posturing, are in his words 'anything but neoliberal'. He points to the continuing significance of the welfare state in these societies as proof that the idea of Western European states being neoliberal is overstated.

In terms of opposition to neoliberalism in Europe, Woltersdorff (2007: 6) argues that anti-neoliberal critics are often imbued with nostalgia for a welfare state that has been criticised for being heteronormative. In Central and Eastern Europe dislocations associated with transition have sometimes focused on sexuality as a marker of the success or failure of the transition process. Discussing the politics of transition in Romania, Carl Stychin (2003: 116) argues that homosexuality has served as a symbol of post-socialist transition, and the transformation of governance in Romania under neoliberalism. Stychin frames law reform in Romania in terms of the EU's disciplining of the country so that its financial and political institutions are reformed for it to be a suitable candidate for EU accession. He notes the key role of the activists from the Netherlands in providing funding and expertise in the development of ACCEPT, the gay rights lobbying group in Romania. This demonstrates the export of a Dutch methodology of human rights work. Stychin is concerned, however, about whether this export of Dutch expertise and knowledge has the imprints of neocolonialism:

> To what extent can European actors avoid the colonial impulse? COC Netherlands [the national gay rights organization in the Netherlands] is now working actively on a lesbian and gay empowerment project in the Republic of Moldova. Will this be a force for 'liberation', or should it be seen as an example of the colonisation of sexuality by the West?
>
> (ibid. 137–8)

Stychin wonders whether the models, tactics and approaches that reflect political history in the Netherlands are appropriate in the Romanian and Moldovan contexts.

In the previous section I noted a recent trend in urban governance – particularly in the UK – to promote gay villages and international LGBT tourism as part of a neoliberal discourse related to heightened intra-urban competition for inward investment (see also Bell and Binnie 2004). This discussion of neoliberalism, sexualised consumption and urban entrepreneurialism was grounded in Manchester where the gay village has been symbolic of the transformation of the city's brand as cosmopolitan consumption leisure space – symbol of its 'successful' economic and aesthetic transformation from industrial to post-industrial city (see also Binnie and Skeggs 2004, for a critique of the way cosmopolitanism was deployed as a discourse in urban governance). However, one of the flaws in this argument is to take these developments for granted and to overstate how these strategies have become generalised. If we consider some examples from Central and Eastern Europe, it is clear that the relationship between urban governance, neoliberalism and sexuality can be configured rather differently in a post-socialist context.

Take, for instance, the case of Krakow in Poland which has experienced a recent boom in international tourism, partly due to the proliferation of low-cost airlines. This has led to Krakow being a focus of British stag and hen parties that bring in significant income to the local economy – but in turn cause problems of alcohol-related disorder. Krakow attracts gay tourists and has an infrastructure for this market (as evidenced by the number of websites developed for the gay tourist market). However, given the extremely conservative nature of the local political climate towards homosexuality, the notion of promoting gay tourism to the city (in a similar way as tourist authorities and city authorities have done in the UK) has been seen as controversial, leading to debate over which form of tourism was most harmful to the city – British stag parties or gay tourism. An article about this debate in the British newspaper the *Observer* quotes from Piotr Kucharski, a spokesperson from a Christian lobby group which launched a campaign against the policy to promote Krakow as a destination for gay tourism: 'I don't know which is worse [. . .] drunken Britons may get their genitals out in public. But we don't want gays performing public obscenities either' (quoted in Davies 2008: 40). The rationale for promoting gay tourism in Krakow follows the familiar script associated with the pink economy. The *Observer* article quotes an official from Krakow's marketing and promotion office: 'Research shows that gays and lesbians spend significantly more on holidays and entertainment than tourists travelling with family and friends. We plan to make money on this' (ibid.). The danger is that the pink economy discourse reinforces the notion that gays are affluent which then feeds a nationalist discourse that pathologises gay men for being immoral and decadent. Support for the populist, nationalist and homophobic Law and Justice Party has been greatest in poor, rural areas as opposed to urban, more affluent metropolitan centres which have favoured other parties such as Civic Platform which is now the governing party since elections in 2007. Naomi Klein has noted that in Poland homophobia has been deployed by nationalist politicians in reaction to the social dislocation caused by economic policies that have caused social unease:

> In Poland you have a new politics that is talking about economic shock therapy as having been a humiliation for the country; that they need to get their nationalist pride back. And part of that nationalist pride is attacking gays and lesbians, attacking women, attacking immigrants.
>
> (2007, quoted in Bedford and Jakobsen 2009: 20)

While the pro-EU discourse is commonplace within LGBT politics in Poland, there are those who challenge the adoption of Western models of politics of LGBT identity. For instance, in a recent call for papers on sexual citizenship in Central and Eastern Europe, Alexander Lambevski argues that Western models of gay identity and politics may have limited application and use in Central and Eastern Europe:

Deep historical distrust in identity based organizations and identity politics, a weak civil society, a fragile rule of law, and the ignorance about, or unpreparedness to use, the legal and political instruments of European citizenship, create a very unique set of challenges for LGBTQ people in post-socialist Europe on their road to freedom and equality.

(2009: 1)

Lambevski goes on to argue:

Transnational LGBTQ rights movements arising from the institutional, legal, social, political, economic and intellectual successes of the gay, lesbian and queer movements in Western Europe, North America, Australia and New Zealand become increasingly aware that a western model of sexual politics and citizenship based on political and economic liberalism is simply unworkable in post-socialist Europe.

(ibid.)

Pro-EU discourses are prominent within pro-gay activists in Poland and their allies in Western Europe. The EU is often represented as a beacon of hope. In far-right nationalist discourses in Poland, anti-EU sentiment often goes together with homophobia: 'In view of the opponents' presentation of homosexuality as something that was marketed by the West and the EU it is not surprising that the aggressive counter-demonstrators shouted "euro-gays", and "the Union is gay" after the homosexuals participating in the march' (Tornquist-Plewa and Malmgren 2007: 20). The embracing of the EU and other European institutions by many LGBT activists in Poland is not surprising given the hope that EU membership would lead to better legal recognition of LGBT people. While challenging simplistic appeals of LGBT lobbyists to notions of European values, identity and EU institutions, Volker Woltersdorff (2007: 5) is however critical of those on the German left who characterise transnational actions of German activists participating in Warsaw equality parades in solidarity with Polish LGBT people as being complicit with neoliberalism:

Interestingly, in Germany it was precisely a radical leftwing newspaper (*Die Junge Welt*) that reported about the participation of German activists at the Warsaw parade of 2006 in an utterly homophobic way. It criticised the German lobby groups for not being left enough, for arrogantly exporting neoliberal EU supremacy and not addressing the real problems of Polish people . . .

Woltersdorff argues that sexuality is trivialised in this discursive formation:

When talking about poverty in the context of global labour division, the call for queer rights is then perceived as an indecent claim that is inappropriate for the people in question, as if sexuality wasn't a basic need for all and necessary for survival.

(ibid.)

It is certainly the case that discussions of social inequality and the class-based politics of sexuality remain marginal within many accounts of the current discussions of LGBTQ politics in Poland. As Sikora et al. note: 'There is no adequate cultural criticism of the remnants of class-based distinctions in our post-communist society, or of the new forms of such distinctions' (2008: 6). The need for a nuanced analysis of the relationships between class politics and the politics of sexuality is particularly imperative given representations of Poland's working-class communities as 'useless, worthless and an obstacle to the "transition" ' (Stenning 2005: 990).

Conclusion: queer solidarities beyond the market?

As the deleterious social consequences and perverse externalities of neo-liberal economic policies become increasingly evident and widespread, the foundations may be inadvertently created for new forms of translocal political solidarity and consciousness amongst those who find themselves marginalized and excluded on a *global* basis.

(Peck and Tickell 2002: 399)

In this chapter, I have sought to understand the ways in which queer theory has addressed questions of economic inequality – specifically in terms of debates on neoliberalism. I have argued that we need to acknowledge that the relationship between neoliberalism and queer, non-normative sexualities is ambivalent and that as Woltersdorff reminds us, anti-neoliberal politics can sometimes reinscribe a romanticised heteronormative and patriarchal notion of the family as a site of resistance to capitalism. In the Polish context neolib-eral economic policies associated with EU membership have created social and economic dislocation. As Klein argues, in periods of social and economic dislocation in Poland, lesbians and gay men have been a convenient target for nationalist politicians. Yet this dislocation is also helping to forge new forms of transnational sexual solidarities. Even the notion of gay tourism can be seen in terms of solidarity activism. On the one hand we could conceptualise a neat distinction between tourism as a gay consumption practice which is apolitical in the eyes of some commentators, and activist solidarity work (which may be framed as ethical and political by others), but we can see a blurring of these boundaries in certain instances. For instance, if we refer to an article in the Dutch gay magazine *Espresso*, which offers a guide for Dutch gay and lesbian tourists visiting Krakow, we do see a blurring of activism and tourism. The article's title 'Tinky Winky and Low Budget

Parties in Krakow' defines a particular set of Western ideas about queer
Poland. This refers to the widely reported comments by a Polish government politician that Tinky Winky (the character in the children's TV programme Teletubbies) could be perverting Polish children's minds and called
for psychologists to study the programme to see whether it was harmful to
children (Bugaric 2008). While covering the usual ingredients of a gay tourist article – where to eat, where to drink, where to stay and where to have
sex – the article also describes the current political situation for Polish
LGBT people. The article is upbeat in celebrating Krakow as an exciting
place for a city break, despite the prevalence of anti-gay posters across the
city. It also notes approvingly that the prices in the shops are cheaper than
in the Netherlands, and invites Dutch lesbians and gay men to graffiti
anti-gay posters, showing a photo of one such poster so decorated with:
'lesbians rule – greetings from Holland'. Such small acts, gestures of support,
could easily be seen as trivial in the same way that gay consumption could
be seen as apolitical, but the development of stronger links in civil
society with LGBTQ people abroad could also been seen as small acts of
transnational solidarity.

Notes

1 See Ratna Kapur's discussion, in this volume (Ch. 3), of the Western specificity of
  queer viewed from the post-colonial setting of India.
2 Compare Nicholas Bamforth's discussion, in this volume (Ch. 10), of the practice
  of applying arguments or precedents about human rights outside their original
  context.

References

Abraham, J. (2009) *Metropolitan Lovers: The Homosexuality of Cities*, Minneapolis,
  MN: University of Minnesota Press.
Badgett, M. V. Lee (2001) *Money, Myths and Change: The Economic Lives of Lesbians
  and Gay Men*, Chicago, IL and London: University of Chicago Press.
Bedford, K. (2009) *Developing Partnerships: Gender, Sexuality, and the Reformed
  World Bank*, Minneapolis, MN: University of Minnesota Press.
—— and Jakobsen, J. R. (2009) *Toward a Vision of Sexual and Economic Justice*,
  New York, NY: Barnard Center for Research on Women.
Beger, N. (2004) *Tensions in the Struggle for Sexual Minority Rights in Europe*,
  Manchester: Manchester University Press.
Bell, D. (1995) 'Pleasure and Danger: The Paradoxical Spaces of Sexual Citizenship',
  in D. Bell and G. Valentine (eds.) *Mapping Desire: Geographies of Sexualities*,
  London: Routledge.
—— and Binnie, J. (2004) 'Authenticating Queer Space: Citizenship, Urbanism and
  Governance', *Urban Studies*, 41(9): 1807–20.
Binnie, J. (2004) *The Globalization of Sexuality*, London: Sage.
—— and Skeggs, B. (2004) 'Cosmopolitan Knowledge and the Production and

Consumption of Sexualized Space: Manchester's Gay Village', *Sociological Review*, 52: 39–61.

Bugaric, B. (2008) 'Populism, Liberal Democracy, and the Rule of Law in Central and Eastern Europe', *Communist and Post-Communist Studies*, 41: 191–203.

Chasin, A. (2000) *Selling Out: The Gay and Lesbian Movement Goes to Market*, New York, NY: St. Martin's Press.

Cornwall, A., Correa, S. and Jolly, S. (eds.) (2008) *Development with a Body: Sexuality, Human Rights and Development*, London: Zed Books.

Cossman, B. (2007) *Sexual Citizens: The Legal and Cultural Regulation of Sex and Belonging*, Stanford, CA: Stanford University Press.

Davies, H. (2008) 'Krakow caught between pink pound and boozy Brits', *Observer*, 17 October: 40.

Duggan, L. (2002) 'The new homonormativity: the sexual politics of neoliberalism', in R. Castronovo and D. Nelson (eds.) *Materializing Democracy: Toward a Revitalized Cultural Politics*, Durham, NC and London: Duke University Press.

—— (2003) *The Twilight of Equality: Neoliberalism, Cultural Politics, and the Attack on Democracy*, Boston, MA: Beacon Press.

Hardisty, J. and Gluckman, A. (1997) 'The Hoax of "Special Rights": The Right Wing's Attack on Gay Men and Lesbians', in A. Gluckman and B. Reed (eds.) *Homo Economics: Capitalism, Community, and Lesbian and Gay Life*, London: Routledge.

Hoggart, L. (2005) 'Neoliberalism, the New Right and Sexual Rights', in A. Saad-Filho and D. Johnston (eds.) *Neoliberalism: A Critical Reader*, London: Pluto.

Hubbard, P. (2004a) 'Revenge and Injustice in the Neoliberal City: Uncovering Masculinist Agendas', *Antipode*, 36: 665–86.

—— (2004b) 'Cleansing the Metropolis: Sex Work and The Politics Of Zero Tolerance', *Urban Studies*, 41: 1687–702.

Lambevski, A. (2009) Call for papers for the inaugural issue of *Sextures*, online: <www.sextures.net> (accessed 2 April 2009).

Lind, A. and Bergeron, S. (eds.) (forthcoming) *Development, Sexual Rights and Global Governance*, London: Routledge.

Milios, J. (2005) 'European integration as a vehicle of neoliberal hegemony', in A. Saad-Filho and D. Johnston (eds.) *Neoliberalism: A Critical Reader*, London: Pluto.

Mizielinska, J. (2009) 'Untitled Thought Piece for Workshop on Anglo-Polish Perspectives on Sexual Politics, Manchester Metropolitan University, 3 July, 2009'.

Moran, L. (1995) 'Violence and the Law: The Case of Sado-Masochism', *Social and Legal Studies*, 4(2): 225–51.

Osterlund, K. (2009) 'Love, Freedom and Governance: Same-Sex Marriage in Canada', *Social and Legal Studies*, 18(1): 93–109.

Peck, J. and Tickell, A. (2002) 'Neoliberalizing space', *Antipode*, 34: 380–404.

Quilley, S. (1997) 'Constructing Manchester's "New Urban Village": Gay Space in the Entrepreneurial City', in G. B. Ingram, A.-M. Bouthillette and Y. Retter (eds.) *Queers in Space: Communities, Public Spaces, Sites of Resistance*, Seattle, WA: Bay Press.

Richardson, D. (2005) 'Desiring sameness? The Rise of a Neoliberal Politics of Normalisation', *Antipode*, 37(3): 515–35.

Robinson, P. (2005) *Queer Wars: The New Gay Right and Its Critics*, Chicago, IL: University of Chicago Press.

Sikora, T., Basiuk, T. and Ferens, D. (2008) 'Introduction', in T. Sikora, T. Basiuk and D. Ferens (eds.) *Out Here: Local and International Perspectives on Queer Studies*, Newcastle-upon-Tyne: Cambridge Scholars Publishers.

Stenning, A. (2005) 'Where is the Post-Socialist Working Class? Working Class Lives in the Spaces Of (Post-)Socialism', *Sociology*, 39: 983–99.

Stychin, C. (2003) *Governing Sexuality: The Changing Politics of Citizenship and Law Reform*, Oxford: Hart Publishing.

Tinkcom, M. (2002) *Working Like a Homosexual: Camp, Capital, Cinema*, Durham, NC: Duke University Press.

Tomsen, S. (2006) 'Homophobic Violence, Cultural Essentialism and Shifting Sexual Identities', *Social and Legal Studies*, 15(3): 389–407.

Toporowski, J. (2005) 'Neoliberalism: The Eastern European frontier', in A. Saad-Filho and D. Johnston (eds.) *Neoliberalism: A Critical Reader*, London: Pluto.

Tornquist-Plewa, B. and Malmgren, A. (2007) *Homophobia and Nationalism in Poland: The Reactions to the March against Homophobia in Cracow*, Trondheim: Trondheim Studies on East European Cultures and Societies.

Wilson, A. (2009) 'The "Neat Concept" of Sexual Citizenship: A Cautionary Tale for Human Rights Discourse', *Contemporary Politics*, 15(1): 73–85.

Woltersdorff, V. (2007) 'Neoliberalism and its Homophobic Discontents', *Interalia*, 2: 1–9.

Chapter 3

De-radicalising the rights claims of sexual subalterns through 'tolerance'

Ratna Kapur

I welcome the opportunity to have 'a conversation' with the other contributors to this collection that is not conducted along the binaries of the West–the Rest, the colonizer–the colonies, the powerful–the impoverished, the here–the there. It is the beginning of a conversation that happens in the unexplored spaces in between these dichotomies. In the arena of sexuality, where pleasure, desire and agency are assumed to be associated with the West, while the third world gendered and sexual subject is constructed almost exclusively through the lens of violence, victimization, impoverishment and cultural barbarism, these binaries are particularly acute. *Slumdog Millionaire*'s bouquet of Oscars in 2009, and similar accolades for Deepa Mehta's film *Water*[1] and Zana Briski's film *Born into Brothels*,[2] all reinforce the idea that while India has arrived on the global political and economic scene, Indians are still largely represented as slumdogs, and Indian women as victims waiting for rescue by their global feminist sisters. I want to challenge the monochromatic lens through which the 'Other', in this case, the sexual 'Other', is viewed along such rigid boundaries.

In the 1942 short story, *The Quilt*, by Ismat Chugtai, a young child witnesses her aunt Begum, a middle-aged sequestered housewife, engage in tempestuous relations of erotic pleasure with Rabbo her female maid-servant in an upper-class Muslim household (Chugtai trans. 1990). The tempest is played out beneath a billowing quilt whose motions are compared by the child to that of a convulsing elephant. Chugtai was charged with obscenity, which precipitated a trial that lasted for two years and triggered a major social and political controversy. The charge was ultimately dismissed. But, as is the effect of most obscenity trials, it left the stain of immorality and stigma on both the sexual speech, as well as the sexual conduct, that was impeached.

The story and the trial reveal how sexuality, in particular female homo-erotic pleasure, cannot be confined to narratives based on 'coming out', which is framed within the logic of visibility and the closet. It pushes one to ask what constitutes 'queer theory' within a post-colonial context? Is it another imposition of the West on the Rest (Tellis 2008: 40)?[3] Is there a queer scholarship that has emerged within the post-colonial context that produces an alternative or different reading of sexuality? While I find it helpful to draw on queer theory associated primarily with the Western academy to advance some of my arguments, I do not use it as the starting point of my analysis. Instead, I decentre queer theory, and stage my arguments by deploying post-colonial theory with a specific focus on the sexual subaltern subject. While such a theoretical location fits more comfortably with both my thinking and work, it simultaneously performs the task of holding back queer theory as the new imperium in legal scholarship.

The Quilt illustrates the complex layering of sexual subjectivities in post-colonial contexts that are not captured in a straightforward 'lesbian' or 'gay' reading.[4] In this chapter, I use the term 'sexual subaltern' to capture this complexity (Kapur 2005). In discussing the sexual subaltern's engagements with law, I draw on subaltern studies scholarship to provide a more complex articulation of the subject position of the sexual subaltern as well as the relationship between law and the sexual subject.

The chapter is divided into two parts. In the first part, I briefly discuss the proliferation of homoerotic imagery, literature and sex talk in the context of sexual subalterns in post-colonial India (John 2008: 560–566; Vanita and Kidwai 2000; Bose and Bhattacharyya 2007). The sexual subaltern has increasingly been accepted within the post-colonial space, and, in the process, has disrupted cultural and sexual norms in the public arena. This disruptive capacity provides space for a more productive and complex politics than can be captured in the notion of 'coming out', or through a focus on non-heteronormative performances.

While the public space has been more amenable to sexual subaltern claims and practices, any declarations of victory may be somewhat premature. In the second part of the chapter I draw attention to some of the contradictory results produced in the sexual subaltern's engagements with law, which has at times diminished the radical potential of sexual subaltern politics. While part of this loss can be attributed to the monochromatic lens through which law regulates the sexual subject, I focus on how there is a flattening out of the sexual subject produced and regulated in and through the discourse of toler-ance. In post-colonial India, tolerance is informed not only by dominant religious norms, most explicitly articulated by the Hindu right, but also nor-mative sexuality, which prescribes norms of behaviour and sexual conduct that are deeply implicated in the identity of the nation. I unpack the compet-ing understandings that structure the concept of tolerance, which has become central to shaping the way in which sexual subalterns are accepted in the public space. I argue that legal engagements have not resulted in the equal treatment of homosexuals and heterosexuals in law, nor have they necessarily been transformative or emancipating (Brown 2006). Instead, sexual sub-alterns are treated as a 'perversion' to be tolerated within the framework of liberal democracy and to deal with the excess that formal equality has failed to accommodate.

Who are sexual subalterns?

The subaltern studies project exposes how certain voices have been excluded from the dominant narratives and the telling of history. The project, as it emerged in India, was initially based on the position and location of the subaltern subject and of writing history from below (Guha 1982: vii–viii; Sarkar 1985). The project was grounded in historical materialism and a search for an essential peasant consciousness. In the 1980s, the project splintered into those who continued to write histories from 'below' and those who adopted a more Foucauldian analysis, focused on contesting the Eurocentric, metropolitan and bureaucratic systems of knowledge (Chakrabarty 1995, 2000). The new focus sought to challenge all traditions and disciplines defined within the logic and rationale of the Enlightenment project, including unmasking the universal subject of liberal rights discourse (Chakrabarty and Bhabha 2002; Lal 2002; Mignolo 2000; Beverley 1999; Bhabha 1994: 171–97).

The term sexual subaltern is at one level intended to capture the extraordinary range and diversity of the counter-heteronormative movement. In India, these counter-heteronormative movements have included a vast array of sexual identities: gay, lesbian, bisexual, transgendered, *kush*, queer, *hijra*, *kothis*, *panthis*, and many more (Sherry 2005; Khan 2001). They have also included sexual practices and behaviours such as adult and consensual pre-marital, extra-marital, non-marital, auto-erotic/masturbatory, promiscuous, and paid-for sex, as well as msm (men who have sex with men). It is this diversity of identities and range of practices that cannot be captured within the abbreviation LGBT (lesbian, gay, bisexual, transgender).

The subaltern subject is not simply a member of a minority group. While they are minorities insofar as they seek to claim formal equal rights, at a more radical level, this subject also brings about a conscious challenge to the dominant normative assumptions about the subject on which law is based. By virtue of her subaltern location and performance in a post-colonial space, the subaltern subject resists the assimilative gestures of the imperial and liberal project. She is a subject who is quite distinct from and unlike the sovereign autonomous subject of liberal rights discourse. The subaltern is a peripheral subject, deployed by post-colonial theory to unmask and challenge the dominant sexual, cultural, gendered and religious assumptions about the 'Other' that continue to inform the law. In the context of the sexual subaltern subject, the dominant sexual, cultural and familial arrangements that are imbricated in law are exposed and disrupted. In the process, new possibilities are produced for excluded subjects, and law is reconceived as a site of power rather than freedom and emancipation. It is this perspective that I bring to my analysis of the sexual subaltern's engagements with law in post-colonial India.

Sexual explosions in law and culture

In the 1990s, there was a significant amount of anxiety over the proliferating discourses on sexual desire and agency in India. The Hindu nationalists, who seek to reconstitute India as a Hindu state, routinely attacked heterosexual couples celebrating Valentine's Day or stores selling Valentine's Day cards. Police raided cybercafés for clients surfing for pornography, or to 'clean up' parks routinely visited by heterosexual couples in large urban centres. These panics continue to feed the sexual shakedowns in the contemporary period. Movements have emerged against public displays of affection, as well as increased surveillance of female sexual conduct in public (*India Today*: 30 January 2009; *Times of India*: 3 February 2009). The harassment on Valentine's Day continues, and homosexual men also continue to be persecuted by legal provisions that criminalize sodomy and other 'unnatural' sexual offences. The Hindu nationalists are key players in the movement to purge India and Indians of sexual agency and sex talk. Its foot soldiers continue to degrade sexuality and banish any overt expression of it outside the model of the good Hindu wife and heteronormative arrangements. In the process, it has projected outward expressions of this degraded sexuality onto its 'Others' (Bacchetta 1999).

Despite these efforts to contain, confine and cabin sexuality, there has been a proliferation of images of alternative sexuality conveying a sense that India has finally arrived. Some declare that the twenty-first century will be the Asian gay century! In the 2008 film *Dostana* (*Friendship*), even Bollywood took the issue of gay sexuality to another level, pulling it from the erratic margins of formula Hindi films, and served up a full-frontal gay performance complete with a 30-second lip-locking kiss involving the hottest superstars of the day – Abhishek Bhacchan and John Abrams.[5] More serious incarnations of the subject, with less beef and brawn, came in *My Brother Nikhil* (2005), a small-budget film sympathetically depicting the discrimination and homophobia experienced by an HIV patient in contemporary Indian society. In 1998, the diasporic film *Fire* rendered same-sex desire intelligible through the performance of queer femininity between two married women in the post-colonial domestic space (Gopinath 2005: 155). There have also been the unlimited subversive readings of the erotic spaces that occur even in the most nationalistic, heteronormative, gender-conforming Bollywood movies – and that too in the domestic arena (Gopinath 2005; Ghosh: Ch. 4, in this volume). These readings attest to the disruptive capacity of queer female desire to complicate the narrative by demolishing the masculinist fortifications and dominant sexual norms that structure the film. The narratives are exposed as being both amenable to queer readings that are momentarily at least subversive, as well as providing space for the recognition of female homoerotic desire.

Alongside the explosion in sexual imagery, there has been a simultaneous proliferation of rights talk in favour of greater sexual expression in public, as well as more heterogeneous sexual identities. In February 2009, the Delhi High Court stayed criminal proceedings against a young married hetero- sexual couple who were charged with obscenity for kissing in public. The Court held that such conduct amounted to nothing more than an 'expression of love' and did not fall within the scope of the obscenity provision of the Indian Penal Code, 1860 (IPC) (Garg 2009). Gay and lesbian groups have successfully challenged the scope of section 377 of the IPC, which makes unnatural sex of any kind illegal, including sodomy between consenting adults (Naz Foundation 2009).[6] The provision was inserted into the IPC by Lord Macaulay as part of the colonial project of regulating and 'cleaning up' native culture in the course of the colonial mission. The provision marked the convergence of colonial, cultural and scientific discourse, to produce a sub- ject where the sexual act was regarded as constitutive of the subject (Foucault 1979). Sodomy was the core identity of this subject who was driven by nothing other than sexual desire (Foucault 1978).

The contemporary use of section 377 has been limited to rare prosecutions for child sexual abuse, rather than to prosecute gay men. It has nevertheless been continuously used as a tool to harass gay men especially in the context of cruising (Peoples' Union for Civil Liberties 2003). The petitioners success- fully argued that the section should be narrowly construed to apply only to non-consenting sexual activity. The case constitutes what Bose has described as the 'eye of the sexuality storm in India' (Bose and Bhattacharyya 2007: xix).

All the forms of resistance discussed have been framed within the overarch- ing claim of human rights. Sex talk and sexual expression are predicated on a universal human rights foundation, and its claim to protect the rights of marginalized groups as well as non-conforming sexual expression. The chal- lenge to section 377 marks the moment when sexual rights claims can no longer be treated as distinct from the larger human rights struggle (ibid. xxix). The persistence of gay rights activists, the enormous publicity afforded to the subject of homosexuality through Bollywood, as well as the successful legal challenges to the sodomy law have shifted the goalposts on what constitutes good sex and bad sex (Rubin 1989: 267–319; Vance 1984: 1–27). It is no longer possible to contain or muzzle the gay subject. Eroticism is claiming a space in law and on the streets, and efforts to eliminate or incarcerate it are being seriously challenged as violations of human rights. In light of what appears to be an explosion of positive imagery through Bollywood and the proliferation of rights advocacy around issues of sexual identity and sexual behaviour, there seems little more to say on the matter. If it is now possible to be gay and *kush* (happy) in India, then surely homosexuals can give them- selves a pat on the back to have realized that which seemed so unrealizable only a decade ago. It's a gay party in India!

While there has been an amplification of voices for more sex and many types of sex, I still wonder if gays and lesbians are feeling more empowered, transformed or emancipated? Is the party premature? The question that arises is whether the court challenges, rights advocacy, civil dissidence and increased sex talk and imagery have actually furthered the cause of sexual subalterns in the direction of more rights or more freedom.

On closer analysis, these actions have not necessarily conferred additional rights on sexual subalterns. In the context of the Delhi High Court's decision upholding the challenge to section 377, the whittling down of the scope of the provision is to ensure that it is not used to prosecute sexually consenting adults. It is a call to tolerate consensual sexual conduct between homosexuals, rather than to confer the right to full, substantive equality. Yet this call for tolerance is a cause for concern, as it becomes a device for social and political control, rather than empowering the groups being tolerated.

Unpacking tolerance

Tolerance means different things to different people. In the context of the colonial encounter, tolerance was the glue that enabled civilizing missions and colonial adventures in the name of taming the barbarous other who was intolerant and uncivil. The colonial project legitimized its rule through the mechanism of tolerance. Tolerance has followed separate types of logic in the post-colonial period. In encounters with indigenous peoples in white-settler colonies, tolerance has taken the form of apologies and claims to reparation by indigenous aborigines such as in Australia. It has emerged in the context of European encounters, with the flow of immigrations from former colonies, and talk of immigration into racially insulated Europe (Brown 2006: 2). In the post-independence period in India, tolerance initially functioned to protect the rights of religious minorities and ensure their security in the immediate aftermath of partition and the process of consolidation of the identity of the modern Indian nation-state.[7] Tolerance has also been central in efforts at conflict resolution in ethnically inflamed societies, as well as in the context of the 'war on terror'.

In the following section, I analyse how tolerance is constituted in the contemporary moment in post-colonial India. I excavate the historical and politically discursive character of tolerance. Beginning with it as a religious norm that has been aggressively and most actively pursued by the Hindu right to advance its own anti-Muslim agenda, I then examine how proposals to expand the majoritarian religious moorings of tolerance, or adopt a more political conception of tolerance, are still unable to dislodge dominant understandings of culture or disrupt normative sexuality. I examine how the use of tolerance continues to inform the post-colonial present and the claims of sexual subalterns. In the context of the colonial encounter, tolerance is a device to deny full legal equality to the native while also managing their claims for greater recognition and empowerment. Tolerance becomes a way of reinforcing dominant norms, while at the same time sustaining an antagonistic posture towards difference and the continuing perception of that difference as threatening or toxic. This discursive aspect of tolerance challenges the normally benign understanding of tolerance as a universal transnational norm or tool to protect the weak against the strong.

Tolerance and the Hindu right

I turn first to the way in which tolerance has in fact been deployed in the context of managing religious minorities in India. The overwhelming view is that tolerance speaks to a protection of minorities against the majority. However, in the context of the emergence of the Hindu right, difference has become a foreign and dangerous identity. Sex workers, migrants, homosexuals and, most overtly, Muslims have become the target of the majoritarian politics of the right wing. And tolerance has become a mechanism for advancing their agenda.

Tolerance in the Indian context has had deeply religious moorings (Cossman and Kapur 2001). Dominant discourses of secularism have emphasized that the principle of tolerance is derived from the cultural traditions of Indian society – cultural traditions that more often than not are equated with Hindu traditions and Hinduism. Although this majoritarian and religious basis of tolerance has been made most explicit in the discourse of the Hindu right, it is also apparent in the constitutional discourse of secularism (Bhargava 1998; Baxi 1999: 211–33). Tolerance is held out by the courts as representing the pluralism of Indian society.[8] Unfortunately, time and again the unstated norm of the majority slips into judicial discourse. The very reason that Indian secularism is said to be different from the Western model lies in the concept of tolerance and the claim that historically, Indian society in general, and Hinduism in particular, has been tolerant of other religions. It has a historical and cultural grounding. It is this grounding that has been taken up by the forces of the Hindu right to develop tolerance in its own distinctive and aggressively nationalistic direction.

Tolerance has a vital place in a liberal democracy for it is the primary defence to assimilation. But to truly be of use to the minority community, tolerance needs to be delinked from its majoritarian and religious foundations – foundations that assert that only Hinduism can be truly tolerant because it does not proselytize. One way out of this dilemma would be to simply pluralize the cultural and religious traditions on which tolerance is based. Rather than emphasizing the exclusivity of Hinduism as a tolerant religion, this pluralizing strategy would search for the historical roots of tolerance in the multiplicity of India's religious traditions.

Such a strategy has been advocated by Ashis Nandy, who argues that secularism as a nineteenth-century import from Europe should be abandoned in favour of a 'tolerance that is religious', and a tolerance that is located 'outside the ideological grid of modernity' (1997: 321–44). In essence, he is arguing in favour of a return to pre-modern forms, uncontaminated by India's encounter with colonialism and modernity. Such an approach has two limitations. The first is that it runs the risks of nostalgic idealism and cultural essentialism – of searching for the elusive authenticity of religious and cultural traditions, of assuming that those traditions can be discovered rather than constructed and negotiated, and of reconstructing those traditions as static, immutable and monolithic. Second, a religious conception of tolerance does not extend beyond tolerance of religious difference. It is unlikely that religious tolerance could speak to the importance of tolerating those who think, act and live differently, if those differences were based on something other than religion. A religious conception of tolerance may not support an argument for tolerance towards sexual sub-groups. It is unclear that such a shift would help sexual subalterns, who may be accorded more space in the polity as members of different religious and cultural communities, but would still be governed by the dominant sexual, cultural, familial and sexual norms that inform tolerance. Such a shift is unlikely to tolerate sex workers or homosexuals, and may continue to encourage incarceration for homosexuality or denial of certain rights and benefits to sexual sub-groups to which heterosexuals are entitled. A principle of tolerance must be one that is up to the challenge, not only of promoting respect for difference along religious lines, but also along a range of other fault lines.

The infusion of religion into the discourse of tolerance needs to be a cause for concern for sexual minorities, and other excluded or marginalized groups. While the dominant understanding of tolerance in India is linked to religious majoritarianism, it is also simultaneously informed by dominant sexual, familial and cultural norms. There is evidence that for the Hindu right, tolerance is shaped by sexual and gender stereotypes that determine the line between those who are a part of Indian culture and society and those who are not. The Hindu right is increasingly defining tolerance according to its own terms. And these terms are partly based on an understanding of female sexuality as heterosexual, chaste, marital, obedient and pure (Sarkar 2001, 1996: 210–38). All other types of sex and sexual conduct that do not fall within this normative arrangement are penalized. Sexual minorities who think, act and live differently challenge dominant sexual and gender norms and remain ostracized in this conception of tolerance. They produce anxiety over the threat they pose to the identity of the nation-state, which resides partly in normative definitions of Indian womanhood and female sexuality (Puri 1999).

This anxiety was expressed in the government's stand in the High Court challenge to section 377, where it stated that Indian society was not as yet ready to extend toleration in the direction of sexual minorities (Naz Foundation 2009: para. 13). Similarly, in a petition filed in the Indian Supreme Court by Baba Ramdev, a popular practitioner of yoga and self-styled guru, seeking a stay of the High Court decision, he states that homosexuality is against Indian cultural values hand the institution of the family and threatens to bring about the collapse of the institution of marriage.[9] The appeal does not provide any space for tolerating this conduct but in fact argues in favour of a 'cure' through yoga (Swami Ramdev 2009: para. 5, dd. 2). It argues that too much of that which constitutes India's identity as separate and distinct (implicitly from the West) is at stake to allow the High Court judgment to stand.

Political conception of tolerance

The claim for greater space and freedom of sexual expression by sexual sub-alterns has been part of an effort to unhinge tolerance from its religious and majoritarian moorings. It is a strategy based on a concept of political tolerance, which acknowledges the irreversible mark that modernity has made on our times, and recognizes that a commitment to living together across differences has to be carved out of this modernity – not in opposition to it. In terms of legal and political discourse, tolerance is no longer derived from ancient, religious sources, but approached as a constitutional value in its own right. This political norm begins from the most basic premise of tolerance – accepting people and their practices despite our disagreements and disapproval. It means not only accepting differences, but accepting those differences that at some level we find unacceptable. It is a conception of tolerance that goes beyond the mere acceptance of different forms of worship or religious differences. It is a normative commitment to accepting a broad range of differences in beliefs, practices and ways of being made necessary by the pluralistic and fragmented world in which we live.

Partha Chatterjee has examined a political conception of tolerance, derived from his Foucauldian analysis of governance and some of the requirements it entails (1997: 345–79). He argues for a reconceptualization of the concept of tolerance as the basis for the recognition and accommodation of group rights in general, and minority religious rights in particular. Chatterjee reframes the kind of treatment that the dominant community will have to extend to subgroups, where tolerance means something more than the right to be different. It requires accepting 'that there will be political contexts where a group could insist on its right not to give reasons for doings things differently provided it explains itself adequately in its own chosen forum' (ibid. 375). He further proposes that cultural minorities will need to ensure that procedures exist through which they can 'publicly seek and obtain from its members consent for its practices . . .' (ibid. 376). In his vision, internal accountability becomes a prerequisite for extending the principle of toler-ance, and in turn, for accommodating a cultural minority's right to do things differently.

But this political conception of tolerance is also fraught with limitations. It may again end up foregrounding religious identity, and relinquishing too much autonomy to highly conservative, even orthodox communities to manage their own affairs without sufficient concern for tolerance within their own ranks. The safeguard in Chatterjee's vision rests in ensuring that there are mechanisms for democratic accountability within the community and respect for persons who differ from the norms within that community. He attempts to formulate a middle ground, 'a somewhere in between' universal principles and the recognition of difference (Chatterjee 1997). It is also difficult to imagine how Chatterjee's propositions could be translated into the legal domain. For example, would courts accept the principle of a right not to give reasons, given that the legal arena is all about giving reasonable argument? Could, or should, courts be called upon to adjudicate issues such as whether cultural minorities have met the minimal requirement of internal accountability? Would we not expect to encounter precisely the same problem of majoritarianism?

A more robust political conception of tolerance moves away from the thin version of tolerance based on mere visibility and the premise of accepting people and their practices despite disagreements and disapproval that is being pursued by sexual subalterns. Yet neither approach necessarily gets the sexual subject out of the trap of Indian culture and normative sexuality that informs dominant understandings of tolerance. There is no disruption of dominant sexual, familial or cultural norms as a result of accommodation through political conceptions of tolerance, which continue to exist untroubled. Indeed the gravitational pull of normative sexuality that informs tolerance can ultimately de-radicalize the subversive potential of rights claims by sexual subalterns.

Chatterjee's position seems to have simply shifted the nature of the problem – from one of tolerance to one of accountability and democracy. The prerequisites of some form of representation, which Chatterjee proposes, may take very different social and political contexts into account. However, his proposal does not completely break out of the imposition of some normative framework on cultural minorities; nor does it address the specific ways in which tolerance is imbricated in power and reinforces dominant sexual, gender and familial norms, together with religious majoritarianism.

Neither Chatterjee nor Nandy addresses the way in which the colonial encounter impacted the discourse of tolerance. Tolerance was one element in the civilizing mission of Empire. If the native could conform to the standards of civilization determined by the colonial power, and demonstrate his fealty to the Empire (the subject was invariably a 'he'), he would be entitled to specific rights and benefits. Yet the move to assimilate was never a complete one. Full legal equality could never be conferred, such as political autonomy, self-rule and governance. The native remained inferior, and cultural arguments, such as evidence of the barbaric treatment of the native women by native men, were deployed to justify the continuation of colonial rule (Sinha 2000). It is in the space between full legal equality and a complete denial of subjectivity that tolerance had a role to play. A subaltern reading of tolerance analyses the complex relationship established between the native and colonial power. It was partly shaped by the desire on the part of the colonized to return a voyeuristic gaze upon the colonial ruler, as well as the desire on the part of the colonial power to civilize and normalize the native subject. By returning the gaze, the native was able not only to expose the distinctions between superhumans, lesser humans and non-humans that informed the discourse of tolerance, but also to illuminate how tolerance was deployed to contain the native and to consolidate colonial rule.

Returning to my earlier discussion, as long as the discussion of tolerance is associated with religion, and freedom of conscience, tolerance appears to be coterminous with equality. It is at least a part of equality. However, a post-colonial analysis of tolerance reveals that tolerance can take shape as a supplement to equality. While claims to equality are intended to be based on a universal logic, tolerance becomes the tool for handling that difference that formal equality is unable to accommodate or address. Tolerance addresses the excess, that which is left out when formal equality is limited or shaped according to dominant norms, such as in the case of homosexuals. In the process, the axis of inclusion and exclusion along which the liberal ideal of equality operates is both exposed, as well as reproduced. The difference and otherness of that which is tolerated is reinscribed, while the regulatory function of tolerance remains hidden. Tolerance in this guise constitutes a compromise, as it permits membership into society, even though this acceptance is just barely able to contain its revulsion of the difference. Tolerance does not operate to dissolve or resolve the hatred (Brown 2006: 28). It simply depoliticizes the issue, while enabling the hatreds to continue to circulate in a more muted fashion.

Tolerance as power

As the question of tolerance in India has been so closely tied to religion, religious majoritarianism and the rights of religious minorities, there has been little scholarly attention over the regulatory and authoritative function of tolerance. As Brown has argued, tolerance no longer has a blessed status, but is revealed as operating as a tool of governance, power and subject production (2006: 10). While the call for tolerance that underscores the legal engagements of sexual subalterns plays an important role in reducing, if not altogether preventing harassment, incarceration, violence and abuse, it has also become an alternative to arguing in favour of full legal equality. The discussion reveals the different roles that tolerance plays, and its imbrication in power. It polices normative borders, while also obscuring the dominant sexual, familial and cultural norms that it sustains. The analysis helps to recast tolerance as a regulatory device that reorganises subjects and further legitimates the liberal project. Tolerance does not offer any vision of transformation, but becomes a substitute for justice, where the difference of the 'Other' is accommodated rather than her injury redressed.

The ruse of tolerance is that it obscures how tolerance emerges from a normative order. Tolerance casts itself as universal, depicts the object or group that is being tolerated as deviant and places it outside of the universal – a lower or inferior form of being. This discursive ruse masks the way in which power operates to produce the dichotomies between the universal and the particular, us and them, the same and the 'Other'. The role of tolerance in the production of heteronormativity and the sustaining of dominant cultural and sexual norms in its encounters with sexual difference remain eclipsed.

Tolerance nestles in with other depoliticizing discourses such as the market and neo-liberalism (ibid. 18). For example, while the explosion of 'gay imagery' and 'gay talk' in popular culture and the media is much in evidence in India, this should not necessarily be equated with greater freedom or politicization. Indeed, even the homosexual is vulnerable to further depoliti-cization through market rationality and the increasing saturation of all features of our lives with entrepreneurial and consumer discourse. In the Bollywood film *Dostana* the 'gay' performance is completely embedded in the market. The sexual subject is defined through his fancy convertibles, bikini babes and penthouse luxury in the heart of Miami. One could read the arrival of the 'gay Indian' as thoroughly constituted by the neoliberal endeavour.

The proliferation of affirmative images and rights talk in India has not necessarily produced an emancipated homosexual subject. Rather this subject is tethered to a specific understanding of tolerance within the post-colonial liberal, democratic context of India. It is a notion of tolerance that does not resolve existing animosities or hatreds. The move towards tolerance is an extension of recognition of the sexual subaltern on terms and in a manner that the state decides. The power, authority and normativity that inform tolerance are concealed or disguised. While there is an appearance of magna-nimity on the part of the majority or the state, in fact the extension of tolerance constitutes a way in which to sustain dominant sexual, familial and cultural norms.

The attempt to move away from a religious-based conception of tolerance, and the appeal to a political conception of tolerance, has not necessarily resulted in the equal treatment of homosexuals and heterosexuals in law. Instead, it has reinforced the difference rather than emancipated it. It is an understanding of tolerance that is informed by the history of the colonial encounter. The native was to be tolerated as incapable of changing. Those who could change did not require tolerance. The homosexual, historically reviled and rejected, can no longer be contained in the contemporary period. Tolerance is therefore deployed to accommodate this subject, but on terms where the dominant cultural, sexual and familial norms remain undisturbed.

Conclusion

The recognition of homosexuality necessarily involves the creation of at least some space that has already challenged the existing heteronormative order. These entry points have been created by an array of controversies, such as around the screening of the film *Fire*, the legal challenge to kissing couples in the public space, or the constitutional challenge to the ban against bar dancing in the western state of Maharasthra.[10] The court decision to reduce the scope of application of section 377 of the IPC was able to build on the wedge already driven into the heteronormative order to continue pushing the boundary between good sex and bad sex.

In India, there is a sense that homosexuals are becoming more empowered through a social justice project being pursued successfully in the name of rights and freedom. Gay and lesbian groups have been able to centre the rights of sexually marginalized groups and identities. Despite these successes, they have not been able to make much headway in the area of empowerment or liberation. As argued, this is partly because legal claims have been largely framed within the discourse of tolerance. While the Hindu right pursues a religious conception of tolerance that is framed by an approach to Indian culture which expunges sexual contaminants, the pursuit of a more expanded religious-based conception of tolerance or political tolerance does not necessarily ensure a more liberating space for sexual subalterns.

While there is indeed a proliferation of space for sexual identities to express themselves, this space is being produced in and through the liberal norm of tolerance, which performs a regulatory function at a time when it is no longer possible to exclude or efface totally the sexual 'Other' with ease. The accommodation of many and more sexualities is a somewhat hollow victory in terms of the freedom that law ostensibly offers. While sexual subalterns are pursuing tolerance as one way to counter the harassment, violence and abuse that they experience, there is a competing and dominant version of tolerance based on religious majoritarianism, coupled with dominant sexual and cultural norms that ultimately holds sway. While it may no longer be possible to incarcerate homosexuals with impunity or to penalize non-heteronormative sexual conduct, tolerance functions as a technique of marginalization and regulation that leaves intact the broader ideological and normative framework within which it operates.

The result is neither complete appropriation nor subversion of tolerance. Both are operating at one and the same time to produce a productive tension (Butler 1993: 128). At one level, the normalizing potential of law is brought about through the dominant sexual and cultural norms that inform tolerance, sacrificing the erotic in the process. At the same time, the sexual subaltern is at times appropriating the terms of domination and remaking these terms (ibid. 137). She is unmasking what is sustained by law, and producing a deeper contest over the meaning of tolerance. In the end, it is perhaps this tension that becomes the space for politics and more power, as opposed to more freedom.

Notes

1 This film won an Oscar nomination in 2007.
2 This film won the Oscar for best documentary in 2005.
3 Compare Nicholas Bamforth's argument in relation to comparative legal materials, in this volume (Ch. 10).
4 I acknowledge that there are distinctions drawn between LGBT scholarship and the field that constitutes queer theory (Butler 1993; Rubin 1989: 267–319; Sedgwick 1990). There are also some moves in post-colonial scholarship in India to distinguish queer theory from LGBT scholarship (Narain 2007). However, these distinctions are often blurred in legal advocacy as well as by those citing the scholarship. The argument remains that both are seen to emanate primarily from 'the West', and neither captures the nuances and complexities of the post-colonial contexts and histories within which the sexual subaltern has emerged.
5 Compare Shohini Ghosh's analysis of such developments, in this volume (Ch. 4).
6 Section 377 states as follows:

> *Unnatural sexual offences:* Whoever voluntarily has carnal intercourse against the order of nature with any man, woman or animal, shall be punished with imprisonment . . . Which may extend to ten years, and shall also be liable to fine.
>   Explanation – Penetration is sufficient to constitute the carnal intercourse necessary to the offence described in this section.

The provision was held not to apply to consenting adult sexual relations in *Naz Foundation v. Government of NCT of Delhi and Others*, Delhi High Court, 2 July 2009 (MANU/DE/0869/2009).
7 The partition of British India in 1947 led to the creation of the separate states of India and Pakistan. Apart from producing one of the biggest refugee movements in history, bloody riots on a large scale also took place between Hindus and Muslims during the period of separation. In 1971, a further partition occurred when East Pakistan seceded from Pakistan and became Bangladesh.
8 *M. Ismail Faruqui v. UOI* (1994) 6 Supreme Court Cases 360 (discussing the meaning of secularism and tolerance in the context of a case challenging the attempt to acquisition land for the purpose of constructing a temple to god Ram in the same place where a sixteenth-century mosque, the Babri Masjid, stood).
9 *Swami Ramdev v. Naz Foundation and Others*, Special Leave Petition, Supreme Court of India, 8 July 2009, paras. 5(a), (h), (i), (t), (u), (cc), (dd.2).
10 *Indian Hotel & Restaurants Ass'n (AHAR) v. State of Maharashtra* (Bombay High Court, 2006).

References

Bacchetta, P. (1999) 'When the (Hindu) Nation Exiles its Queers', *Social Text*, 17(4): 141–66.
Baxi, U. (1999) 'The Constitutional Discourse on Secularism', in U. Baxi, A. Jacob and J. Singh (eds.) *Reconstructing the Republic*, Delhi: Har-Anand Publications.

Beverley, J. (1999) *Subalternity and Representations: Arguments in Cultural Theory*, Durham, NC: Duke University Press.

Bhabha, H. (1994) *The Location of Culture*, London: Routledge.

Bhargava, R. (ed.) (1998) *Secularism and Its Critics*, Delhi: Oxford University Press.

Bose, B. and Bhattacharyya, S. (eds.) (2007) *The Phobic and the Erotic: The Politics of Sexualities in Contemporary India*, Calcutta: Seagull.

Brown, W. (2006) *Regulating Aversion: Tolerance in the Age of Identity and Empire*, Princeton, NJ: Princeton University Press.

Butler, J. (1993) *Bodies That Matter: On the Discursive Limits of 'Sex'*, New York, NY: Routledge.

Chakrabarty, D. (1995) 'Radical Histories and Question of Enlightenment Rationalism: Some Recent Critiques of Subaltern Studies', *Economic and Political Weekly*, 30(14): 751–9; reprinted in V. Chaturvedi (ed.) (2000) *Mapping Subaltern Studies and the Postcolonial*, London: Verso.

—— (2000) *Provincializing Europe*, Princeton, NJ: Princeton University Press.

—— and Bhabha, H. (2002) *Habitations in Modernity: Essays in the Wake of Subaltern Studies*, Chicago, IL: University of Chicago Press.

Chatterjee, P. (1997) 'Secularism and Toleration', in R. Bhargava (ed.) *Secularism and its Critics*, New Delhi: Oxford University Press.

Chugtai, I. (1990) *The Quilt and Other Short Stories* (trans.) T. Naquvi and S. Hameed, Delhi: Kali for Women.

Cossman, B. and Kapur, R. (2001 reprint) *Secularism's Last Sigh? Hindutva and the (Mis)Rule of Law*, Delhi: Oxford University Press.

Foucault, M. (1978) *The History of Sexuality, Volume 1: An Introduction*, New York, NY: New York Vintage.

—— (1979) *Discipline and Punish: The Birth of the Prison* (trans.) A. Sheriden, New York, NY: Vintage.

Garg, A. (2009) 'Kissing in Public by Married Couples not Obscene', *Times of India*, 2 February. Online: <www.indiatimes.com/articleshow/msid-4066941,prtpage-1.cms> (accessed 15 April 2009).

Gopinath, G. (2005) *Impossible Desires: Queer Diasporas and South Asian Public Cultures*, Durham, NC: Duke University Press.

Guha, R. (ed.) (1982) *Subaltern Studies I: Writings on South Asian History and Society*, Delhi: Oxford University Press.

India Today (2009) 'Pub culture against Indian ethos, must stop: Ramdoss', 30 January. Online: <http://indiatoday.intoday.in/index.php?option=com_content&task=view&id=26843&sectionid=4&secid=0> (accessed 9 June 2009).

John, M. (2008) *Women's Studies in India: A Reader*, New Delhi: Penguin Books.

Kapur, R. (2005) *Erotic Justice: Law and the New Politics of Postcolonialism*, London: Cavendish.

Khan, S. (2001) 'Culture, Sexualities, and Identities: Men Who Have Sex with Men in India', *Journal of Homosexuality*, 40(3 & 4): 99–115.

Lal, V. (2002) *Empire and Knowledge: Culture and Plurality in the Global Economy*, Sterling, VA: Pluto Press.

Mignolo, W. (2000) *Local Histories/Global Designs*, Princeton, NJ: Princeton University Press.

Nandy, A. (1997) 'The Politics of Secularism and the Recovery of Religious Tolerance', in R. Bhargava (ed.) *Secularism and Its Critics*, New Delhi: Oxford University Press.

Narain, A. (2007) 'Queer Journey', *Indian Journal of Gender Studies*, 14(1): 61–71.

Peoples' Union for Civil Liberties (2003) *Report on Human Rights Violations Against Sexual Minorities.* Online: <http://www.pucl.org/Topics/Gender/2003/sexual-minorities.htm> (accessed 9 June, 2009).

Puri, P. (1999) *Women, Body, Desire in Post-Colonial India: Narratives of Gender and Sexuality*, New York, NY: Routledge

Rubin, G (1989) 'Thinking Sex: Notes for a Radical Theory of the Politics of Sexuality', in C. Vance (ed.) *Pleasure and Danger: Exploring Female Sexuality*, reprint, Boston, MA: Routledge.

Sarkar, S. (1985) *A Critique of Colonial India*, Calcutta: Papyrus.

Sarkar, T. (1996) 'Colonial Lawmaking and Lives/Deaths of Indian Women: Different Readings of Law and Community', in R. Kapur (ed.) *Feminist Terrains in Legal Domains: Interdisciplinary Essays on Woman and Law*, New Delhi: Kali for Women.

—— (2001) *Hindu Wife and Hindu Nation*, New Delhi: Permanent Black

Sedgwick, E. (1990) *Epistemology of the Closet*, Berkeley, CA: University of California Press.

Sherry, J. (2005) *Social Work Practice and Men Who Have Sex with Men*, New Delhi, Thousand Oaks, London: Sage Publications.

Sinha, M (ed.) (2000) *Kathernie Mayo: Mother India: Selection from the Controversial 1927 Text*, Ann Arbor, MI: University of Michigan Press.

Tellis, A. (2008) 'The Revolution Will Not be Funded', *Himal Southasian*, March: 39–41.

Times of India (2009). 'Muthalik's Sene turns wrath on Valentine's Day', 3 February. Online: <http://timesofindia.indiatimes.com/articleshow/msid-4068955,prtpage-1.cms> (accessed 15 April 2009).

Vance, C. (1984) 'Pleasure and Danger: Toward a Politics of Sexuality', in C. Vance (ed.) *Pleasure and Danger: Exploring Female Sexuality*, reprint, Boston, MA: Routledge.

Vanita, R, and Kidwai, S. (eds.) (2000) *Same Sex Love in India*, New York, NY: St. Martin's Press.

Part 2

Representation

Chapter 4

Bollywood cinema and queer sexualities

Shohini Ghosh

It may not be inaccurate to suggest that at the close of the twentieth century in India, the media including television, radio, print and cinema, emerged as an authoritative archive of contemporary cultural sensibilities. The same moment also witnessed an efflorescence and rapid circulation of speech and representation on issues of sex and sexuality. In this chapter, I look at how cinema becomes available to us as a site of competing discourses around sexuality, thereby providing us perceptive, even controversial, insights into the articulation of desire. For the purposes of this chapter, I will look at the expansive landscape of Bombay cinema (or Bollywood as it is now popularly called), in an attempt to understand how it may have archived our journeys of desire.[1]

Bombay cinema as an archive of sexuality

India is the largest film-producing country in the world and has recorded a steady growth over the years (PriceWaterhouseCoopers and FICCI 2007).[2] Bombay cinema, whose phenomenal popularity with audiences cuts across class, caste, ethnicity, religion, region, linguistic groups, gender and sexual orientation, commands a 40 per cent share in the Indian market, while the rest is dominated by regional language cinema. In the last two decades, 'Bollywood' has established a global presence but the majority of its audience still comprises people of South Asian origins. The difficulty of 'crossing over' to an international audience may well be attributed to Bombay cinema's rather unique cinematic style. For many years, Bombay cinema's spectacular popular success was considered to be incompatible with recognition as 'serious cinema'. It was largely perceived to be escapist, exaggerated and artificial. For example, writer Andrew Robinson approvingly quoted film critic Chidananda Das's description of Bombay cinema as the:

> [c]inema of the lumpen proletariat, the unemployed half-educated or uneducated vagrant youth, nouveau riche with more money than educa-tion, the hoarder, the black marketeer, the children and adolescents

brought up on the pavements of large cities living in the shadow of high-rise [buildings].

(1982: 16–18)

A serious reassessment of Bombay cinema began only in the late 1980s. In 1989 psychoanalyst Sudhir Kakkar wrote that when 'dogmatic rationalists dismiss [Bombay] films as unrealistic and complain that their plots lack credibility and their characters stretch the limits of the believable, this condescending judgement is usually based on a restricted vision of reality'. He argued that 'to limit and reduce the real to that which can be demonstrated as factual is to exclude the domain of the psychologically real . . .'. On the contrary, he insisted, the very tropes of artificiality, including the song and dance sequences provide greater space for the expression of subjectivity than a rigid fidelity to 'realism'. The cinematic universe propelled by desire and imagination, he says, 'provides us with an alternative world where we can continue our longstanding quarrel with reality' (Kakkar 1989: 30).

Song and dance sequences have been perhaps the most popular and distinctive trope of Bombay cinema. These ubiquitous sequences are elaborately staged fantasies that allow for the free play of conscious and unconscious desires. To this end, song and dance sequences have frequently provided space for the play of forbidden love and transgressive desires. The impossible jumps in space, time and situations are key to Bombay cinema's affinity to dreams and fantasies. By disrupting the linear movement of storytelling, song sequences facilitate a departure from and a return to the narrative. As powerful vehicles of desire, songs and dances often play out Bakhtin's (1984) notion of the carnivalesque. For Bakhtin, the carnival is an expression of people's 'second life' that shatters, symbolically at least, all oppressive hierarchies. The transporting into art of the spirit of popular festivities allows people a brief entry into a symbolic sphere of utopian freedom. It is 'a joyful affirmation of change, a dress rehearsal for utopia' (Shohat and Stam 1994: 306; see also Stam 1989: 122–56) that allows those on the margins to move to the centre of the narrative.[3] For this reason, song and dance sequences allow female protagonists a centrality that film narratives usually deny them. It is with this understanding of cinema as a fantasmatic space that I will attempt to illustrate how Bombay cinema has functioned as an archive of sexual subjectivities.

Queering the popular media

The 1990s witnessed a radical restructuring of India's urban mediascape. The liberalization of the economy, globalizing imperatives, the rapid proliferation of satellite television channels, new media and telecommunications technologies all catalyzed wide-ranging cultural transformations. The rise of the Hindu right during the period, accompanied by an aggressive cultural nationalism, contributed to creating a censorious climate. The increasing space devoted to expressions of sex and sexuality in the print and electronic media fuelled public anxieties. The efflorescence of sexual speech, the very source of public anxieties, was inspiring for those who had little to gain from the tired aspirations of heteronormativity. Just as dissident speech around heterosexuality challenged its compulsory location within marriage and monogamy, queer sexuality challenged heterosexuality itself. This discursive conversation found space on film, television, print, cyberspace, real conversations and tentative whispers.

The 'coming out' of cinematic queerness at the turn of the new millennium gathered force as film and queer studies began to receive scholarly attention. The emergence of queer studies facilitated a revisiting of canonical and marginal texts.

The changing contours of the 1990s mediascape were accompanied by representational shifts and disruptions in the narratives of Bombay cinema. Male and female protagonists no longer found themselves confronted with predictable moral choices, instead they were caught in a world of moral flux and ambiguity. In a clear disruption with the past, the female protagonist began to reconcile in her character the persona of the vamp and the heroine. The moral binaries of good–bad, moral–immoral no longer defined the worlds of the heroine (good woman) and the vamp (bad woman). I have argued elsewhere that the moral panics of the 1990s were actually anxieties around the shifting moral framework around women's sexuality (Ghosh 1999).

Public anxieties notwithstanding, the print and electronic media continued to create spaces for diverse articulations of genders and sexualities. For the first time, female bonding and suggestions of queerness began emerging in the world of representation. In the 1990s television also foregrounded a theme that was underrepresented in pre-1990s films and television – female friendship and female bonding. Television serials like *Adhikar* (Rights), *Mujhe Chand Chahiye* (I Want the Moon), *Kabhi Kabhi* (Once in A While) and *Hasratein* (Desires) depicted female friendships of varying intensity. In *Mujhe Chand Chahiye*, a young girl falls in love with a woman teacher.[4] One of the longest-running and critically acclaimed serials, *Adhikar*, revolves around the relationship between a Muslim woman, Shama, and a Hindu woman, Amita. Their male partners notwithstanding, the relationship between the two women remains the most privileged. In one episode, a crisis is precipitated when Amita's boyfriend, Narendra, jealously accuses her of loving Shama more than she loves him. In another episode, an anguished Amita tells her father that she and Shama are one and inseparable.

The women are not oblivious to their mutual attraction, as is evident from a sequence in the 23rd episode. This sequence is located in Shama's marital home after Amita has testified confidently in a rape trial. The sequence begins with Amita and Shama gazing into each other's eyes. Amita raises her mouth and blows a kiss to a delighted Shama. The conversation proceeds as follows:

Shama: You are unmatched. Only you could have said what you did in that crowded courtroom. When I look at you, I wonder – what am I? I am probably beautiful, my complexion is fair – what else do I have? But look at you – I so feel like kissing you.

Amita: Don't! You will spoil me. Narendra has already kissed me.

Shama: What? You shameless woman . . .

Amita: Why shameless? If he doesn't kiss me on such an occasion . . .

Shama: What nonsense you speak . . .

Amita: Even when I speak nonsense, I speak the truth. Really – if I were a man, I swear, I would have married you.

Shama: [laughing] Earlier, I only suspected it but now it's confirmed.

Amita: What?

Shama: That you are not a woman. There is nothing womanlike in you. There is a man inside you.

Amita: [delighted] Wah! How well you have spoken. That's precisely the point, my friend. You have described me absolutely right. Now, what prize should I give you? Should I kiss you? [Leans over and kisses her on her lips]

Amita: There, I've kissed you.

Shama: [Happy and laughing] You've polluted me!

Amita: Pollution is part of our religion – not yours. You people drink from the same cup.

Shama: I don't want to drink from everyone's cup.

Amita: Not everyone – just two! [Holds up two fingers.]

Shama: [amused] Two?

Amita: Yes. First it was only me. [Your husband] arrived much later.

Shama: [Amused, looks toward the door of the room to see if anyone has heard]: Idiot! You don't care about your own reputation. At least care about mine. [She gets up and shuts the door. Returns and sits in front of Amita.] What would have happened if someone had heard?[5]

The first major public debate around queer sexuality was triggered by the release of Deepa Mehta's *Fire* (1998) about two married sisters-in-law in a Hindu middle-class family, who fall in love with each other. Starring well-known actress Shabana Azmi and debutante Nandita Das, the theatrical release of *Fire* was accompanied by widely exhibited posters wherein the lesbian lovers occupied the same visual space that had conventionally belonged to heterosexual lovers. Two weeks after the film was released, the Hindu right went on a rampage against the film. They ransacked cinema halls, destroyed property and accused the film of endangering 'Indian culture' and the institution of marriage.

The Hindu right's violent offensive against *Fire* met with counter-protests from feminists, artists, film-makers, human rights activist and other members of the civil society thereby precipitating the first major public debate in India on queer sexuality. Circulated extensively through the media, this debate saw the emergence of a new constellation of interlocutors – the self-identified queer. Fortuitously, Nishit Saran's autoethnographic documentary *Summer in My Veins* (1998) made its timely debut. Using an informal, home-video style, the film records Nishit's coming out to his mother. It was a reply, as it were, to the Hindu right's insistence that homosexuals did not exist in India.

Fire is a significant film because it places queer sexuality at the centre of the narrative. Most importantly, by explicitly crossing the line between female bonding and female homosexuality it allows a new interpretative strategy to come into play. Mundane homosocial activities like cooking together, hanging up clothes to dry, oiling each other's hair or a foot massage become invested with sexual and erotic energy. No longer can it be assumed that things are as 'straight' as they *appear* to be. Consequently, an interpretative strategy commonly used by queer subcultures enters public spectatorial practices thereby opening older texts to retrospective queering. Not only do we learn to see the queer, we learn to see queerly.[6]

Retrospectively queering Bombay cinema

An exercise in 'retrospective queering' would reveal that while homosexuality was rarely addressed explicitly, many films bore the markers of queer suggestions. In my earlier work, I maintained that perhaps one reason why Bombay cinema has always had a special attraction for queer subcultures is because it privileges romantic love as an exalted emotion (Ghosh 2002). While explicit depictions of homosexual love have been absent except in minor sub-plots or comic relief, Bombay cinema has had a long-standing tradition of male friendship films. These films about intense friendship and fierce loyalties between two male friends can be read as being connotative of homoerotic love. Homoeroticism is suggested through overlapping boundaries between love and friendship.

In *Namak Haram* (The Traitor, 1973), a story of passionate male friendship, one protagonist declares: 'Without friendship there is no love. Without love there is no friendship'. In a popular song from *Dosti* (Friendship, 1964), another buddy melodrama, love and friendship are invoked as inseparable siblings. Moreover, since Bombay cinema rarely represents romance through sexual explicitness, the cinematic tropes deployed to represent love are similar, even identical, to those depicting friendship. *Dosti* is the story of love between two poor and physically disabled young men who live and struggle together in the city. This story of passionate friendship is narrated through established tropes of romance, separation and eventual reconciliation extrapolated directly from the conventions of heterosexual love in popular cinema. As I have suggested elsewhere, *Dosti* can be read as addressing the

issue of homosexuality through the deployment of disability as a metaphor for difference (ibid.).[7] Similarly, *Anand* (Joy, 1970) places two men in
the diagetic space conventionally occupied by heterosexual couples. *Namak
Haram* and *Anand* are parables of intense love and eventual loss where,
at the end of the film, one man dies in the arms of the other. In both
films, the men have heterosexual love interests (either in the past or in
the present) but these remain resolutely marginal to the narrative of male
friendship.

Heterosexual involvement notwithstanding, men choose other men as
their most important partners in films like *Sholay* (Embers, 1975), *Anurodh*
(Request, 1977), *Yaraana* (Friendship, 1981), *Naam* (The Name, 1986), *Main
Khilari, Tu Anari* (I Am an Expert, You're an Amateur, 1994) and *Dosti:
Friendship Forever* (2005). Bombay Cinema's most successful blockbuster
Sholay revolves around the friendship of two men. While both men have
heterosexual love interests their most intense bonding is with each other.
In one sequence, one friend sends the other to fix his match with a village
woman who has taken his fancy. The friend negotiates with the woman's
maternal aunt ('Mausi') and the conversations proceeds as follows:

Mausi: What kind of family does he come from? I need to find out.
          What kind of man is he? And what does he earn?
Jai: As far as income is concerned . . . well, once he has a family he
          will start earning.
Mausi: You mean he has no income?
Jai: When did I say that, Mausi? Now look . . . no one can win every
          day, you see . . . so sometimes he loses.
Mausi: Loses?
Jai: Gambling is like that. What can I say?
Mausi: Is he a gambler?
Jai: No, no, Mausi . . . what are you saying? He is a straightforward,
          honest man. But when one drinks, one does lose one's sense of
          good and bad.
Mausi: He's a gambler, he's an alcoholic, yet you continue to say he's a
          nice man.
Jai: You don't know Veeru. He's a simple and honest man. Just let
          him marry Basanti and you will see, once he is married he will
          stop visiting the courtesan.
Mausi: That's all that was left. So he visits a courtesan as well?
Jai: So what's wrong with that? Even kings and emperors used to
          visit courtesans.
Mausi: I see! Now will you tell me what lineage your meritorious friend
          descends from?
Jai: As soon as we get to know, we will let you know, Mausi.
          [Pause]. Should I consider the proposal accepted?

Understandably, Mausi drives Jai away. This comic sequence is commonly read as a clever manoeuvre to subvert a hasty wedlock. However, it can also be read as one in which the relationship between the two men is protected from any permanent heterosexual intrusion.

In popular cinema, love between women has not enjoyed the same narrative centrality as love between men. Female bonding, while appearing around the margins, has almost always lacked the vitality of male bonding. Female homoeroticism appeared fleetingly in films like *Razia Sultan* (Queen Razia, 1983), *Mere Mehboob* (My Beloved, 1963), *Humjoli* (Beloved Friend, 1970) and *Yeh Aag Kab Bujhegi* (When Will this Fire Be Quenched? 1991) and more self-consciously in Shyam Benegal's *Mandi* (Brothel, 1983) but rarely did it become central to the narrative. The most obvious reason for this lack is the male centeredness of popular cinema's narratives. Barring genres that privilege the female protagonist, such as the courtesan genre, women never enjoyed the same central significance that male protagonists did. Once again, it was the 1990s that self-consciously inaugurated representations of female bonding.[8]

False appearances and mistaken identities

Radical ideas have frequently emerged first in the realm of independent films before making their way into mainstream cinema. For instance, it was Riyad Wadia's experimental film *BomGay* (1996) that inaugurated queer-identified films in India. Starring the now-popular star Rahul Bose, *BomGay*, a highly stylized avant-garde film, structured around six poems by R. Raj Rao, circulated widely in queer circles and international film festivals. His next film, *A Mermaid Called Aida*, was a portrait of well-known transsexual Aida Banaji.

In the early 1990s, the films of Pratibha Parmar, a UK-based film-maker of Indian origin, exerted considerable influence on the emergent gay and lesbian movement in India. From the mid-1980s, Parmar started making films about queer South Asian people and concerns. *Khush* (1991), a 24-minute documentary exploring queer South Asian identities, won innumerable awards and is now a cult classic. She made a diverse range of films including *Sari Red* (1988), a video poem about the violence faced by South Asian women, and *Flesh and Paper* (1990), an experimental film on lesbian writer Suniti Namjoshi. The telecast of *Flesh and Paper* inaugurated the first occasion for a sari-clad woman to talk about being Asian and lesbian on UK prime-time TV. Parmar then made *A Place of Rage* (1991) about the struggles and achievement of African-American women, starring Angela Davis, June Jordan and Alice Walker, followed by *Double the Trouble Twice the Fun* (1992) about gay people with disability, featuring writer Firdous Kanga. In 1996, she made *Jodie* about actress Jodie Foster's transatlantic status as a gay icon. Almost single-handedly Parmar traversed a wide range of formalist devices and styles to address the many concerns of South Asian queers in the diaspora. Working both from the margins and the centre, Parmar introduced non-mainstream ideas into the mainstream. Her first feature film, titled *Nina's Heavenly Delights* (2006), is about a Scottish-Indian woman struggling to retain a family restaurant. In this self-confident and cheerful film, queer identities are not a 'problem' but a usual part of everyday life. Queerness in the film is as ubiquitous, sensual and pleasurable as the food that Nina so passionately prepares.

Film texts and television narratives are always imbricated within the discursive universe within which they are born. At the start of the new millennium, the public discussion around queer sexuality became fraught. In 2001, a petition was filed in the Delhi High court asking for the decriminalization of homosexuality. In 2003, the government argued against decriminalization, stating that Indian society's disapproval of homosexuality was strong enough to justify it being treated as a criminal offence even where adults indulge in it in private. Subsequently, the Supreme Court instructed the government to reconsider the constitutional validity of the matter. In a landmark judgment delivered on 2 July 2009, the Delhi High Court decriminalized homosexuality. The judgment received widespread appreciation across the country but also met with strong criticism from small but vocal quarters. The public continues to be split on the issue as the arguments next get heard before the Supreme Court.

As queer sexuality becomes impossible to elide or overlook at the start of the new millennium, two new currents begin to emerge. The first is the beginnings of a new queer cinema that displaces conventional cinematic codes of masculinity and femininity. Inspired by independent film movements and emergent sexual politics, films such as *Shabnam Mausi* (Shabnam Aunty, Yogesh Bhardwaj, 2005) and *My Brother Nikhil* (Onir, 2005) are bold incursions into queer lives. Inspired by an actual story, *Shabnam Mausi* is the story of a hijra who goes onto to win the elections to become a member of the state legislative assembly.[9] *My Brother Nikhil* is about state swimming champion Nikhil Kapoor's (Sanjay Suri) painful marginalization as he tests positive for HIV. Both films broke new ground by featuring queer protagonists and reimagining new gender and sexual identities, plunging heterosexual masculinity into a state of profound flux, thereby reshaping conventional notions of manhood and male desire.

The second, and more predominant, current signals the emergence of an ambivalent narrative strategy that invokes queer desires through a simultaneous address to the erotic and the phobic. Signalling the public dilemma around emergent sexualities, the latter approach, as I have suggested elsewhere, is inaugurated by Gurinder Chaddha's *Bend It Like Beckham* (2002). Released in both Hindi and English all over India, the film features Jaswinder (Parminder Nagra) and Juliet alias Jules (Keira Knightly) as football buddies whose gestures of buddy bonding and passionate fights (over the attentions of a male football coach) create much confusion in their respective families. Parminder's family (Indians settled in Britain) mistake Jules for a boy and raise hell. The matter is laid to rest when the 'boy' in question turns out to be a girl! Meanwhile, Juliet's mother is hysterical because she is convinced that her daughter is a lesbian. 'I am not blaming you', she tells her husband and Juliet's indulgent father, 'but it is the football'. Parminder's family, on the other hand, is blissfully oblivious to the possibility of homosexuality. When Juliet's angry mother hurls the word 'lesbian' at Parminder during a family wedding, an elderly aunt says, 'Lesbian? But she's born in March. I thought she's Piscean!'. Another adds, 'She's not Lebanese, she's Punjabi'.

The mistaken sexual identities of the two women, and the reaction of their respective families, account for much of the humour in the film. Yet the film is careful not to blur the lines between homosocial bonding and homoeroticism.[10] Consequently, sexual ambiguity is displaced in favour of unambiguous straightness on the part of the two women. The suggestion seems to be that contrary to all appearances, these smart, masculine women playing a butch game are actually *femmes*. An irate Juliet tells her mother: 'Just because I wear trackkies and play sports does not make me a lesbian'.

In *Bend It Like Beckham*, it is the homophobic mother's 'misreading' that precipitates the comedy of errors. The trope of the homophobe 'sighting' the queer gets repeated in several Bombay films but most notably in *Kal Ho Na Ho* (Tomorrow May Never Come, 2004) by Nikhil Advani. A triangular love story involving two men and one woman, the film plays self-consciously on the slippage between friendship and eroticism. However, it also retains ambivalence about homosexuality by introducing homophobia as a possible (perhaps even legitimate) response through the figure of Kantaben, a disapproving and paranoid housekeeper. The horrified Kanataben is convinced that the two men (played by Saif Ali Khan and Shah Rukh Khan) are lovers. Once again, the 'misreading' hinges on the idea of false appearances and mistaken identities. In one sequence, the character played by Saif jumps up to answer the phone when Shah Rukh tries to restrain him by holding him from the back. Kantaben enters the room to find one man clinging to the posterior of the one who shouts, 'Give it to me . . . I want it . . .'. Predictably, the horrified woman flees the room.[11] Similarly, the homophobic sexologist in *Masti* (Fun and Games, Indra Kumar, 2004) is scandalized by a series of queer misreadings. Since the misreadings hinge on the idea of false appearances and mistaken identities, the motivation for laughter remains resolutely ambiguous. Are we laughing at homophobia? Or at homosexuality? While the text allows viewers to occupy a variety of reading positions, it is worth noting that it is the homophobe who becomes the interpreter of 'queer readings'.

In June 2004, a public debate was triggered by the film *Girlfriend* (Karan Razdan), which once again mobilized the phobic in order to articulate the erotic. The film is about two women who share a house, friendship and, as is later revealed, a history of sexual intimacies. Trouble begins when one woman falls in love with a man and the other (more butch) woman morphs into a rampaging killer. Queer activists justifiably enraged by the film's sexual politics met the release of *Girlfriend* with strong but peaceful protests. *Girlfriend*'s lesbian protagonist's metamorphosis from a fond friend into a psychopath is accomplished through mobilizing an array of prejudicial assumptions about lesbian women. The film ends with the queer killer falling to her death and heteronormativity being restored as the heterosexual lovers reunite. In a widely circulated open letter to the director, a queer artist wrote that if Hindu right groups went on a 'rampage yet again, to protest [the] film *Girlfriend*, ask for the film to be banned or sent back to the censor board, I might even forgive you' (Shah 2004). That's exactly what happened! Soon after, the foot soldiers of the Hindu right mounted a violent protest against the film alleging that it sought to introduce 'ideas like homosexuality' that 'was responsible for new diseases like AIDS'. They demanded that the film be returned to the censors so that shots that were 'objectionable and against Indian culture' could be removed.

How could the same film outrage two such opposing constituencies? I have suggested elsewhere that the possible answer lies in the narrative being positioned on the precarious fault line of the phobic and the erotic (Ghosh 2007). The homophobic storyline notwithstanding, the film is able to 'render visible' the romantic and sexual possibilities of women loving women including two extended lesbian lovemaking sequences. The first sequence appears in flashback as the reluctant lesbian (now reformed hetero) confesses to an evening of intoxicated (and intoxicating) lesbian sex. When the vividly narrated flashback comes to an end, she claims that the next morning, she remembered nothing! The second, equally explicit, lovemaking sequence turns out to be a bad dream from which the hero wakes – now determined to save his girlfriend by marrying her. Interestingly, both lovemaking sequences appear through the imaginings, not of the self-proclaimed queer protagonist, but of the professedly straight, even homophobic, characters. It was as though homophobia were standing alibi for homosexual desires.

In contrast, *Men Not Allowed* (Shrey Srivastava, 2006), a lesbian love story with a happy and affirmative ending, shows no explicit lovemaking between the two women. This fact would have been unremarkable had the film not been punctuated by 'sex scenes' featuring heterosexual couples including the two female protagonists and their male lovers. While the straight-sex sequences are resonant of soft-porn film conventions, lesbian love is represented through the classic tropes of the romantic melodrama. The conclusion of *Girlfriend*, unlike that of *Men Not Allowed*, reaffirms heterosexuality and punishes the lesbian woman with death. Yet, it is able to create a narrative space for a visibilizing of lesbian sexual pleasure. *Men Not Allowed*, its privileging of lesbian love notwithstanding, invisibilizes lesbian sex. Paradoxically, the trope of phobia and reprimand, it would seem, extends the permission to visibilize sexualized queer love.

Dostana (Friendship, Tarun Mansukhani, 2008) marks a significant shift in visibilizing the queer by building the gag of 'misreading' into an integral plot element while decentring the key role played by the homophobe. The film explores the pleasures of both homosocial and heterosexual friendships and suggests that heterosexuality may not be inevitable. The 'gag' of 'false appearances', proudly announced in the trailers of the film, is an integral plot element. The story is about Sameer (Abhishek Bachchan), a nurse in Miami, and Kunal (John Abraham) who pretend to be a gay couple in order to rent an apartment from a paranoid aunt who won't let straight men live with her beautiful niece, Neha (Priyanka Chopra). The masquerade of performing the gay couple for almost the entire length of the film allows the narrative to be queered quite definitively even when the two men compete to grab the attentions of their object of desire, Neha. The film incorporates queer extra-textual references, in-the-know queer jokes, photo traditions of gay men's magazines and high camp. The opening credit sequence is a fascinating play with a range of sexual subjectivities inviting the audience to occupy many spectatorial positions.[12]

Dostana is also significant because it disrupts the trope of 'false appearances and mistaken identities'. First, the simultaneous address to the phobic and the erotic is ruptured. It is no longer the on-screen homophobe who misreads (or reads) but the on-screen queers! The earlier preoccupation with simultaneously invoking the phobic and the erotic is displaced when the homophobic mother, who fails to exorcise the ghost of 'gayness' from her son ends up accepting his imagined (or real) sexuality. Moreover, the queer track moves out of the masquerade thereby destabilizing the certitudes around heterosexual inevitability. This happens when the 'masquerade' is bust and the men are dared to kiss in public. The crowd chants 'kiss, kiss' as though Bombay cinema were being persuaded to 'come out' of the closet. First the men are reluctant and awkward, then the more hesitant of the two, grabs the other and kisses him while the camera goes into a kinetic frenzy. This rapturous climax features the first kiss between male protagonists in any Bombay film.

In the epilogue, Neha asks the two men about whether they ever felt attracted to each other while pretending to be gay. The men snort in denial. Then the kiss appears – like a thought bubble over their heads. It is likely that the spectators (like the on-screen protagonists) will be 'haunted' by the spectre of the kiss, and a sneaking suspicion that things may well be what they appear to be.

Queer conclusions

Like all cinematic conventions, Bombay cinema teaches the devoted cinephile the art of 'looking'. To this end, I would like to conclude with an example from the 1964 blockbuster hit *Mere Mehboob* (My Beloved, H. S. Rawail), which is plotted around a matrix of complicated relationships. The central protagonists Anwar (Rajendra Kumar) and Husna (Sadhana) are lovers. Anwar has been raised and educated by his sister Najma (Nimmi) who is a tawaif (courtesan). Anwar and Najma's devotion to each other has to remain a secret so that the brother's reputation is not tarnished by his sister's occupation. The relationship is unknown to even Nawab Bulund Akhtar (Ashok Kumar), Najma's wealthy long-time lover, who happens to be Husna's brother. When Anwar gets engaged to Husna, Najma is called to dance at the celebrations. Later that night, Najma holds Anwar in a tight embrace. She caresses his face and asks whether anyone had ever seen a bridegroom so handsome. At this point, Nawab Akhtar walks in and finds the couple in embrace. He hears Najma tell Anwar, 'It is late in the night, why don't you sleep over tonight?'. Anwar agrees, and the two walk up the stairs with their arms around each other. Nawab Akhtar is in shock. He has no doubt that Anwar and Najma are lovers. He staggers home and collapses in front of Husna. This 'misreading' destabilizes all relationships in the film. Later, in an attempt to clear the misunderstanding, Anwar asks Nawab Akhtar: 'Would it be wrong if you expressed your affection for Husna in this manner?'. The perplexed Nawab reminds Anwar that Najma is his sister. 'Exactly', replies Anwar, 'so is Najma my sister'. The film ends with all misunderstandings cleared and the two pairs of lovers reunited.

To my mind, the sequence in which the embrace between the siblings is mistaken for the embrace of lovers is vital to understanding how Bombay cinema articulates forbidden desire. The sequence is a reminder that the business of 'seeing' is tricky. Things are not what they appear to be, and what appears to be can mean many things. Most importantly, this sequence 'teaches' us how to read (or misread) forbidden love. The business of 'looking' has never been easy but looking at queer cinema may be particularly fraught as the narrative logic of visibilizing the queer may, on occasion, run counter to the logic of sexual politics. Film scholar Ellis Hansen argues that every film with a queer theme, notwithstanding the sexuality of its director or the origin of its funding, is still embattled in a highly moralistic debate over the correctness of its politics, 'as though art were to be valued only as sexual propaganda' (1999: 11). Therefore, queerness is rendered visible through an array of diagetic strategies many of which may appear to be oppositional to our sexual politics and beliefs in the world of lived experience. More importantly, the diagetic strategies come with a history of conventions that may not slide and 'cross over' cinematic cultures very easily. The cinema of queer desires is a cultural product, an art work, a political intervention and, most importantly, a cinematic text deploying a range of representational strategies. This demands of queer cinephiles a more complex engagement with not just the 'story' but the 'telling' of it. In this telling is archived our many journeys of desires.

Notes

1 Compare Ratna Kapur's reading of cultural productions chosen from the same field, in this volume (Ch. 3).
2 For example, the year 2004 saw the largest box-office sales in the world. Admissions (ticket sales) reached a record figure of 3.1 billion, whereas the USA (which includes films made in Hollywood) sold 1.5 billion admissions. The rest of the Asia Pacific region sold only 1 billion admissions.
3 This is not to suggest that song and dance sequences are necessarily subversive. On the contrary, these sequences are often deployed to privilege dominant discourses.
4 *Mujhe Chand Chahiye* is based on the 1993 Hindi novel of the same name by Surinder Verma.
5 This sequence appears in Episode 23 of *Adhikar*. The translation from Hindi to English is mine.
6 Compare Leslie Moran's effort to read the silence and gaps in judicial swearing-in speeches, in this volume (Ch. 6).
7 For an analysis of *Dosti* and *Tamanna* along these lines, see Vanita (2001).
8 Film and TV in the 1990s saw a marked increase in the number of female leads and protagonists. It also witnessed the emergence of India's first female superstar, Madhuri Dixit who, in films like *Ansoo Baney Angarey* (Tears Turn to Fire, 1993), *Anjaam* (Consequence, 1994) and *Mrityudand* (Death Penalty, 1997), occupied the diagetic space reserved for the male hero. The Bombay film industry's first significant transgender film *Tamanna* (Desire, 1997) was scripted by a woman, Tanuja Chandra, who subsequently directed two major woman-centred films *Dushman* (Enemy, 1998) and *Sangharsh* (Struggle, 1999). The controversial song sequence from the film *Khalnayak* (Villain, 1993), which started a cycle of anxieties around transgressive images of women's sexuality, was choreographed by a woman, Saroj Khan, the leading choreographer of the 1990s.
9 The real-life Shabnam Mausi was born as Chandra Prakash in a Brahmin family in 1995 and was handed over to eunuchs. She took up acting in Hindi films and starred in bit roles in various films. Later, she moved to Madhya Pradesh and took up social work. In 1999, she stood for state legislative elections and won.
10 It is said that Gurinder Chaddha originally conceived the film as a lesbian love story but had to change the script to make it more 'marketable' for producers.
11 That the 'misread' couple is played by two of Bombay's leading superstars Shah Rukh Khan and Saif Ali Khan is indicative of the growing legitimacy to expressions of on-screen queerness.
12 The publicity surrounding the film primed the audience to 'read' the narrative queerly. In a pre-release interview on TV, Abhishekh Bachchan says that while the industry was fighting over who the King of Bollywood was, John Abraham and he were the undisputed Queens!

References

Bakhtin M. (1984, originally 1941) *Rabelais and His World* (trans.) H. Iswolsky, Bloomington, IN: Indiana University Press.

Ghosh, S. (1999) 'The Troubled Existence of Sex and Sexuality: Feminists Engage with Censorship', in C. Brosius and M. Butcher (eds.) *Image Journeys: Audio-Visual Media and Cultural Change in India*, Thousand Oaks, CA: Sage Publications.

—— (2002) 'Queer Pleasures for Queer People: Film, Television and Queer Sexuality in India', in R. Vanita (ed.) *Queering India: Same Sex Love and Eroticism in Indian Culture and Society*, New York, NY: Routledge.

—— (2007) 'False Appearances and Mistaken Identities: The Phobic and the Erotic in Bombay Cinema's Queer Vision', in B. Bose and S. Bhattacharya (eds.) *The Phobic and the Erotic: The Politics of Sexualities in Contemporary India*, New York, NY: Seagull Books.

Hansen, E. (1999) 'Introduction', in E. Hansen (ed.) *Out Takes: Essays on Queer and Film*, Durham, NC: Duke University Press.

Kakkar, S. (1989) *Intimate Relations: Exploring Indian Sexuality*, New Delhi: Penguin.

PriceWaterhouseCoopers & FICCI (2007) *The Indian Entertainment & Media Industry Report: A Growth Story Unfolds*, India: PriceWaterhouseCoopers/FICCI.

Robinson, A. (1982) 'The New Indian Cinema', *Films and Filmmaking*, 338 (November): 16–18.

Shah, T. (2004) 'From the Fire into the Frying Pan', *Countercurrents*. Online: <http://www.countercurrents.org/gender-girlfriend160604.htm> (accessed 31 August 2009).

Shohat, E. and Stam, R. (1994) *Unthinking Eurocentrism: Multiculturalism and the Media*, New York, NY: Routledge.

Stam, R. (1989) *Subversive Pleasures: Bakhtin, Cultural Criticism and Film*, Baltimore, MD: Johns Hopkins University Press.

Vanita, R. (2001) '*Dosti* to *Tamanna*: Love between Men in Hindi Cinema', in S. Lamb and D. Mines (eds.) *Everyday Life in South Asia*, Bloomington, IN: Indiana University Press.

Chapter 5

Post-apartheid fraternity, post-apartheid democracy, post-apartheid sexuality

Queer reflections on Jane Alexander's *Butcher Boys*

Jaco Barnard-Naudé

> If the term 'queer' is to be a site of collective contestations, the point of departure for a set of historical considerations and future imaginings, it will have to remain that which is, in the present, never fully owned, but always and only redeployed, twisted, queered from a prior usage and in the direction of urgent and expanding political purposes.
>
> (Butler 1993: 228)

Preface

With your permission, then, these three permanent residents of the South African National Gallery in Cape Town. Their mother – if you would prefer to call her that – is South African artist Jane Alexander (Powell and Alexander 1995). They came to life in 1985, at a time of turmoil and during a state of emergency in their country of birth (Bedford 2008: 125). Some will say that they have long been dead, and others that they never really lived. In the main room of the gallery they sit next to each other on a modest wooden bench, overlooking from three different directions the daily comings and goings of visitors from all over the world who have come to the national gallery to see them. Collectively, they are called *The Butcher Boys*.

One visitor to the gallery describes her experience of encountering *The Butcher Boys* for the first time as follows: '[T]he Boys hit you in the chest when you are standing right there in front of them, forbidden to touch'.[1] Their unusual appearance – to put it mildly – has earned them quite a reputation. Author Mike Nicol, in his book *The Waiting Country*, describes *The Butcher Boys* as '[m]alificents' (1996: 21). Erin Mosley, in turn, comments on them as follows: 'Alexander's piece stands as a testament to darker days, a time in which boys became butchers – and, by extension, a time in which people were butchered – and because of this it serves an important role in the context of South Africa's transition to democracy' (2007: 98–9). Clearly, Jane Alexander's *Butcher Boys* are read as the artist's statement about the brutality of apartheid totalitarianism.

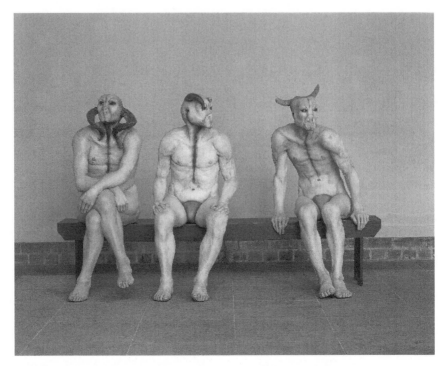

Plate 5.1   The Butcher Boys, by Jane Alexander; photograph by Mark Lewis.

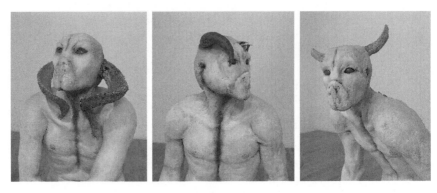

Plates 5.2–5.4   The Butcher Boys (details), by Jane Alexander; photographs by Eileen Costa.

However, the dimension that appeals to me about *The Butcher Boys* is one that has only been very quietly or silently implied up to this point, yet it is the dimension that is assumed by, and undergirds, every single aspect of their 'interpretation' or their 'reading' as an artistic statement about apartheid. It is the dimension that is always already bounded up with what they are said to represent. It is strictly the dimension that not only ties them to apartheid but that also ties them to each other, or, to put it slightly more accurately: it is the dimension that ties them together and consequently, inevitably, ties them to apartheid. It is of course the dimension of blood and of resemblance and the family, because, as you can clearly see, *The Butcher Boys* are undoubtedly brothers.

Introduction

In antiquity, political philosophy (and particularly the discourse on democracy) begins with the thought of friendship (Hutter 1978: 2). In his *Politics of Friendship*, Jacques Derrida asserts that, since ancient Greece, this thought of the figure of the friend in politics relentlessly makes its appearance with the features of the brother (Derrida 1997: viii). This friend-as-brother 'seems spontaneously to belong to a *familial, fraternalist* and thus *androcentric* configuration of politics' (ibid.). *Politics of Friendship* asks the reader to 'dream of a friendship which goes beyond this proximity of the congeneric double . . . what would then be the politics of such a "beyond the principle of fraternity"', Derrida asks; 'Would this still deserve the name politics?' (ibid.). Derrida points particularly to the fact that it is *democracy* as a political regime that is 'rarely determined in the absence of confraternity or brotherhood' (ibid.).

I believe that the most important dimension of the dream Derrida asks us to dream here is the dimension of the sexual or sexuality within democracy–as–friendship. It is clear from the above that the aspect of sex or of the sexual is implicit in Derrida's questioning of the democracy–friendship–fraternity triad. In effect Derrida is asking us to imagine a democracy (in the broadest sense of that term)[2] no longer conceived of in terms of identity, nation or sameness, but rather 'structured' by radical alterity. I want to suggest that Derrida is asking us the question, radically formulated, of what the terms 'post-apartheid' fraternity, 'post-apartheid' friendship and 'post-apartheid' democracy can or should mean. How indeed does the invocation of 'post-apartheid' affect the triad of Western political thought? Specifically, can we align the strategies of queer theory with the dreams of the 'post-apartheid'?

In order to explore some possible answers to the questions raised above, I want, in what follows, to read Jane Alexander's *Butcher Boys* (as a negative statement about apartheid) in the light of Derrida's critique of a political founded in friendship which is, in turn, founded in fraternity. I want to look specifically at the influence that the fraternal configuration of the political exerted in post-apartheid South Africa on the same-sex marriage debate and the eventual formal legalization of same-sex marriage.[3] To this extent I am explicitly and directly involving the question of the sexual within democracy (Robson 2005), for I consider this involvement crucial in coming to terms with a transformative, trans-fraternal understanding of the political in South

Africa. If we heed Jean-Luc Nancy's affirmation that 'it is always a question of the body' (1993: 66) – male body, female body, body politic, body of the people – then the way in which these bodies are involved with each other and the way in which these bodies transform each other, continuously, is more clearly visible and the crucial role this involvement of bodies plays in democratic politics, more discernable.

Fraternity, friendship, democracy and *aimance* (lovence)

In *Politics of Friendship* Derrida asserted that the questioning of a notion of friendship founded in fraternity first of all involves a problematization of the Aristotelian assertion that friendship consists in loving rather than in being loved (Derrida 1997: 8). What is at stake when one is questioning and reconsidering the centrality of fraternity in the 'politics' of friendship or the role of friendship in politics, according to Derrida, is the concept of *aimance* or lovence, the middle voice between loving and being loved, between activity and passivity (ibid. 7). Derrida firmly asserts that if we want to know what lovence means, 'one must know that the only way to find out is by questioning first of all the act and the experience of loving rather than the state or situation of being loved' (ibid. 8). This particular questioning of loving (active) rather than being loved (passive) is necessary because it is the act of loving (rather than being loved) that has been prioritized in the history of friendship – for Aristotle preached that the good friend is the one who loves, not the one who is being loved. Since democracy is this association of the friends who are loving, we must rethink the prioritization of the act of loving in order to rethink fraternity, friendship and democracy itself.

The act of loving implies an autonomous decision *to* love. As Alex Thompson has indicated, Derrida's concept of *aimance*, draws attention to what precedes and for this reason makes any friendship (conceived as the act of (fraternal) loving) possible (2005: 85). Thompson argues that Derrida in effect associates *aimance* with 'a calling of/for a politics beyond friendship modelled on fraternity' (ibid.). He continues that for Derrida friendship is constitutively split between *aimance* and fraternity. To quote Thompson:

> Friendship, as election by decision, is made possible by the multiplicity of possible friends among whom I choose, with whom I am already in a relationship of neither active nor passive affection, but *aimance*; but I betray this multiplicity of possible friends by preferring my friends, even by calling them friends. The necessity of this betrayal and exclusion is what Derrida calls the logic of fraternization, and which he claims dictates the relationship between friendship and brotherhood.

(ibid. 16)

If heeded, the concept of *aimance* thus complicates, as Derrida argues in *Adieu to Emmanuel Levinas*, a *necessary* deduction of 'a politics and a law from ethics. This deduction is necessary in order to determine the ' "better" or the "less bad" ' (Derrida 1999: 115). Derrida introduces *aimance* then in order to radicalize the notion that the work of the political, 'the properly political act or operation comes down to creating (producing, making, etc) the most possible friendship' (Derrida 1997: 199).[4] As Thomson indicates: 'If the [Schmittian] friend–enemy choice were to be taken as the definition of politics, we could describe *aimance* as the politicization of the decision, and brotherhood . . . as its inexorable and inevitable depoliticization' (2005: 167).

Apartheid and fraternity

If we consider apartheid South Africa against the backdrop of these insights, it is clear that apartheid was conceived as, and thus undergirded by, the most perverse, exclusive and murderous understanding of the political as fraternal. Apartheid was, to use Derrida's term, a horrendous 'fraternocracy' (Derrida 1997: 50), opposed to the very heart of political life. Here we must bear in mind Hannah Arendt's insight that totalitarian systems, such as apartheid, attempt a complete end to political life as constituted by plurality: 'the fact that men, not Man, live on the earth and inhabit the world' (Arendt and Canovan 1998: 1). Totalitarian systems make, as Arendt famously put it, of all men, One Man (1985: 467). One could say that apartheid, as one permutation of such a totalitarian system, ceaselessly attempted a depoliticization of the decision in relation to the friend. It was a system predicated on sameness, on the resemblance of brothers, on a specific identity, a self-present subjectivity and thus the collective subjectivity of nation – an order utterly neglectful (even hateful) of radical alterity and thus of *aimance*.

It is in fact no coincidence then, that as an artistic statement about apartheid, Jane Alexander portrays her *Butcher Boys* as brothers. As such they provide a vivid portrayal of the perverse fraternity on which apartheid – as a legal order – was predicated. *The Butcher Boys* vividly represents the dictatorship of brothers, the law of brothers. Their beastly, deformed, non-human physical features draw attention to what we could call the 'inhumanity' of apartheid fraternity, for, when all was said and done, apartheid's sons-as-brothers were responsible for nothing less than a crime *against* humanity. It is quite literally true that this inhuman fraternity attempted the total eradication of everyone and everything that was not like them, that did not resemble them. For Derrida the same problem is always already situated at the very heart of democracy. Derrida's account of the history of fraternity as a juridico-political principle led him to insist that there is 'never any danger for the democracy to come, except where *there are brothers* . . . where the fraternity of brothers *dictates the law*, where a *political dictatorship* of fraternocracy comes to be imposed' (2005: 50). Going forward we should, therefore, bear in mind that for Derrida fraternalism is first and foremost the problem of democracy, because fraternocracy is simply nothing but the becoming totalitarian of democracy – it represents democracy's most unfriendly gesture.

Of rainbows and marriage: post-apartheid democracy and post-apartheid sexuality

How do we read, then, *The Butcher Boys* still as a negative statement about apartheid, but here specifically, in terms also of the possibility of apartheid within democracy and (the possibility of) apartheid within the sexual in South Africa? As a starting point it is useful to consider the many repressive laws in relation to the sexual that the apartheid government passed during its reign. Examples included the Immorality Act, the Prohibition Against Mixed Marriages Act and the criminalization of consensual sodomy between men. All these were attempts to regulate the sexual in accordance with a very specific nationalist and racist ideology that posited a very specific preferred identity. The minimum markers of this identity were whiteness, heterosexuality and an unwavering devotion to conservative Calvinist Christianity. Come the end of apartheid, the birth of democracy and the abolition of these measures to police sexual activity, come the consideration of the sexual now, not within apartheid, but within democracy.

The transition from totalitarianism to democracy in South Africa could be characterized as having necessitated an aesthetic shift: from the 'One Man aesthetic' of apartheid to the 'plurality aesthetic' of democracy. Politicians, freedom fighters and cultural icons alike expressed this aesthetic shift through an affirmation and celebration of South Africa's 'rainbow nation' – a term coined by that icon of peace, tolerance and goodwill (now emeritus) Archbishop Desmond Tutu (Cock and Bernstein 2002: 47). Given the obvious connection with the international rainbow motif in gay culture, it was hardly surprising that gay rights activists saw this 'rainbow nation' rhetoric as holding particular potential for the achievement of freedom on this front in South Africa – especially given that section 9(3) of the 1996 Constitution prohibits discrimination on the grounds of sexual orientation.

To evaluate critically this new dawn of the sexual within democracy, it is important to consider the history of emancipation on the grounds of sexual orientation in South Africa. To this extent, I would like to consider specifically the question of the sexual within the question of marriage and how this has influenced the importance of the sexual to democracy. Answering this question will require us to look very closely at the 'debate' regarding the legal recognition of same-sex marriage in South Africa. Is the sexual emancipation narrative in South Africa true to Derrida's dream of the democracy to come, true to a politics no longer closed in upon itself according to the logic of fraternal friendship, but open and reopening? Or are we once more at a juncture where the sexual within democracy comes to mean nothing more than the exclusive and excluding fraternization of (heterosexual) brothers?[5]

Let us consider then the way in which the issue of sexual minority emancipation came to the South African courts and also the way in which the Constitutional Court of South Africa dealt with it. This methodology is justified if we accept (as I do) Robson's argument that '[t]he debate regarding judicial review is especially pronounced when the substantive controversies are sexual ones' (2005: 413). Of course the debate is 'especially pronounced' because (from a democratic point of view) the question remains whether these matters should not be dealt with through direct ballot measures, as has been the case in parts of the United States (Robson 2008: 196).

One reason why emancipation was fought for primarily through the courts is, of course, because the Constitution of South Africa prohibited discrimination on the basis of sexual orientation from the outset. Since the Constitution is justiciable, it made sense (from a minority point of view) to turn to the courts instead of the legislature. The story famously starts in what we colloquially refer to today in South Africa as the first 'National Coalition case' in which the Constitutional Court declared unconstitutional the common law crime of private, consensual adult male sodomy (National Coalition 1999) as well as certain other pieces of statute that had relied on the common law criminalization of sodomy.[6] South African queer theorist Pierre De Vos explains that the driving force behind the litigation in this case – an NGO (non-governmental organization) called the National Coalition for Gay and Lesbian Equality – used the inclusion of sexual orientation as a ground of unfair discrimination in the South African Constitution to argue that the criminalization of consensual male sodomy was unconstitutional (2007: 447–8). De Vos argues that the strategic decision to bring a case in which the remedy would be decriminalization of sexual conduct, as opposed to, for instance a case that involved legal protection of same-sex couples, was part of a conservative, disciplinary strategy of the National Coalition which festered with concessions to (rather than defiantly challenged) the heteronormative (or shall we say, fraternal) hegemony (ibid. 446). According to De Vos, the Coalition was concerned that a public backlash might occur if the Constitutional Court were to make a decision on a more controversial topic such as same-sex marriage or adoption by same-sex couples (ibid. 443–4).

What De Vos suggests here is that the National Coalition was from the outset bound to walk a treacherous tightrope: it was well aware that it had to ensure that its struggle continued to fit with the struggle against apartheid. In other words, the struggle for sexual emancipation had to fit with, or be aligned to, a broader struggle against a political order founded in the most inhospitable fraternity imaginable. In order to guarantee this fit, the Coalition was particularly committed to being uncontroversial by showing that gays and lesbians were also 'normal' human beings, that they were also brothers (or, perhaps, sisters *as* brothers). Otherness, one could argue, was sacrificed for an insistence on sameness. In a significant sense it could be said that the Coalition's strategy around the first case, National Coalition 1999, smacked of what Johnson calls the phenomenon of passing (2002: 257): the sexual emancipation struggle had to match, sufficiently closely, the struggle for political emancipation, it had to pass as part of the political anti-apartheid struggle. The strategy of the Coalition was thus, ironically so, predicated on the belief that, in order to succeed, it had to be sufficiently obedient to the heteronormative discipline – and thus in this sense sufficiently tied to the fraternal – in order to avoid a public backlash that could have disastrous consequences.

Given the fact that the decision to bring the first National Coalition case was enframed by the heteronormative hegemony, it is surprising and of course commendable that the Constitutional Court in its decision went out of its way to challenge heteronormativity and its role in the emergence of the discourse. As De Vos writes in a recent contribution, the Court's adoption of a broad and generous interpretation of the phrase 'sexual orientation' might well have qualified as a first queer moment in the jurisprudence (2008: 255). To quote the Court:

> sexual orientation is defined by reference to erotic attraction: in the case of heterosexuals, to members of the opposite sex; in the case of gays and lesbians, to members of the same sex. Potentially a homosexual or gay or lesbian person can therefore be anyone who is erotically attracted to members of his or her own sex.
>
> The concept 'sexual orientation' as used in section 9(3) of the 1996 Constitution must be given a generous interpretation of which it is linguistically and textually fully capable of bearing. It applies equally to the orientation of persons who are bi-sexual, or transsexual and it also applies to the orientation of persons who might on a single occasion only be erotically attracted to a member of their own sex.
>
> (National Coalition 1999: para. 21)

The Court here adopted a broad and generous interpretation of sexual orientation – an interpretation that made it quite clear that homosexual relations did not necessarily have to mimic stereotypical heterosexual relations in order to qualify for legal recognition. The Court adopted a markedly radical interpretation of the phrase which accorded with existing radical literature on the topic (Sedgwick 1994: 7–8). In this sense, it is ironic that the National Coalition's conservative litigation strategy in fact led, in the judgment, to a subversion of the very fraternal hegemony in the terms of which that strategy had been conceived. It turned out that the Court appeared to be far more open and receiving of queer sexualities than the National Coalition had expected. The first National Coalition case thus came to signify more than just the decriminalization of the crime of sodomy. Instead it actually affirmed the importance of plurality and difference for the sexual within democracy. It emphatically stated that democracy is not consistent with repressive state practices regarding sexuality and that such practices would not be tolerated under a democratic dispensation. This much was clear from the opening lines of the separate concurring judgment delivered by Justice Sachs:

> Only in the most technical sense is this a case about who may penetrate whom where. At a practical and symbolical level it is about the status, moral citizenship and sense of self-worth of a significant section of the community. At a more general and conceptual level, it concerns the nature of the open, democratic and pluralistic society contemplated by the Constitution.
>
> (National Coalition 1999: para. 107)

Given the profoundly anti-heteronormative approach that the first National Coalition judgment took to the rights of members of sexual minorities within the context of the emergence of democracy, one would have hoped that further cases would be decided with reference to this apparently strong queer and indeed anti-essentialist 'foundation'. Yet, as De Vos indicates, when the Court was faced for the first time with the question of legal *protection* (as opposed to decriminalization) of same-sex partnerships in the second National Coalition case (National Coalition 2000), it lapsed back into the more comfortable rhetoric of heteronormative fraternity and the politics of passing (2008: 266–71).

The first concession to heteronormativity occurred when the Court decided that the word 'spouse' could not, in its context in the relevant legislation,[7] be construed as including a partner in a permanent same-sex life partnership (National Coalition 2000: para. 23). According to the Court such a construction would 'distort' the meaning of the expression. The Court relied explicitly on what it called the 'ordinary' meaning of the word spouse as denoting a husband or a wife (ibid. para. 25). Clearly the Court played its ideological hand when it unproblematically conflated the heteronormative meaning of the word with its so-called 'ordinary' meaning, thereby sending the message that what is ordinary – or normal – is what is heteronormative. This was further emphasized when the Court held that the word 'marriage', as used in the relevant legislation, did not extend 'any further than those marriages that are ordinarily recognized by our law' (ibid.). Given these arguments, the unconstitutionality of the relevant legislation could only be cured by reading words into the statute that would afford partners in same-sex life partnerships the same rights as spouses in legally recognized marriages (ibid. para. 82).

Although this judgment clearly vindicated further the constitutional right not to be discriminated against on the basis of sexual orientation, this vindication had a price. It turned out that, when it came to something more than decriminalization of private homosexual conduct, the sentiments of concern for difference and anti-fraternal non-essentialism that so centrally operated in the foreground in the first National Coalition case had their limits. Not only did this judgment convey the heteronormative sentiment that the same-sex life partnership was not sufficiently ordinary to warrant protection under the existing institutions of family law, the Court also imposed a politics of passing on this partnership when it came up with a list of factors which would help a court to decide whether the same-sex life partnership before it was worthy of protection (National Coalition 2000: para. 88). These factors were basically made up out of the characteristics of a heterosexual marriage. Their use implied that the type of same-sex life partnership that the law would protect had to approximate as closely as possible the idealized, ordinary – and I would add mythical – heterosexual, monogamous marriage. Yet by separating the same-sex life partnership from the legal institutions of 'marriage' and 'spouse', the Court conveyed the sentiment that 'marriage' had to be insulated from possible intrusions by queer relationships – no matter how unqueer they are – because, after all, queer relationships are still, well, queer. This was evident in the very fact that the Court used the language of protection in its judgment: 'protecting the traditional institution of marriage as recognized by law may not be done in a way which unjustifiably limits the constitutional rights of partners in a permanent same-sex life partnership' (ibid. para. 55).

The point to be made here is that the Court still considered it necessary to 'protect' the traditional institution of marriage, albeit that it added the caveat that this protection of marriage may not fall foul of the Constitution. The obvious question is, of course, why it was still necessary to protect traditional marriage if the new democratic constitutional order required the affirmation and celebration of difference and plurality (see National Coalition 1999). On this reading, the Court's creation of the legal institution of a permanent same-sex life partnership conveyed the message that a separate but equal dispensation was not only warranted but also constitutional. Considered against the background of the particularly unfortunate history of 'separate but equal' dispensations in apartheid South Africa, it could be argued that the Court failed in this judgment to affirm and live up to its own embrace of plurality, difference and anti-fraternal insights in National Coalition 1999.

Unfortunately, it was the second National Coalition case that won the day in the end, as it set the precedent for other cases in which the Court would deal with the question of affirmative legal protection for same-sex partnerships as well as for partnerships unconsummated by a legally recognized marriage. If these decisions are closely analysed, one unfailing theme emerges: the legal sanctity of a formal marriage concluded in terms of the 1961 Marriage Act. Two brief examples will illustrate the point.

In the 2005 judgment in *Volks v. Robinson*, the Constitutional Court decided that a woman who had, for all intents and purposes, lived with a man as his wife for more than 20 years, could not benefit from his estate as the surviving spouse in terms of the Maintenance of Surviving Spouses Act of 1990. The reasoning of the Court was that Mrs Robinson could have entered into a marriage in terms of the 1961 Act, but chose not to do so and therefore could not claim benefits from Mr Volks' estate in death that she did not enjoy while he was still alive (*Volks* 2005: paras. 55–6). In the *Du Toit* case, the Court similarly thought it necessary to stress that the status of the applicants as unmarried persons precluded them from adopting a child:

> [T]he applicants' status as unmarried persons which currently precludes them from joint adoption of the siblings is inextricably linked to their sexual orientation. But for their sexual orientation which precludes them from entering into a marriage, they fulfil the criteria that would otherwise make them eligible jointly to adopt children in terms of the impugned legislation.
>
> (2002: para. 23)

Given the remedy in National Coalition 2000, precedent dictated that the unconstitutionality in this instance had to be cured again by reading into the Act words recognizing and protecting the same-sex life partnership under consideration (ibid. para. 29).

A few years and a few cases later, it was evident that the narrative of inclusion despite difference proffered by the first Coalition judgment had been eclipsed. The understanding of the priority of protection of *all* minorities in post-apartheid South Africa, specifically entitlement to equality precisely because or on the basis of difference, or what Jean-Luc Nancy would call the absence of common substance (1993: 72), had been subverted. Instead, the master narrative that took hold in – or enframed – the emergence of protection for non-marital erotic relationships in South Africa was heteronormativity or a politics of fraternity. It was, undoubtedly, a more generous and open heteronormativity and fraternity, but a heteronormativity and a fraternity nevertheless.

It would be understandable if, in response to the above mentioned contentions, reference would be made to the Constitutional Court's now famous judgment in *Fourie v. Minister of Home Affairs*, in which the 1961 Marriage Act was declared unconstitutional and Parliament ordered to cure the unconstitutionality within a year of the judgment. This judgment sparked the enactment of the Civil Union Act of 2006, which effectively legalizes same-sex marriage as a species of a civil union. Some might argue that this would never have been possible in the absence of the advances achieved through the recognition of the same-sex life partnership as a legal institution. This is not necessarily the case. I, for one, would reply that such a conclusion is one that takes an insufficiently critical position of the disciplinary effect of heteronormative power. I hope that the reasons for such a reply will become clear from what follows.

The *Fourie* judgment undeniably represents an attempt to reinvoke the queer rhetoric deployed in the first National Coalition judgment (1999). In this sense, the judgment simultaneously attempts to return the discourse to the narrative advanced in the first National Coalition case, namely the anti-apartheid, anti-fraternocratic struggle. This is evident when one considers the opening paragraphs of the judgment, where Justice Sachs writes:

> In the pre-democratic era same-sex unions were not only denied any form of legal protection, they were regarded as immoral and their consummation by men could attract imprisonment. Since the interim Constitution came into force in 1994, however, the Bill of Rights has dramatically altered the situation ... Legislative developments ... have ameliorated but not eliminated the disadvantages same-sex couples suffer. More deeply, the exclusionary definition of marriage injures gays and lesbians because it implies a judgment on them. It suggests not only that their relationships and commitments and loving bonds are inferior, but that they themselves can never be fully part of the community of moral equals that the Constitution promises to create for all.
>
> (2006: paras. 4, 17)

As it did in 1999 in the first National Coalition case, the Court clearly (re)connects here the sexual emancipation discourse with the anti-apartheid struggle, while making it clear that judicial relief granted through the recognition of same-sex life partnerships was not enough. Strategically, the redeployment of the rhetoric of the first National Coalition case could not have been more crucial. After all, the Court was about to declare the 1961 Marriage Act – that untouchable idol of the South African family – to be unconstitutional. It thus had to illustrate clearly that the declaration of constitutional invalidity of the Marriage Act formed part and parcel of the ideology that informed and sparked the anti-apartheid struggle.

The Constitutional Court consequently decided that the 1961 Marriage Act and the common law definition of a marriage on which it relied were unconstitutional because they excluded same-sex couples from their reach. Instead of immediately reading words into the statute to cure the unconstitutionality, the Court decided to suspend the order of unconstitutionality. It gave Parliament one year to come up with legislation that would afford same-sex life partners the same legal protection as their heterosexual counterparts (ibid. para. 156). The rationale behind this decision seems to have been that the issue of same-sex marriage was 'of great public significance' and involved such 'deep sensitivities' that it was 'appropriate' for the legislature to address the matter (ibid. para. 147). However, this scant justification makes little sense if one considers the matters 'of great public significance' in which the Court had already intervened – the glaring example of course being the abolition of the death penalty in the case of *S v. Makwanyane*.

Be that as it may, the matter went to Parliament with the warning that, should it fail to meet the deadline, there would be an automatic reading in of the words 'or spouse' into the relevant section of the Marriage Act in order to cure the unconstitutionality (ibid. para. 157). (Finally, the jurisprudence had reached a stage where the definition of a spouse included a partner in a same-sex life partnership.)

The *Fourie* judgment also sent the issue of same-sex marriage to the legislature with some clear guidelines it was supposed to follow when considering how to recognize same-sex marriage. The most important of these guidelines stated that whatever legislative measures Parliament eventually adopted, it had to ensure that the legislation would not lead to a separate but equal dispensation (ibid. para. 150). With this statement the Court in fact implied that its own creation – the same-sex life partnership – was unsatisfactory in the absence of the choice to marry. To this extent it overruled its own earlier judgment in the National Coalition 2000 case. Marriage, held the Court, is a unique institution and constitutes 'much more than a piece of paper' (ibid. para. 70). Well aware of the centrality attributed to marriage and its consequences in our culture, and indeed affirming it, the Court held that to deny same-sex couples a choice in this regard 'is to negate their right to self-definition in a most profound way' (ibid. para. 71). As Sachs J. put it:

> The exclusion of same-sex couples from the benefits and responsibilities of marriage, accordingly, is not a small and tangential inconvenience resulting from a few surviving relics of societal prejudice destined to evaporate like the morning dew. It represents a harsh if oblique statement by the law that same-sex couples are outsiders, and that their need for affirmation and protection of their intimate relations as human beings is somehow less than that of heterosexual couples. It reinforces the wounding notion that they are to be treated as biological oddities, as failed or lapsed human beings who do not fit into normal society, and, as such, do not qualify for the full moral concern and respect that our Constitution seeks to secure for everyone. It signifies that their capacity for love, commitment and accepting responsibility is by definition less worthy of regard than that of heterosexual couples.
>
> (ibid.)

The 'democratic' process that followed unfortunately and disappointingly smacked of a fraternal conception of the political in at least two senses. First, Parliament came up with a first draft of the Civil Union Bill that totally ignored the guidelines for legislation set in the *Fourie* judgment (Civil Union Bill 2006). The aim of this Bill was ironically to create a separate but equal institution for same-sex partnerships which the Bill termed 'civil partnerships' (Civil Union Bill 2006, s. 1). No wonder that this move was equated to an 'Apartheid Grand Re-Opening' by a cartoonist in the national press

(Shapiro 2006). Marriage was not at all available in terms of this Bill even though the Constitutional Court had clearly indicated it should be. The Parliamentary Portfolio Committee, tasked with the responsibility to conduct a public participation process regarding the proposed legislation, continued to conduct this process on the basis of a Bill that completely ignored what was said in the *Fourie* judgment (Barnard 2007). This opened the door for a plethora of fraternocentric, fascist and often fundamentalist religious submissions arguing that same-sex marriage is an abomination (De Vos and Barnard 2007: 813). Submission after submission contended that Parliament should not pass the Bill because it would signify democracy's darkest day in South Africa. These submissions of course failed to see the irony that in its first draft this Bill was in and of itself already a concession to fraternocracy for the simple reason that it did not allow for the recognition of same-sex marriage. Instead of asking the question whether the proposed Civil Union Bill met the requirements of the Constitutional Court's judgment, the public participation process became a platform for an unmediated parade of hate speech against homosexuals (Barnard 2007: 517).

It was left to LGBTI (lesbian, gay, bisexual, transgender, queer, intersex) NGOs to make this point over and over until the Committee finally noted this and redrafted the Civil Union Bill at the eleventh hour in order better to approximate what was envisaged in the *Fourie* decision. This was done by affording marriage in terms of the Civil Union Act as a species of civil union. The 1961 Marriage Act, however, remains on the statute books, inaccessible to same-sex couples. Whether the ghost of the second National Coalition case is to be blamed for this state of affairs is an open question.

Conclusion: the sexual within democracy – to come

Even though a marriage of sorts, or a marriage as civil union, can now be concluded validly by a same-sex couple in South Africa, it is clear that the shadow of a conception of democracy founded in fraternity and in the most inhospitable of friendships remains with us. The history of the litigation on sexual emancipation illustrates how easily even a well-meaning, self-conscious, pro-queer discourse can lapse back into the language and institutions of fraternocentrism. It is of course true that all opposition to same-sex marriage is not necessarily fraternocentric, but the point that this piece tries to make is that one should be constantly aware of the power of disciplinary, fraternal heteronormative influence, and that this can present a significant obstacle when one considers matters as vexed as queering the empire.

This piece also wishes to illustrate that when it comes to sexuality, South African society remains deeply conservative, exclusionary, prejudiced, and even murderous – that is to say, there are definite limits to democracy when it comes to the sexual in South Africa. The brutal, hate-inspired murders of Sizakele Sigasa, a gay and lesbian rights activist, and her friend

Salome Masooa in Soweto in 2007, as well as the murder of lesbian activist and footballer, Eudy Simelane, on 28 April 2008 in Kwa Thema, near Johannesburg, testify unequivocally to this (Ndaba 2007). These murders take us right back to Jane Alexander's *Butcher Boys* and the statement this work makes about the inhuman dimensions of apartheid and fraternocentrism. These murders testify to the fact that today it is still more important than ever to think of democracy – founded on the notion of philia, or friendship – in a way that is 'no longer an insult to the friendship we strive to think beyond the homo-fraternal and phallogocentric schema' (Derrida 1997: 306). Jane Alexander's *Butcher Boys* ultimately testify to this terrible fact, a fact that is as empowering as it is burdensome. Today, more than ever, it is the 'to come' of *aimance* – the democracy to come – that must guard the space and the spacing of the sexual within democracy. Such is the responsibility of any post-apartheid ~~fraternity~~. Such is the responsibility of a post-apartheid sexuality.

Acknowledgements

I would like to sincerely thank Kim Brooks and Robert Leckey for organizing the Queer/Empire workshop at McGill University where this work was first presented. I have benefitted enormously from the rigorous discussions between, and the intellectual eloquence of, the participants in the workshop.

Notes

1 <www.tanyapretorius.co.za/content/art/artists/jane%20alexander.htm>.
2 As Ruthann Robson (2005: 410) indicates, democracy is 'not simply a form of state, but is an état social which is as much about the "mores" constituting social relations as about political organizations of the government'.
3 Compare discussions of similar issues, in different national contexts, by Margaret Denike and Nan Seuffert, both in this volume (Chs. 9 and 11 respectively).
4 There are numerous agreements with this reading. See, for example, Fenves 1999: 142, who indicates that *Politics of Friendship* is written in the name of the democracy to come. Also see Critchley 1998: 266; Wills 2005: para. 30.
5 'What happens when, in taking up the case of the sister, the woman is made a sister? And a sister a case of the brother?' (Derrida 1997: viii).
6 It should be noted that the Cape High Court, in the earlier case of *S v. K* 1997 (4) SA 469 (C) had anticipated the abolition of sodomy when it refused to uphold a conviction by the magistrates' court on a charge of sodomy. However, the decision, holding that the crime of consensual, private, male sodomy ceased to exist with the coming into operation of the Interim Constitution of 1993, only applied in the jurisdiction of the Cape High Court.
7 The relevant legislation was the Aliens Control Act of 1991, s. 25, which provided that only the 'spouse' or 'dependent child' of a person who is permanently and lawfully resident in South Africa can apply for an immigration permit. The applicants complained that the section is unconstitutional because it did not allow the partners of permanently resident South Africans in permanent same-sex life partnerships to also apply for such permits.

References

Arendt, H. (1951, 1994 edn) *The Origins of Totalitarianism*, New York, NY: Harcourt.
—— and Canovan, M. (1998) *The Human Condition*, Chicago, IL: University of Chicago Press.
Barnard, J. (2007) 'Totalitarianism, (Same-Sex) Marriage and Democratic Politics in Post-Apartheid South Africa', *South African Journal on Human Rights*, 23: 500–25.
Barnard-Naudé, A. J. (2008) 'Beyond the Brother: Radical Freedom', *Acta Juridica*: 273–97.
Bedford, E. (2008) 'Translation and the Media: Media and the Arts', in C. Villa-Vicenzio and F. Du Toit (eds.) *Truth and Reconciliation in South Africa: 10 Years On*, Cape Town: Institute for Justice and Reconciliation.
Butler, J. (1993) *Bodies That Matter: On the Discursive Limits of 'Sex'*, London: Routledge.
Cock, J. and Bernstein, A. R. (2002) *Melting Pots and Rainbow Nations: Conversations about Difference in the United States and South Africa*, Chicago, IL: University of Illinois Press.
Critchley, S. (1998) 'The Other's Decision in Me. (What Are the Politics of Friendship?)', *European Journal of Social Theory*, 1: 259–79.
De Vos, P. (2007) 'The "inevitability" of same-sex marriage in South Africa's post-apartheid state', *South African Journal on Human Rights*, 23: 432–65.
—— (2008) 'From Heteronormativity to Full Sexual Citizenship', *Acta Juridica*: 254–72.
—— and Barnard, A. J. (2007) 'Same-Sex Marriage, Civil Unions and Domestic Partnerships in South Africa: Critical Reflections on an Ongoing Saga', *South African Law Journal*, 4: 795–826.
Derrida, J. (1997) *Politics of Friendship* (trans.) G. Collins, London: Verso Books.
—— (1999) *Adieu to Emmanuel Levinas* (trans.) P.-A. Brault and M. Naas, Stanford, CA: Stanford University Press.
—— (2005) *Rogues: Two Essays on Reason* (trans.) P.-A. Brault and M. Naas, Stanford, CA: Stanford University Press.
Du Toit and Another v. Minister for Welfare and Population Development and Others (2002) (10) BCLR 1006.
Fenves, P. D. (1999) 'Politics of Friendship – Once Again', *Eighteenth Century Studies*, 32(2): 133–55.
Hutter, H. (1978) *Politics as Friendship*, Waterloo, ON: Wilfried Laurier University Press.
Johnson, C. (2002) 'Heteronormative Citizenship and the Politics of Passing', *Sexualities*, 5: 317–36.
Minister of Home Affairs v. Fourie and Others (2006) (1) SA 524 (CC).
Mosley, E. (2007) ' "Visualizing" Apartheid: Contemporary Art and Collective Memory during South Africa's Transition to Democracy', *Antipoda*, 5: 98–120.
Nancy, J.-L. (1993) *The Experience of Freedom* (trans.) B. McDonald, Stanford, CA: Stanford University Press.
National Coalition for Gay and Lesbian Equality and Another v. Minister of Justice and Others (1999) (1) SA 6 (CC).
National Coalition for Gay and Lesbian Equality and Another v. Minister of Home Affairs (2000) (2) SA 1 (CC).

Ndaba, B. (2007) ' "Hate Crime" against Lesbians Slated', *Star*, 12 July, page 2.

Nicol, M. (1996) *The Waiting Country: A South African Witness*, London: Gollancz.

Parliament of the Republic of South Africa (1961) Marriage Act 24 of 1961, Pretoria: Government Printer.

—— (1990) Maintenance of Surviving Spouses Act 27 of 1990, Pretoria: Government Printer.

—— (2006) Civil Union Bill 26 of 2006, Pretoria: Government Printer.

—— (2006) Civil Union Act 17 of 2006, Pretoria: Government Printer.

Powell, I. and Alexander, J. (1995) *Jane Alexander: Sculptures and Photomontages*, Johannesburg: Standard Bank National Arts Festival (South Africa).

Robson, R. (2005) 'Sexual Democracy', *South African Journal on Human Rights*, 23: 409–31.

—— (2008) 'On Rupture and Rhyme: Perspectives on the Past, the Present, and Future of Same-Sex Marriage', in M. Judge, A. Manion and S. De Waal (eds.), *To Have & to Hold: The Making of Same-Sex Marriage in South Africa*, Johannesburg: Fanele.

Sedgwick, E. K. (1994) *Tendencies*, New York, NY: Routledge.

Shapiro, J. (2006) 'Cartoon', *Cape Times*, 21 September, page 4.

Thomson, A. (2005) *Deconstruction and Democracy: Derrida's Politics of Friendship*, London: Continuum.

Volks NO v. Robinson and Others (2005) (5) BCLR 671.

Wills, D. (2005) 'Full dorsal: Derrida's politics of friendship', *Postmodern Culture*, 15(3). Online: <http://pmc.iath.virginia.edu/text-only/issue.505/15.3wills.txt>.

Chapter 6

The judicial virtue of sexuality

Leslie J. Moran

Early in the course of undertaking empirical research on the sexual diversity of the judiciary in Australia, South Africa and England and Wales, I had to address a particular challenge that appeared to differentiate sexual diversity from other strands of diversity such as race, ethnicity, faith, disability and gender (Moran 2006). Sexuality, I was repeatedly told, was unlike the other strands of diversity. In short, sexuality is not, and ought not, to be taken into account. Other strands of diversity, informants told me, must be recorded and benchmarked, both being essential to monitor progress towards the desired (and in some instances legally required) objective of a more diverse judiciary. In sharp contrast, the message about sexuality was that it is and ought to remain absent. Some strands of diversity, these key informants seemed to suggest, have a desirable quality; they have come to represent a virtue of the institution. Sexual orientation does not.

This research landscape generated a number of challenges. How do you research and make sense of sexuality that key informants insist is and ought to remain absent and irrelevant? How do you research the operation and effects of that which is apparently not spoken about? How do you research the sexual norm when its existence and operation is denied? Queer theory was one theoretical tool that provided me with a number of insights that enabled me to respond to these methodological challenges. I offer an overview of some of the key queer theory insights that helped me to engage with and make sense of the research data. Thereafter, I use these insights to analyse data generated through my ongoing project to examine the formation and operation of sexuality in the judicial institution. But first, a few words about the data I want to examine.

Swearing-in ceremonies

The data set at the heart of this essay may for some be surprising and unexpected. It is a collection of documents that record the proceedings of judicial swearing-in ceremonies heralding the beginning of a judicial appointment. The individuals are newly appointed to positions in the Supreme Court of New South Wales, Australia. The sample is taken from ceremonies that span the years 1974 to 2008. Each document records the formal proceedings including the presentation of the new commission of appointment, the swearing of the oath of office, as well as the text of the speeches given for the occasions; by the Attorney-General (or his appointee and more recently the President of the Bar Association); the President of the Law Society; the new judge. The ceremonies have been described as 'civic occasions' (Spigelman 1998: 6), as a 'ceremony of welcome' (Loxton 1973: 5) and a 'celebration' (Macken 2008: 7). They take place in the Banco Court, on the 13th floor of the Supreme Court building in downtown Sydney, at the heart of the legal community. The courtroom is the largest, most elaborately and expensively furnished court in the building. It is the court of the Chief Justice, the head of the judiciary. While a functioning courtroom, the presence of key ceremonial objects (the portraits of the Chief Justices) highlights the particular ceremonial and symbolic role of the space. And the performance of the swearing-in events in this location highlights their symbolic significance for the institution. The public nature of the event is in part reflected in the face-to-face interactions between speakers and the audience that attends these ceremonies, made up of fellow judges of the Supreme Court, fellow judges from other courts, men and women of the legal profession, friends and family of the new judge and 'the public' more generally (Spigelman 1998: 4). However, it probably remains the case that, while the audience has the potential to be diverse and widespread, in practice these are ceremonies that predominantly attract a 'legal audience' (Allsop 2008: 11). Technology, in particular the printing press and more recently digitalisation has potentially changed this, widening the audience, if not by categories then by balance and number, making these ceremonial events more readily accessible to the public.[1] This technological accessibility also transforms the nature of the interaction from face-to-face to mediated 'quasi-interactions' (Mawby 2002: 73).

Public sex

A few words are in order about aspects of queer theory that helped to make sense of the gaps and silences that emerged as a recurring theme in my early research data on sexuality in the judiciary. The first insight is queer theory's insistence that sexuality is a matter of 'culture' (Berlant and Warner 1998: 548, fn 2), a 'sexual regime'. Seidman describes it as, 'a field of sexual meanings, discourses and practices that are interlaced with social institutions and movements' (1994: 169). As such, sexuality, Berlant and Warner explain, is always in play. It is always in public. Thus, the perceived and proposed absence of sexuality from the institution of the judiciary in general, and judicial diversity debates, in particular, needs to be treated with considerable caution. More specifically, a requirement to be silent about sexuality is not the absence or disappearance of sexuality from individual and institutional relations and settings but a key dimension of its mode of public appearance and operation.[2]

Under the conditions of heteronormativity, silence is a device by which sexuality appears in public and more specifically it is one of the devices through which heterosexuality as the norm is reproduced in society in general and, I want to suggest, in the institution of the judiciary in particular. Sexuality in general, and gay or lesbian sexuality in particular, is not so much a troubling new addition, a threatening invasion, an inappropriate incivility or an irrelevant matter in judicial settings. It is always already a very public and relevant dimension of the institution of the judiciary.

Silence, absence and invisibility all play a key role in the public fabrication of the heterosexual as privileged sexual subject. It is as the unmarked that heterosexuality is fashioned as the basic idiom of the personal, and the social. Heterosexuality is in some respects like the air we breathe, a diffuse all-pervasive presence (a sense of rightness) but at the same time out of mind, unnoticed, unrecognisable, often unconscious, and immanent to the practice or to the institutions.

The attribution of absence to the pervasive presence of heterosexuality plays a central role in linking certain qualities and values to that subject position. One characteristic attributed to heterosexuality as the unmarked is that of 'a state of nature' which gives rise to a multitude of positive connotations; truth, sincerity, unaffected, unprejudiced and so on. Another is the link between heterosexuality and the ideal. And another is the assumption that heterosexuality is the very pinnacle of moral accomplishment. In short the heteronormative regime produces heterosexuality as a rather paradoxical phenomenon, which is always present and generating a superabundance of meaning while at the same time being absent.

Thinking sexuality as a regime or culture, rather than an identity, requires us to recognise the diffusion of heterosexuality: it has no centre. There is no singular moment of operation or final moment of realisation. But its social, temporal and spatial diffusion potentially makes it much more difficult to recognise its forms of operation (Berlant and Warner 1998: 556). At best, Berlant and Warner suggest, it is never more than a fragile, provisional unity. Finally, the study of heteronormative culture requires that we take seriously 'the metacultural work of the very category of heterosexuality' which, as Berlant and Warner explain, this works to consolidate, 'as a sexuality widely differing practices, norms and institutions' (553). In response sensitivity is needed both to the way the purported totality of heterosexuality fashions and displays cohesion and singularity and at the same time marks and exposes its fragility. With all these thoughts in mind let me return to the data I want to analyse.

'May it please the court . . .'

The texts of the judicial swearing-in ceremonies that make up my data set are very uniform, suggesting that there has been little formal change to the structure of the ceremony during the period studied. In turn, the nature and tenor of the speeches by the government law officers (the Attorney-General and Solicitor-General), the Presidents of the Bar and the Law Society demonstrate a remarkable consistency of general content and tone. These speeches take the form of what might best be described as life writing (biography) that has a strong hagiographic quality. More specifically, the speeches identify and map the qualities of the newly made judicial subject. They have a double function, formulating and fashioning the subject not only as an exemplary individual life but also as an exemplary life that embodies the virtues of the judicial institution. As such the speeches are a very specific form of life writing, being biographical accounts dedicated to the portrayal of State officials (Moran 2008, 2009). The new appointee's response in the first instance is framed somewhat differently, being a statement of thanks. But it also has strong life-writing qualities (this time autobiographical). As one of the newly appointed judges explained, 'Preparing [the speech] was like preparing my own eulogy' (Fullerton 2007: 6). Like the speeches that precede it, the judge's response also has a double function as a form of textual self-fashioning that is also an institutional self-fashioning. Each speech offers a textual portrait that makes and makes public the values and virtues of the institution of the judge. The objective of this essay is to explore how, if at all, sexuality is made in these texts and, more specifically, how the judicial subject's sexuality is figured as an institutional ideal, as a judicial virtue, in this important public setting.

Sexuality is present in all the swearing-in texts studied. It appears most regularly in biographical and autobiographical references to the judicial subject's family. For example, at the ceremony to swear-in Justice Priestley, Attorney-General Landa commented, 'Perhaps the most outstanding characteristics you have exhibited are intellectual honesty and a deep and abiding devotion to your family' (1983: 5). While in this instance there is no further information about the nature of this family, under conditions of heteronormativity the cultural assumptions and expectations make it heterosexual by the very absence of a reference to sexuality. In an example taken from the following year, the swearing-in of Justice Ash, the heterosexual nature of the family is more explicitly reported, 'The step your Honour has taken is a major one . . . for your Honour, but it is also an important one in the lives of your Honour's family – Mrs Ash especially and your four children' (Loxton 1975: 8). In 2008, at the swearing-in of Justice Allsop as the new President of the Court of Appeal, hetero-familial sexuality is attached to a particular emotional quality of the subject, 'devotion'. The Attorney-General explains, 'One central aspect of your life which has not been mentioned is your devotion to your children . . . and your wife . . .' (Hatzistergos 2008: 5). The appearance of the family and family values in a hagiographic text devoted to writing the life of the subject as the embodiment of the qualities of judicial office is far from arbitrary. They are chosen because they work to shape the subject's individual *and* official persona in the image of the ideal moral accomplishments that the hetero-familial represents.

A second family haunts these texts. This 'other' family is the sum total of intimate social relations that make up the professional life of a legal practitioner. In some instances the connection between the biological family and the social (professional) family is literal: the two families coincide. In the case of Justice Clarke, the President of the Law Society explained, 'Your Honour is one of a long line in the legal profession . . . your grandfather was a solicitor . . . subsequently a leading member of the Tasmanian Bar . . . your Honour's father was called to the Bar in London' (McLachlan 1983: 4). Another example is from the Attorney-General's speech at the swearing-in of Justice Windeyer, 'Your Honour's appointment continues a proud family tradition of service to the law. You are a member of the sixth generation of Windeyer lawyers in Australia' (Coombs 1992: 1). Again, in the absence of explicit reference to the sexuality of these familial relations (both biological and social), the cultural assumption and expectation is that they are heterosexual. More specifically, the coincidence highlighted in these examples facilitates the mapping of the virtues of the biological hetero-family onto the social relations of the family that is the legal profession. It is the social family that has nurtured the new judicial subject.

While the image of the profession as a 'family' and the biological–social family nexus are abiding themes of the swearing-in texts, the literal coincidence of the biological and professional families is exceptional. Beyond this link, the connection between the biological and the social family is made by way of metaphor. Family metaphors abound in descriptions of professional relationships. One example is Justice Fullerton's reference to fellow judges as, 'my sister and brother judges' (Fullerton 2007: 6). In general, the biographical and autobiographical accounts are littered with references to the metaphorical familial ties that bind the subject to the legal professional family. They catalogue the history and nature of the incumbent's relationship with judges, barristers, clerks and solicitors. One important family moment that recurs is the intimacy between the new incumbent and now senior judges who occupy the role of 'mentor'. As the Attorney-General explained at the swearing-in of Justice Priestley, 'It must be of singular pleasure to you, Chief Justice, that his Honour was the first person to read with you when you were in fact junior counsel . . . he could not have had a better mentor' (Landa 1983: 2). Another family moment that regularly dots the speeches is participation in family events: professional committees. A third is participation in manly sports with other legal colleagues, particularly 'tennis' (ibid. 2), and 'golfing and cricket' (Gaudron 1983: 2). The family metaphors take on a slightly different form in the following comment on the professional life of the new appointee Mr Justice Meagher, by the President of the Law Society. He declared, 'I must express the view that you have been in love not only with the law, but also with the Bar and its traditions, its camaraderie, its pursuit of excellence and the skills of advocacy' (Thornton 1989: 8). Here the sentimental romantic characteristics commonly associated with the hetero-familial are mapped onto the professional world. Justice Simpson gives this a slightly different spin, but one that naturally follows on from being in love with the law and the Bar. In her reply to the welcoming speeches she explained that, 'appointment to this, or any other court . . . was properly seen as the last stage of a legal career – the professional equivalent of marriage' (Simpson 1994: 12–13).[3]

I want to linger a little longer over Justice Simpson's use of the metaphor of 'marriage'. Let me begin with a few general observations on the meaning of the term 'marriage'. Judith Butler describes marriage as a relation of kinship and, more particularly, as a recognizable form of kinship that organises sexuality, 'in the service of reproductive relations' (Butler 2002: 14). The legal status of marriage, she explains, gives this mode of sexual reproductive kinship a privileged status. Where same-sex reproductive relations are excluded from the legal definition of 'marriage' the latter is made to stand for reproductive relations as heterosexual. In Justice Simpson's use of 'marriage' as a metaphor of the social relations that achieve their objective in judicial appointment, these sexual (and other) qualities transfer onto the social relations that make up the legal career, and the office of the judge, making them in that image. As a particularly celebrated and privileged form of 'kinship', and more specifically, in an image of 'reproductive kinship', and a kinship that has a particular sexual form, the legal professional social relations fit neatly into Butler's definition of 'kinship' which goes as follows:

> a set of practices that institutes relationships of various kinds which negotiate reproduction of life and the demands of death . . . kinship practices will be those that emerge to address fundamental forms of human dependency, which may include birth, child-rearing, relations of emotional dependency and support, generational ties . . . (to name a few)
> (2002: 15)

Justice Simpson's use of the marriage metaphor transfers these characteristics onto professional social relations, making professional relations into relations of reproductive kinship. What is the sexual nature of the legal profession as reproductive kinship? And, more specifically, how does it fashion the sexuality of the judiciary?

While neither Bench nor Bar can continue to be defined by reference to gendered kinship relations characterised by the terms 'fraternity' or 'brotherhood' (by reference to a single sex/gender–male/masculine), it remains the case men have dominated (and in many instances continue to dominate) these professional kinship relations. More specifically, legal professional kinship reproduction is not hetero-sexed but mainly same-sex reproduction. The depiction of men (in a variety of roles, as teachers, pupil masters, head of chambers, judicial mentors, clerks, etc.) as the dominant players in institutional reproduction (both professional and judicial) is a key feature of the majority of the swearing-in speeches in my sample. In the overwhelming majority of the speeches relating to male members of the judiciary the role of women in professional reproduction is formally abolished. Their role is confined to domestic/biological reproduction.

In thinking through the implications that this raises for the sexual fashioning of the judicial subject, I want to turn to Eve Sedgwick's pioneering work on homosociality. Homosociality, she explains:

> is a word occasionally used in history and the social sciences, where it describes social bonds between persons of the same sex; it is a neologism, obviously formed by analogy with 'homosexual' and just as obviously meant to be distinguished from 'homosexual'. In fact, it is applied to such activities as 'male bonding', which may, as in our society, be characterized by intense homophobia, fear and hatred of homosexuality. To draw the 'homosocial' back into the orbit of 'desire' . . . is to hypothesize the potential unbrokenness of a continuum between homosocial and homosexual – a continuum whose visibility, for men in our society, is radically disrupted.
>
> (1985: 1–2)

I resort to Sedgwick's 'homosocial' not to put genital homosexual desire at the root of other forms of male homosociality, but to draw attention to the significance of same-sex desire in professional reproduction and to highlight one of the effects this has on sexuality in that context: the production and reproduction of a demand for the radical dislocation of genital homosexual desire. In short, the institutionalisation of homosocial desire in professional kinship relations of reproduction works to secure the sexual culture of those same-sex professional relations as formally exclusively heterosexual. Resort to those professional kinship relations in the public formation of the subject's judicial qualities and virtues is a means by which the sexual virtues of the judicial subject are also formed as heterosexual.

Same-sex professional reproduction is not a kinship theme unique to male judges. In the case of women judges, the importance of all female reproductive kinship is noted by the female judges themselves, as well as by the other speakers. The first woman appointed to the bench of the Supreme Court was the Honourable Carolyn Chalmers Simpson, QC. In her speech she thanks, 'those many women who have preceded me in the legal profession' (Simpson 1994: 15) and singles out Mrs Jan Joy (her clerk in chambers) and her secretary, Julie Briese. In later examples women judges are identified in a manner now familiar from the swearing-in speeches of male judges: as mentors. For example, the Attorney-General explains that Justice Fullerton came from a social context in which she had no contacts with the Bar, making a career at the Bar difficult if not impossible. He continued, all changed when, 'In an act of generosity . . . Justice Virginia Bell, then a junior, took an interest . . .' (Slattery 2007: 2). In her own inauguration speech Justice Virginia Bell identified a slightly different familial role: that of 'role model'. She identified figures such as Justice Matthews, Justice Gaudron, Justice O'Connor, Justice Simpson, as important, 'not just because they have served as role models . . . but particularly for their personal qualities of unfailing warmth and support for women members of the profession'. She concludes, 'I have been a beneficiary . . .' (Bell 1999: 3).

If the analysis offered so far paints a picture of the cohesion and the singularity of the sexual virtues of the judicial subject made under the conditions of heteronormativity, then I must also add that the data offers evidence of a more diffuse and multiple heterosexuality – a heterosexuality that is more fragile. Let me begin by drawing upon comments Justice Meagher made in his response to the usual laudatory biographical speeches that inevitably preceded the judge's reply. He begins in terms that are familiar, 'Finally I must thank my wife and daughter . . .', but at that point his comments break with convention. He thanks them, 'for performing handsomely the tasks for which they as women were designed; namely to provide me with domestic comfort; and also for their fortitude in embracing the new challenge which confronts them – to supply me with financial assistance' (1989: 11). How are we to make sense of what appears to be something of a celebration of the subordinate position of the female members of the judge's family? Justice Meagher offers a guide to the meaning of these comments. It comes from an observation he makes about the nature of the swearing-in speeches. The generous remarks, central to the hagiographic tone of the speeches, he explains are, 'nonsense . . . [f]lattery . . . heavily laced with mendacity' (ibid. 9). One reading of his harsh and barbed comments about the burdens, trials and tribulations suffered by his wife and daughter is that they expose the hagiographic fiction for what it is; challenging the sentimental romantic family ideal as the metaphorical template for the institutional ideal of judicial office.

Speeches from the earlier period in my sample provide another example of challenges to the homogenous sentimental romantic hetero-familial ideal. Comments commonly focus upon the impact of career on family. For example, at the swearing-in of Justice Priestley, the Attorney-General begins in the usual way by making institutional virtues out of the subject's heterosexual family, and by making the man/judge in the image of, 'A dedicated but truly contemporary family man . . .' (Landa 1983: 3). The tenor changes a little when he goes on to note the impact of professional life upon family life, which takes the form of, 'the sacrifice of time available to family and loved ones inherent in any successful and distinguished barrister's life . . .' (ibid.).

The familial/institutional virtues of the hetero-family as the moral apotheosis are not so much fully realised in the institution of the judge but threatened by the career pathway that terminates in the self same institution that is built upon long periods of absence by the father/judge from domestic life and biological family. This comment both acknowledges the failure and the fragility of the heterosexual ideal (the threat is connoted by way of the reference to the 'sacrifice of time' – the absent father). But at the same time the threat is quickly glossed over and the link between the moral virtues of the heterosexual family and the judicial institution are remade by reference to the pride (the self awareness of moral superiority) experienced by the family, which follows the elevation of the husband/father to the office of judge. As the Attorney-General explains, 'I am confident that they will feel the sacrifice . . . has been well rewarded by his appointment' (ibid.). And it is a recuperative theme that continues to be resorted to. As the Attorney-General explained in the 2008 swearing in of Justice Allsop as President of the Court of Appeal, 'Your family share in the honour you receive today' (Hatzistergos 2008: 5).

I now want to consider the texts of the ceremonies of three particular judges. The first is Michael Kirby. In 1984 he was appointed as President of the Court of Appeal. In 1999, some three years after leaving the Court of Appeal to take up an appointment to the High Court of Australia, he announced his long-standing relationship with a man, Johan, in the pages of the Australian edition of *Who's Who*. In response to a question I put to him during the course of an interview, 'Would you agree that [1999] was the first moment in your professional life that everybody knew that you were gay?' he replied, 'Certainly not'. He explained, prior to that date:

> It was commonly known that I was homosexual because I had a partner from the 11th of Feb 1969 and lived together with him in the suburbs of Sydney. We lived quite openly. We went shopping and did other things that ordinary people did. Australia is quite a small society, 20 million people, and concentrated in a few cities, therefore I think it was generally known that I was gay. But that was not asserted. Remember, in the early days, from 1969 till 1974, homosexual acts even between consenting adults in private were still illegal. Mind you, they hadn't for many years been prosecuted and it was something of a dead letter. They were used occasionally to harass people. But it wasn't the subject of very many criminal prosecutions. But that was a reason for a certain degree of discretion. As well as that, I'm quite a discreet sort of a person. Most people who end up on the judiciary are. So, that was a period in my life and the life of my partner when we were not, as it were, in your face.
>
> (2006)

The second judge is Justice Virginia Bell (1999). While she has made no formal announcement about her sexuality, others have described her as 'an openly lesbian lawyer' (Marsden 2005: 171), and the entry for her in the free encyclopaedia *Wikipedia* explains (giving newspaper reports as its sources), 'Bell lives in inner Sydney with her female partner, a barrister' (Anon, undated). The third judge is Justice Elizabeth Fullerton (2007).

The texts of the swearing-in ceremonies of all three of these judges have much in common with all of the other texts that make up this case study. The biographical expositions show all the signs of the hagiographic mode of representation noted above. All of these judicial subjects are depicted as the embodiment of exemplary legal careers, and evidence of their investment in professional relations is presented. Befitting the senior post being occupied by Michael Kirby, the Attorney-General summed up the new incumbents' exceptional achievements in the comment that, 'Few curricula have demonstrated so much *vita*' (Landa 1984: 3). Likewise, the lives of all three judges are fashioned in hyperbolic form according to the established need to evidence the particular cognitive qualities of the judicial subject. Kirby is 'one of the nation's ablest legal minds' (ibid. 1–2). Bell is, 'more skilful and entertaining than other colleagues at the Bar' (Barker 1999: 1), and Fullerton is 'pre-eminent . . . in the present generation' of leading counsel (Slattery 2007: 1). In turn the speeches map their many emotional and cultural qualities onto those attached to judicial office; of their erudition, independence, dedication, passion, generosity, fearlessness, to name but a few.

What of references to sexuality? References to family are to be found in all three cases. One difference in the texts that relate to these judges is that in two texts (Kirby 1984; Bell 1999) family is only mentioned by the judge, maybe in response to the lack of biographical references in the other two speeches. In all instances where the nature of that family is expanded upon it is by reference to parents, siblings, aunts, nephews. Heterosexuality is the unspoken of these figures of reproductive kinship that is the biological family.

References to the other family – the profession as family – are more prominent aspects of the biographies of all three lives. President Kirby (as he then was) makes use of a kinship analogy in his comment that his, 'original home' is in, 'the bosom of the law' (1984: 12). He also notes the proximity of the domestic and professional family in his aside that, 'there is my family: a close and loving home environment, whose only error in fact was to spawn so many lawyers' (ibid. 13). If neither family nor home necessarily excludes his long time male partner Johan, the absence of a reference to him and the reference to the coincidence of biological and professional families (Kirby's brother is Justice David Kirby a judge of the Supreme Court of New South Wales since 1998) at least formally leaves the heterosexual assumption undisturbed. There is a noticeable difference in the way reference is made to the familial role of judicial mentor between these three swearing-in texts. There is no explicit reference to the gender of the reproductive kinship network that Kirby is part of. However, in the biographical and autobiographical accounts relating to the two women the gender of the professional kinship networks is explicitly

stated. If male same-sex reproductive kinship produces the male judicial subject as heterosexual, there is nothing in the references to female same-sex
reproductive kinship to suggest that these female judges are fashioned as
anything other than according to the same heterosexual assumptions.

So far the biographical and autobiographical fashioning recorded in the
texts of the swearing-in ceremonies of Justices Kirby, Bell and Fullerton form
their individual and institutional persona according to the requirements of
heterosexuality as a judicial virtue. Is this the end of their sexual formation in
that context? The swearing-in texts of both women contain reference to other
sexualities. In both instances it occurs by way of a reference to Sydney's gay
and lesbian event, the Mardi Gras. In the case of Justice Bell it is introduced
by the President of the Law Society, forming a part of Justice Bell's professional pedigree, as a sign of her exceptional professional qualities. Justice Bell's
first professional appointment was as a lawyer with the Redfern Legal Centre,
'a pioneer of the community legal service'. The President of the Law Society
continues, 'The centre was known for taking cases that few others would. This
includes the now historic civil liberties case involving those arrested at the
first Gay Mardi Gras in mid-1978' (Hole 1999: 2). In the speeches of Justice
Fullerton's inauguration it is used to fashion her civic credentials and virtues.
The President of the Bar Association explained that Justice Fullerton was, 'a
director of the Gay and Lesbian Mardi Gras Board and ... chaired the
Mardi Gras Festival committees' (Slattery 2007: 4).

Now for some references that intrigue me. The first is a comment by the
Attorney-General made during his acclamation of Michael Kirby. It appears
in the context of a reference to Kirby's prolific writing that takes the form of,
'a ceaseless production of papers, articles, speeches and reviews'. Commenting on Kirby's preference for using opening quotes, the Attorney-General
observes, 'the author may remain hidden in the obscurities of erudition ...'
(Landa 1984: 5). As this comment suggests, the very public persona produced
through his copious scholarship leaves the subject surprisingly hidden from
view. During the course of his speech at the swearing-in ceremony of Justice
Bell, the President of the Bar Association concluded that he, 'would have to
agree with [Justice Bell's] own assessment of [her personality] you are a very,
very private extrovert ...' and he concluded, 'being enigmatic can be an
attractive quality in a judge' (Barker 1999: 2). How are we to make sense of
these? Do the references to a violent disjunction of the private and public
persona of these two judges allude to their different sexuality?

I end with two extracts from the swearing-in ceremony of Justice Fullerton.
Both come from Justice Fullerton's speech. But first, I want to offer this in
the context of a statement made to me by a judge of the District court who
described the speech as an overt statement of the judge's lesbianism. In clos-
ing her speech, Justice Fullerton thanked her parents for their joint and
different wisdom, ethics and their, 'peculiar sense of the vaudeville and for
your approval for the choices I have made in my life'. The second extract

contains a reference to hairstyles, and more specifically 'the mullet' haircut. Justice Fullerton, explains, 'I was totally uneducated in the codes of decorum expected of a barrister. Losing the mullet came first. Getting morning trousers to fit was next, but I am not sure that I've taken much in since then' (Fullerton 2007: 7). How are we to make sense of these comments? Is the 'choice' the decision to come out? Justice Fullerton's comment on her status as an outsider at the start of her career at the Bar may be a reference to sexuality, but is not reducible to it. Another indicator of sexuality is the haircut. The third might be clothing, and more specifically a rather archaic type of men's trousers worn by barristers. But can any of these comments, in the hagiographic context of the swearing-in statements, be read as a reference to a non-heterosexual fashioning of the judicial subject?

In short the answer I offer is 'yes' and 'no'. In a different context and a different medium, painted judicial portraits, I have argued that there is a need to resist the idea that the whole meaning is in the image (either visual or I would now add textual) (Moran 2008). The wider context and the knowledge, history, experience, assumptions and expectations of the audience are also crucial to making sense of the swearing-in ceremony and the biographical and autobiographical objectives that shape the speeches. For example those who do not know about the aesthetic, cultural and political significance of the mullet haircut[4] may not be capable of reading sexuality into Justice Fullerton's speech. But if you are 'in the know' it can be read as a sign of sexuality.

Conclusions

The biographical and autobiographical texts studied here are produced through an intense process of selection and organisation informed by the need to make the subject an exemplar of the institution of the judge. A study of these texts provides an insight into the biographical and autobiographical techniques through which the institution and the institutional values of judicial office are made and made public through the process of embodiment in the individual office holder. This process of embodiment through life writing is a public process of formation of the subject, the individual who occupies judicial office. Moreover it is a very public practice that forms that person's subjectivity by way of the virtues and values of that office. The analysis offered here suggests that sexuality, and more specifically heterosexuality, is always a key dimension of that project of individual and institutional formation.

There may be some evidence that the sexuality that may be capable of being formed as a judicial virtue is changing. And that change is taking place through shifts in what might be described as 'minor details' such as a reference to a haircut or involvement with an organisation. But the analysis of these texts also warns against any simplistic assumption that sexuality and sexual difference is reducible to that which is to be found in the performance or the text of the swearing-in ceremony. The analysis offered here warns against the 'illusion of immanence'; that the totality of meaning is to be found in the image itself. While what appears in the speech or on the pages of the text is important, the meaning of the text is as much a product of the social relations that are produced in and through the text – they may be key to its sexual meaning. The life writing of the individual subject/institution does play a key role in making and making public sexuality as a virtue of judicial office but attempts to make and change the sexual virtues of that institution to not end with that process. They are also made in and through the social relations produced through the face-to-face interactions with the judge and the quasi-interactions with the text.

Acknowledgements

The early stage of the research for this essay was undertaken with the financial assistance of the University of Sydney. I was a visiting fellow in the Faculty of Law from January to April 2007, undertaking a research project on sexual diversity in the judiciary. Special thanks to Jenni Millbank and Gail Mason, who played a key role in supporting this research.

Notes

1 Post-1998 swearing-in texts are published on the website of the Supreme Court of New South Wales. Those pre-1998 are in the Law Library of the Supreme Court of New South Wales in the collection of Judges Papers filed under the relevant name.
2 Compare the readings of sexuality's presence in Indian cinema by Ratna Kapur and Shohini Ghosh, both in this volume (Chs. 3 and 4 respectively).
3 Justice Simpson prefaces her comments on 'family' with the following remark: 'I have reached the point at which thank you's are delivered to parents, spouses and children. I have none of these' (Simpson 1994: 15).
4 Under the title *How to know if someone is a lesbian*, 'Step 3 explains, 'Mullet haircuts and hair clipped or shaved close to the head, have been traditional stereotypes for the butch lesbian. This doesn't mean that everyone with the hairstyle is gay, nor does it mean that all lesbians have that type of hairstyle. Female mulletheads wear the look as a symbol' (eHow Relationships & Family Editor undated).

References

Allsop J. L. B. (2008) 'Swearing-in Speech of Allsop P.', *Swearing-in ceremony of the Honourable James Leslie Bain Allsop as a judge of the Supreme Court of New South Wales and President of the Court of Appeal of the Supreme Court of New South Wales*, Sydney: Supreme Court New South Wales. Online: <www.lawlink.nsw.gov.au/ lawlink/Supreme_Court/ll_sc.nsf/vwFiles/Allsop020608.pdf/$file/Allsop020608.pdf> (accessed 2 June 2009).

Anon. (undated) 'Virginia Bell', *Wikipedia*. Online: <http://en.wikipedia.org/w/index.php?title=Virginia_Bell> (accessed 20 May 2009).

Anon. (1996) *Eulogy for Mr Justice Yeldham*. Library Supreme Court of New South Wales. Copy on file with the author.

Arena, F. (2002) *Franca: My Story*, East Roseville, New South Wales: Simon & Schuster.

Barker I. (1999) 'Swearing-in Speech, Ian Barker Esq., QC, President, New South Wales Bar Association', in *Swearing-in ceremony of the Honourable Virginia Margaret Bell, SC as judge of the Supreme Court of New South Wales*, Sydney: Supreme Court New South Wales.

Bell, V. (1999) 'Swearing-in Speech, Bell J.', *Swearing-in ceremony of the Honourable Virginia Margaret Bell, SC as judge of the Supreme Court of New South Wales*, Sydney: Supreme Court New South Wales.

Berlant, L. and Warner, M. (1998) 'Sex in Public', *Critical Inquiry*, 24(2): 547–66.

Butler, J. (2002) 'Is Kinship Always Already Heterosexual?', *Differences: A Journal of Feminist Cultural Studies*, 13(1): 14–44.

Coombs, J. (1992) 'Swearing-in Speech of J. Coombs Esq., QC President New South Wales Bar Association', *Swearing-in ceremony of the Honourable William Victor Windeyer AM RFD ED as a judge of the Supreme Court of New South Wales*, Sydney: Supreme Court New South Wales.

Davies T. (1996) 'Silence of the lambs', *Sydney Star Observer*, 11 May, page 8.

eHow Relationships & Family Editor (undated), 'How to Know If Someone Is a Lesbian', online: <www.ehow.com/how_2106673_know-someone-lesbian.html> (accessed 2 June 2009).

Fullerton E. (2007) 'Swearing-in Speech of Fullerton J', *Swearing-in ceremony of the Honourable Elizabeth Fullerton SC as a judge of the Supreme Court of New South Wales*, Sydney: Supreme Court New South Wales. Online: <www.lawlink.nsw. gov.au/lawlink/Supreme_Court/ll_sc.nsf/pages/SCO_fullerton190207> (accessed 2 June 2009).

Gaudron M. G. (1983) 'Swearing-in Speech of Miss M. G. Gaudron, QC Solicitor-General', *Swearing-in ceremony of the Honourable Matthew John Robert Clarke as a judge of the Supreme Court of New South* Wales, Sydney: Supreme Court New South Wales.

Hatzistergos, J. (2008) 'Swearing-in speech the Honourable John Hatzistergos MLC, Attorney-General of New South Wales' *Swearing-in ceremony of the Honourable James Leslie Bain Allsop as a judge of the Supreme Court of New South Wales and President of the Court of Appeal of the Supreme Court of New South Wales*, Sydney: Supreme Court New South Wales.

Hole, M. (1999) 'Swearing-in Speech, Ms Margaret Hole, President, Law Society of New South Wales', *Swearing-in ceremony of the Honourable Virginia Margaret Bell, SC as judge of the Supreme Court of New South Wales*, Sydney: Supreme Court New South Wales.

Kirby, M. (1983) 'Swearing-in Speech, Kirby P.' *Swearing-in ceremony of the Honourable Michael Donald Kirby C. M. C. as a judge of the Supreme Court of New South Wales, a judge of Appeal of the Court of the Supreme Court of New South Wales and President of the Court of Appeal of the Supreme Court of New South Wales*, Sydney: Supreme Court of New South Wales.

—— (2006) *Interview with Justice Michael Kirby*. (On file with the author.)

Landa, D. P. (1983) 'Swearing-in Speech the Honourable D. P. Landa, MLC Attorney-General', *Swearing-in ceremony of the Honourable Lancelot John Priestley as a judge of the Supreme Court of New South Wales and as a judge of appeal of the Supreme Court of New South Wales*, Sydney: Supreme Court of New South Wales.

—— (1984) 'Swearing-in Speech the Honourable D. P. Landa, MLC Attorney-General', *Swearing-in ceremony of the Honourable Michael Donald Kirby C. M. C. as a judge of the Supreme Court of New South Wales, a judge of Appeal of the Court of the Supreme Court of New South Wales and President of the Court of Appeal of the Supreme Court of New South Wales*, Sydney: Supreme Court of New South Wales.

Loxton, A. H. (1974) 'Swearing-in Speech, A. H. Loxton Esq, President, Law Society of New South Wales', *Addresses on the swearing-in of the Honourable Mr Justice David Albert Yeldham*, Sydney: Supreme Court of New South Wales.

—— (1975) 'Swearing-in Speech A. H. Loxton Esq, President, Law Society of New South Wales', *Swearing-in of the Honourable William Percy Ash as a justice of the Supreme Court of New South Wales*. Sydney: Supreme Court New South Wales.

Macken, H (2008) 'Swearing-in Speech Mr H. Macken, President, Law Society of New South Wales', *Swearing-in ceremony of the Honourable James Leslie Bain Allsop as a judge of the Supreme Court of New South Wales and President of the Court of Appeal of the Supreme Court of New South Wales*, Sydney: Supreme Court New South Wales. Online: <www.lawlink.nsw.gov.au/lawlink/Supreme_Court/ll_sc.nsf/vwFiles/Allsop020608.pdf/$file/Allsop020608.pdf> (accessed 2 June 2009).

Marsden, J. (2005) *I Am What I Am: My Life and Curious Times*, Camberwell, Victoria: Penguin.

Mawby, R. C. (2002) *Policing Images: Policing, Communication and Legitimacy*, Cullompton: Willan Publishing.

McLachlan, D. E. (1983) 'Swearing-in Speech D. E. McLachlan, Esq., President of the Law Society of New South Wales', *Swearing-in ceremony of the honourable Matthew John Robert Clarke as a judge of the Supreme Court of New South Wales*, Sydney: Supreme Court New South Wales.

Meagher, R. P. (1989) 'Swearing-in Speech, Meagher JA, *Swearing-in ceremony of the Honourable Roderick Pitt Meagher as a justice of the Supreme Court of New South Wales and as a judge of appeal*, Sydney: Supreme Court New South Wales.

Moran, L. J. (2006) 'Judicial Diversity and the Challenge of Sexuality: Some Preliminary Findings', *Sydney Law Review* 28(4): 565–598.

—— (2008) 'Judicial Bodies as Sexual Bodies: A Tale of Two Portraits', *Australian Feminist Law Journal*, 29 (December): 91–108.

—— (2009) 'Judging Pictures: A Case Study of Portraits of the Chief Justices, Supreme Court of New South Wales', *International Journal of Law in Context*, 5(3): 61–80.

Sedgwick, E. K. (1985) *Between Men: English Literature and Male Homosocial Desire*, New York, NY: Columbia University Press.

Seidman, S. (1994) 'Queer-ing Sociology, Sociologizing Queer Theory: An Introduction', *Sociological Theory*, 12(2):166–77.

Simpson, C. C. (1994) 'Swearing-in Speech Simpson J.', *Swearing-in ceremony of the Honourable Carolyn Chalmers Simpson QC as a judge of the Supreme Court of New South Wales*, Sydney: Supreme Court New South Wales.

Slattery, M. (2007) 'Swearing-in Speech Mr M. Slattery, QC President, New South Wales Bar Association', *Swearing-in ceremony of the Honourable Elizabeth Fullerton SC as a judge of the Supreme Court of New South Wales*, Sydney: Supreme Court New South Wales.

Spigelman, J. J. (1998) 'Swearing-in Speech', Sydney: Supreme Court New South Wales. Online: <www.lawlink.nsw.gov.au/lawlink/supreme_court/ll_sc.nsf/pages/SCO_speech_spigelman_250598> (accessed 2 June 2009).

Thornton, B. E. (1989) 'Swearing-in Speech, B. E. Thornton Esq., President, the Law Society of New South Wales', *Swearing-in ceremony of the Honourable Roderick Pitt Meagher as a justice of the Supreme Court of New South Wales and as a judge of appeal*, Sydney: Supreme Court New South Wales.

Part 3

Regulation

Chapter 7

Reproductive outsiders – the perils and disruptive potential of reproductive coalitions

Jenni Millbank

Scholarship and activism concerning reproduction and parenting evinces a distinctly bifurcated trend. Lesbian and gay issues and those of heterosexual parents are usually addressed entirely separately, by different people writing to, and speaking with, different audiences. Mainstream family law texts and courses in universities continue to barely acknowledge the existence of gay and lesbian families (Parkinson 2009), while major scholars on reproductive rights are more likely to mention gay or lesbian cases in passing as evidence of a wider point (such as the role of intention in determining parentage) rather than to centre their issues in analysis, or explore them in any detail (Dolgin 2008: 360). Meanwhile, gay and lesbian family-related scholarship has had a far greater focus on family *recognition* issues specific to gay men and lesbians, rather than on issues of reproductive rights related to family *formation*. Perhaps because many gay and lesbian families conceive in collaboration with each other in informal circumstances, access to family formation avenues has not been felt to be as pressing an issue as the legal recognition of families already in existence. Yet, there is a sizable portion of gay and lesbian intending parents who are either unable or unwilling to reproduce in concert with each other and thus need fertility services and adoption. Both of these avenues have traditionally been, and often continue to be, highly discriminatory against same-sex couples. While commentators have pointed out the lack of reasoned basis for exclusion from fertility and adoption services, and identified avenues for challenging exclusions (Storrow 2007; Millbank 2006), discussion has tended not to extend beyond quite formalistic in-or-out parameters. Moreover, when challenges have been brought, or campaigns waged, for change by gay and lesbian parenting groups or individuals, there has been little sense of common cause with straight people who are also prospective parents and who need to use these same avenues of family formation. In short, gay and lesbian attention has focused on the exclusion of gay men and lesbians by virtue of their sexuality, and has too frequently assumed that heterosexual people are *included* by virtue of their heterosexuality. We are out and they are in; over-looking the fact that heterosexual prospective parents often suffer harmful and discriminatory forms of exclusion from both fertility services and adoption avenues for a wide range of reasons – because they are single, or don't wish to marry, are under or over a certain age, had cancer in recent years, or want to select a genetically matched embryo to try to heal an existing child.

In a recent paper, I concluded with a call to reproductive outsiders of all kinds to 'recognise and draw on their commonalities, while being respectful too of differences, in order to work for a legal regime that can fully accommodate both their parental aspirations and functional parent–child relationships' (Millbank 2008a: 165). In this chapter, I want to consider what it could mean, not just for scholarship, but for activism and social change, if we try to forge real coalitions between gay and straight non-genetic families.[1] The examples I draw on are largely Australian, but most of the arguments made are applicable also to the United Kingdom (UK), Canada and New Zealand (NZ), which have broadly similar approaches to reproductive regulation and adoption. Very few, if any, of the examples that I draw upon have application to the United States (US).[2] The US is entirely anomalous because it has:

- high numbers of children available for domestic adoption;
- largely unregulated fertility services offering assisted reproductive technology (ART);
- widely available payment for donor gametes;
- widely legal, and in several states legally enforceable, paid surrogacy.

The context for Australia, the UK, NZ and Canada is literally the reverse of the above. While family formation options in these countries have much in common with each other, they have little in common with the US.

Who are reproductive outsiders and what do they have in common?

By reproductive outsiders I mean all individuals and couples who are pursuing a desire to parent outside the confines of the hetero-nuclear, sexually reproductive family. This includes all lesbian and gay parenting units, but also heterosexual people who are unable to have children without assistance.[3] For these groups, family formation involves a loss of autonomy through the need for contribution by others, a move away from normative modes of family formation, and the creation of non-traditional family units. At a minimalist level, for heterosexual people, outside input could simply involve the provision of a fertility process (such as in vitro fertilisation – IVF) in place of sex. By still utilizing both partners' genetic material, the end result is still a normative bio-genetic family, even though the process of family formation varied. At the 'outside', for heterosexual 'outsiders', family formation could involve the adoption of a genetically unrelated child, or conceiving with the genetic contribution of a third party through the use of donor sperm, eggs or embryos, or with the gestational labour of another person in the instance of surrogacy. At this reach, the loss of autonomy, departure from 'the natural' and often non-matched genetic make-up of the heterosexual family is much more analogous to the experience of gay and lesbian reproduction.

The cultural context in which this discussion takes place is one of distinct tension between, on the one hand, a growing visibility of a wide variety of non-genetic family forms, and on the other, increasing emphasis on genetic identity in public discourse and in social and legal policy. The rise of what has been termed 'genetic essentialism' – the idea that genes are constitutive of self and family (Dolgin 2000, 2008) either to the exclusion of or as a trump over social relationships (Diduck 2007) – has occurred through a process by which increasingly perfectible access to genetic information has translated into the *right* and *need* for us all to know the 'truth' of our genetic origins (Donovan 2006). In turn access to this genetic 'truth' (or history or roots) is laden with cultural values of identity formation and self-understanding such that this genetic knowledge is understood to be essential for 'completeness' as an individual. (Witness for example the UK 'Who Do You Think You Are?' television series where genealogy is depicted as a voyage of self-discovery and personal growth on camera: BBC 2004–ongoing, Series 6, 2009. There was an Australian-made series in 2008: SBS 2008. See also Smart 2007.)

In family and reproductive policy, this right to knowledge has gradually been transformed from the mere identification of progenitors to an increasingly unquestioned assumption that identification of genetically related individuals inexorably results in contact with them, leading inevitably to an ongoing social relationship between once lost and now reunited 'relatives'. For example, when the state of New South Wales (NSW) in Australia passed the Assisted Reproductive Technology Act in 2007, introducing a compulsory centralized donor register for the first time, it also explicitly included a right for donors to direct their donation towards, or more likely *away* from, certain 'classes of women' (s. 19(b)), effectively legislating in favour of what would otherwise be unlawful discrimination. The discriminatory donation provision was justified by the government on the basis that when the child and their 'genetic parent' meet, it is:

> in the best interests of the child for the genetic parent to have given consent to the circumstances surrounding the child's birth and upbringing.
>
> To put this in another way, it will not be in the child's best interests to discover later in life that their genetic parent has a fundamental objection to their existence or the social and cultural circumstances in which they were raised.
>
> (Kelly 2007: 4383)

So not only must gamete donors (who become here 'genetic parents') be able to relate to the child but they must also be able to connect with and approve of the child's 'social and cultural circumstances' (elsewhere known as, but not here named as, their 'family').

Moreover, the expectation of family reunification with donors implies that the absence of such connection will (always?) be experienced by offspring as a *loss* or *lack*. In this trope, intact functioning genetically unrelated families of mutual care and support are, and always will be, *incomplete*. Importantly, Alison Diduck indentifies a further recent trend in family law, which is that genetic relationships are collapsed into the discourse of child welfare such that biological relationships are granted 'priority, *in the name of welfare*, over social ones' (2007: 471, emphasis in original). Thus, children's welfare or best interests are not separate or additional considerations to those of genetic relatedness; rather they are inseverable and mutually reinforcing, as the above example illustrates. In this context, non-genetic families of all kinds face very serious challenges; troubles, I suggest, that are better shared than faced alone.

A key difference between gay and straight experiences, which explains to some extent the vast disconnect between these two groups in the political arena, is their collective identification and, consequently, their modes of public engagement. Gay and lesbian communities in the countries under discussion have in the past 30 years developed a strong sense of collective identity, gathered together in both social and lobbying organizations, and achieved a relatively high level of political impact within a short period of time. While heterosexual people who face barriers to family formation through infertility do have representation and lobbying resources, these tend to be limited and fragmented, with a relatively low and un-unified public profile (for example, small adoptive parents or international adoptive parents groups, and even more marginal surrogacy groups). Yet, both numerically, and ideologically, heterosexual intending parents ought to be relatively more powerful than gay and lesbian parenting groups. I suggest that perhaps the reason they are not is because, at a very basic level, infertile heterosexual people do not have a collective identity, or cohesive social support systems, to generate activism and enable action from the ground up. In this sense, I think they have a lot to learn from lesbians and gay men – and a lot to gain.

Infertility is often characterized as a highly personal experience. There are strong connotations of infertility as an integral aspect of the sexual relationship, and also as a disease or illness, both of which have traditionally been framed as private matters not suited to discussion in the public realm. Infertility may engender feelings of abnormality, failure or shame in the individuals who experience it. For many people, infertility comes to them at some point in adult life as an unexpected and unpleasant discovery that sets them apart from their friends and family (van den Akker 2001). In calling for consideration of a positive collective coalition around the experience of infertility, I am not saying these feelings are unimportant or these barriers are irrelevant.

Yet in the preceding paragraph one could substitute 'homosexuality' for 'infertility' and the remarks would still make sense. In the face of historical tropes of homosexuality as a form of disease or abnormality, and continuing contemporary pressures to conceal lesbian and gay sexuality as 'private', lesbians and gay men have formed strong collective identities and activist coalitions to positively pursue relationship and parenting rights. This is not to suggest that lesbian and gay identity is cohesive. Like infertile heterosexual people, we may in fact have nothing else in common with our allies – being divided by socio-economic class or other factors such as race or ethnicity. But we have been relatively successful in terms of collective organization and achievement of reform agendas. We are united by what we *seek* as well as who we *are*. That is why I speak here of *coalition*s – it is a working together around common goals, and need not involve uniformity of experience or assimilation to a common identity (and see Binnie, this volume (Chapter 2), on the idea of sexual solidarities).

At first blush, there may seem to be much more difference than commonality between the position of lesbian and gay families and those of straight people using assisted reproduction or surrogacy. In particular, the prioritization of genetic connection to both parents by straight couples (van den Akker 2007: 55, 57–8), and/or the framing of their claims by reference to 'normal' family, or as close a facsimile as they are able to achieve, act to reinforce both genetic essentialism (Dolgin 2008: 367–71) and heteronormativity, and thus potentially undermine or devalue claims to non-genetic family based on caregiving and functionality. (Although I acknowledge that lesbians and gay men are not immune from genetic essentialism and other normalizing impulses, they are rather less likely to invoke them successfully.) Yet even claims that arise from, or are cloaked in, the discourses of genetic essentialism and the primacy of the hetero-nuclear family, may nonetheless have unexplored or unexpected commonality with the goals and interests of other reproductive outsiders. Two examples to explore this point briefly are:

1   heterosexual couples who want to have a child with the help of a surrogate and
2   heterosexual women who want to have a dead male partner's child.

In both of these examples, the parties are eschewing other family formation options, such as the use of donated sperm or adoption, in favour of their own and/or their (former) partner's genetic connection with a child: *their* child.[4]

Yet surrogacy involves the close involvement of another person in a couple's reproductive endeavour, often not at arm's length but up close. This kind of collaborative relationship has some parallels with that of lesbian couples conceiving with known donors, in that they need the input of another person, for months or sometimes years in a negotiated understanding of family and connectedness that defies traditional expectations. Of course known sperm donation to a lesbian couple is not analogous to surrogacy, as it does not involve the same degree of bodily commitment as a gestational relationship. However sperm donation, while physically simple, can entail a high degree of emotional investment and complexity, and for some known donors at least can entail feelings of loss or relinquishment (Dempsey 2004; Riggs 2008). Storrow notes that feminist accounts of surrogacy have tended to 'ossify the dichotomy of gestational function and gametic contribution, with gestation being associated with nurture and gametes with raw materials, body parts, and property' (2005: 313). While feminist accounts are deeply concerned about exploitation in surrogacy, there has been considerably less analysis of egg donation, and an almost complete disregard for the experience of known sperm donors (for an exception, see Dempsey 2004).

What unites these situations of third-party assistance is the complex sense of gift, or loan, or investment, of self in the reproductive endeavour of others. In both surrogacy and known donor situations, intended parents may be (or feel) vulnerable on the basis that if they end up in conflict about their respective roles with a genetic or gestational contributor to their family it is that person who will be received as a more 'natural' parent by courts or other arbiters (Millbank 2008a: 163–4). Moreover, when surrogacy does not involve the intended mother's own egg, both kinds of family form entail a mother whose claim to maternal status is made through her post-birth care giving alone, and who therefore faces the imputation that she is not a 'real' mother because of her lack of gestational and genetic link.

Another unexpected, perhaps more tenuous, commonality with lesbian families and those formed through surrogacy arises from recent research into the experiences of heterosexual commissioning parents and surrogates, particularly in the UK, which suggests that surrogacy may be very much a *female collaboration*. While men's genetic connection was centred in these family forms, in that all of them involved use of the commissioning father's sperm and less than half (MacCallum et al. 2003: 1137) involved the commissioning mother's egg, men's involvement in the reproductive endeavour as a whole was marginalized. In contrast to early feminist concerns that infertile women would be pressured into surrogacy by a male partner's desire to preserve at any cost his own genetic tie with children (Storrow 2005: 308–9), one study found that roughly half of the commissioning mothers reported that the decision to try surrogacy was a joint one, with over 40 per cent of women reporting it as *more* their decision than their partner's (MacCallum 2003: 1337). Commissioning mothers were also much more involved than fathers in the pregnancy and birth; many of them attended all medical appointments with the gestational mother (with the implicit provision of mutual emotional support), and the great majority also attended at the birth, compared to only a minority of the fathers (81 per cent compared to only 31 per cent) (ibid. 1338–40). Two studies also found that mothers were somewhat more likely to engage in regular ongoing contact with the surrogate in the future than the father was (ibid.: 1338; Jadva 2003: 2200).

Finally, it is notable that unlike most heterosexual families formed through donor sperm and many formed with donor eggs, surrogacy families, like lesbian families, overwhelmingly *tell* their children the circumstances of their conception (compare e.g. Golombok et al. 1999, 2006a). Surrogacy families are also far more likely than heterosexual families formed with donor gametes to share their circumstances with family, friends and other social contacts. They don't try to 'pass' as 'normal' and in this sense heterosexual families formed through surrogacy don't reinforce traditional hetero-nuclear family paradigms and do contribute to a visible diversity of family forms.

In the second example, that of heterosexual women who are determined to have the child of a comatose, dying or dead male partner, while it is entirely possible that they may be motivated by an idea of fatherhood as purely or primarily genetic, or a fantasy of the eternal biological family that stretches beyond the grave, there are nonetheless interesting common threads with lesbian interests. Women in this situation are not unlike lesbians in the result- ing family form: they are intentionally creating fatherless families that do not, and cannot, resemble their genetic origins. In doing so they defy the demand of heteronormativity for dual-sex parenting, and face the wrath of many who posit fatherlessness as the source of all social ills. They also breach an aspect of the 'natural' in reproduction that is incredibly provocative – conceiving with the dead, which brings with it connotations of abject/unwholesome sexuality such as necrophilia. Thus, like lesbians, they are confronting both sexual and social taboos in pursuing their chosen family form.

Women wanting to reproduce with dead male partners and lesbians seek- ing access to fertility services are also both uncomfortably placed in relation to often disapproving ethics bodies and fertility regulators. At the same time as their claim rests on the idea of autonomy of decision making in family formation, it is also, necessarily, a claim for *assistance* in achieving this end. These claims are therefore not ones that can be understood simply in terms of rights to privacy, reproductive autonomy or freedom from state interference. They must also be understood at some level as claims for *inclusion, assistance* and, in some sense, *approval*.

Defying nature and the 'natural' best interests of children

Both of the above examples connect to the next point, which is that every form of non-coitally formed family, no matter how differently situated, is united in 'defying nature'. In this context, all prospective parents face the condemnation of increasingly vocal religious (and occasionally secular) opposition to non-genetic family forms, and also must brook the intrusion of medical and/or governmental bodies into their family formation. While this could crudely be characterized as a 'common enemy' argument, I think it goes much deeper.

First, both religious opponents of non-genetic families *and* government regulatory agencies justify their intervention largely, even primarily, on the basis of child welfare claims, and both claim to represent the interests of as yet unborn children in reproductive policy making and debates (see also Storrow 2007, on the child's best interests principle in self-regulated clinical 'gatekeeping' practice in the US). The second, and related, bedrock principle which unites both religious and government agencies in the countries under discussion is the unwavering belief that any form of labour-based payment (other than limited compensation for medical expenses) for reproductive contributions by a third party – be they sperm or egg donor, surrogate mother – is a harm to the person receiving payment, to the community as a whole, and to the child who may be born as a consequence of the arrangement.

The enmeshing of the ideals of child's best interests and the ethos of reproductive volunteerism, and their elevation to the realm of unquestioned common good, has severely constrained the ability of reproductive outsiders of all kinds to form families in the way they wish, or the way they are most able. The wishes of prospective parents who are pursuing assisted means to form a family, or avenues such as inter-country adoption, are commonly characterized in public discourse as 'selfish', 'desperate' or consumerist (Crabb and Augoustinos 2008, 309–310). Yet selfless altruism and constant child-centredness are not required of, or imposed upon, adults in the sexual reproduction context, where the unquestioned role of parents involves deciding for themselves the best setting for their children to be born into (see Storrow 2007 for a neat comparative table of best interests analysis in reproductive technology, child welfare, and adoption contexts).[5]

Indeed, at one extreme there is the view that it is an *abuse of children's rights* to conceive them with use of donor gametes at all (see Somerville 2007; Laing and Oderberg 2005; Appell 2008), while a more common expression of the best interests principle is that it is a breach of children's rights to conceive them in circumstances which might prevent access to identifying information about their genetic origins (Shanner 2003). While secular scholars and government regulatory agencies have recently pursued the latter, religious groups are more likely to pursue the former version of this child's best interests argument, valorizing the marital–genetic family as the best or only family form. Religious groups also advocate for direct and extreme forms of intervention such as completely banning all forms of third party conception through donor gametes or surrogacy, which while they have not eventuated in the countries under discussion, have been influential elsewhere (Italy, Egypt: see Storrow 2005). In recent times governments and their regulatory agencies more commonly espouse pluralism – or at least agnosticism – regarding family forms. Governments are both more indirect and more moderate in their aims, promoting 'responsible reproduction' within circumscribed limits such as banning payment, preventing the import or export of gametes, tightly controlling access to fertility treatment in surrogacy and requiring the centralized collection and compulsory release of donor information.

In some respects, the practical result of government regulation may not be that dissimilar to that of mooted prohibitions. Notably New Zealand, the UK, Canada and some Australian states have all introduced compulsory gamete donor disclosure regimes in which the donor cannot, in the future, refuse the release of identifying information about themselves. In the UK and Australia, this was predicted to lead 'initially' to a halving of the numbers of sperm donors, and then to a shift into a different demographic of donor (Ripper 2008; Godman et al. 2006; Daniels 2007). But thus far, there has been an ongoing crisis in semen supply, leading many providers to close their waiting lists or even programs (ABC 2008; Reuters 2008). Yet disclosure regimes are still regarded as a universal good (see e.g. Cahn 2008) because they grant the non-derogable right to children to know their genetic origins – even if those children appear considerably less likely to come into existence now. It is virtually *unthinkable*, and certainly unspeakable, in this context to argue for positive rights to reproductive freedom or opportunity from the perspective of the involved adults – donors and intended parents – or to argue that one could prioritize or even balance their interests and decision-making capacity in a model of 'good enough' parenting (Turkmendag et al. 2008).

The second and related hegemonic norm is that assisted reproductive endeavours should be a 'labour of love' for all of the individuals involved – and thereby resemble as closely as possible the (ideal) sexual family, and most especially the ideal of maternal sacrifice. While not advocating an 'open market' of commercial reproductive labour such as exists in much of the US, I am concerned that exploration of *any* form of payment or compensation is, in the context of the UK, Canada, Australia and NZ, considered outside the bounds of discussion.[6] Like the discourses of child welfare, this silences the claims of intending parents, reduces their range of choices, as well as those of donors and surrogates, and imposes upon them a higher standard of selflessness than that expected of parents elsewhere.

Doctors, nurses, social workers, counsellors, scientists, technicians, storage facilities, receptionists, delivery men and shareholders involved in assisted reproduction are all paid. Indeed some of them make extraordinary profits. Yet in Australia, for example, monetary payment to reimburse an egg donor for lost wages when she takes time off work, and assumes not insignificant health risks, to undergo egg retrieval surgery, or the arrangement of a 'reciprocal donation' arrangement swapping sperm and eggs between a heterosexual couple with female infertility who need donor eggs and a lesbian couple who need donor sperm through a clinical service, may be unlawful if held to constitute 'valuable consideration' or an 'inducement, discount or priority' (Prohibition of Human Cloning Act 2002 (Cth), s. 21; Human

Cloning for Reproduction and other Prohibited Practices Act 2003 (NSW), s. 16). There is a certain irony when fertility companies valued at hundreds of millions of dollars can develop their own loan arms so that patients can borrow money to begin or continue treatment (Repromed 2008; South 2009), but are prohibited from facilitating gamete exchanges on the basis that this will 'commercialise' human reproduction. Equally ironic is the fact that a number of these for-profit fertility services produce 'how-to' booklets for patients (including appendices with draft advertisements and lists of questions for potential donors) so that their patients can go forth into the community to personally seek egg and sperm donors themselves (Repromed 2008) – effectively outsourcing the cost and labour of donor recruitment to patients. Blanket bans on all forms of payment or 'benefit' mean that intending parents must be beggars and not choosers in what is a marketplace by any other name.

In making these arguments, I do not advocate some unmediated version of reproductive 'liberty', unmindful of structural power imbalances and the potential for economic and other abuses. Rather, I argue that restrictive regulation based on ideals of the child's best interests through 'responsible reproduction', such as discriminatory eligibility criteria, lack of access to donor gametes and unrealistically 'perfect' prerequisites for surrogacy[7] can cause both individual *and* structural harm. This happens through evasion, in so-called fertility tourism, in which 'responsible' highly regulated jurisdictions effectively ensure the outsourcing of their reproductive markets.[8] As Richard Storrow notes:

> local laws that purport to outlaw socially irresponsible forms of procreation have extraterritorial effects that violate the spirit of those same laws. By importing oppression in the form of infertile individuals who travel abroad to exercise what they perceive to be their reproductive rights in the destination country in ways that oppress women there, these laws turn public oppression in one country into private oppression in another.
>
> (2005: 329)

Differences and difficulties

Notwithstanding the above arguments, I am conscious of the fact that each of these groups of reproductive outsiders may experience very serious clashes or conflicts of interest, with fractures cutting across straight–gay, gender and genetic–non-genetic lines. Such conflicts may occur both across and within these groups – who, after all, can only be called 'groups' loosely if at all. I briefly touch on some of these fractures, although there are potentially many more, to give a sense of what challenges we may have to face in forming coalitions and working together.

Gay/straight

A much discussed schism between gay and lesbian claims to family, and those of heterosexual non-traditional families, has occurred through claims for same-sex marriage, primarily in the US but also elsewhere. Numerous litigation briefs filed on behalf of gay and lesbian individuals and organizations have made claims to equal access to marriage based on the assertion that marriage, and marriage alone, represents the optimal environment for the raising of children (see e.g. *Goodridge v. Massachusetts Department of Public Health* 798 NE2d 941 (2003)). Such claims have also arisen outside the litigation context. For example in Australia, the lobby group Australian Marriage Equality promoted '19 reasons' for gay marriage including, 'All children should enjoy the tangible and intangible benefits that marriage can bring' (Reason 12). Further reasons included that 'gay parents want marriage in order to be good role models to their children' (Reason 13) and that marriage is needed to provide a 'stable and committed environment for their family' (Reason 14).[9] These kinds of claims either implicitly or explicitly posit that children whose parents are unmarried suffer not only legal, but social, emotional and educational disadvantage (Polikoff 2005), and thereby contribute to the demonization of female sole parent households as well as hampering claims for adaptive and flexible approaches to recognition for a broader array of both heterosexual and same-sex family forms (see e.g. Ettlebrick 2001; Polikoff 1993). Yet claims of 'marriage superiority' continue to be made, placing gay and lesbian claims to one method of family recognition directly at odds with the interests and needs of a broader range of non-traditional families.

Gender

Another fracture occurs along gender lines when gay men who are, or are seeking to be, fathers identify themselves with fathers' rights discourses that are largely hostile to lesbian mothers and female primary caregivers more broadly. In the past this has arisen in donor-father claims to parental status or contact with children born into lesbian-led families. In these cases gay men have framed their claims to children in a manner that asserts the primacy of genetic ties (Boyd 2007; Millbank 2008b; Kelly 2002). Moreover, they have constructed the genetic tie in a gendered way which privileges men's contributions to parenting over women's (Riggs 2008; Diduck 2007). While motherhood *does* fatherhood just *is*.

A recent example of this dimension to gay men's parenting aspirations arose in the process of achieving parental rights for lesbian co-mothers in NSW in 2008. Coalition community groups, such as the Gay and Lesbian Rights Lobby, worked for several years to extend existing laws that grant parental status to the consenting male partner of a woman conceiving a child through assisted reproduction to now include a mother's female partner.[10] The reforms were retrospective in operation, covering children already born before the reforms as well as those born since. The law requires both mothers to be listed on the birth register and certificate and includes provision for the amendment of old birth certificates to add co-mothers who were previously excluded, including if necessary the removal of sperm donors previously listed. At the point where legislation was actually before Parliament, a small number of gay men who identified themselves as members of a gay father's group (Gay Dads NSW) joined voices with conservative, religious and father's rights groups in opposing the reform on the basis that it 'abolished' or 'devalued' fatherhood. Parliamentary debates quote Anthony O'Brien, a gay father, claiming that the reform:

> DIMINISHES THE RIGHTS OF OUR CHILDREN by removing the recognition of our role – not just in being the biological parent but also in our parenting role in the lives of our children . . . THE FATHER HAS A RIGHT TO BE RECOGNISED ON THE BIRTH CERTIFICATE.
> (Rhiannon 2008: 7886. Capitalization in original. See also Smith, 2007 on comparable changes and remarkably similar rhetoric in the UK)

Yet sperm donors, whether known or unknown, and whether listed on the birth certificate or not, do not, and did not, have parental status in any Australian jurisdiction. The legal position of gay men who are known sperm donors, or even actively co-parenting with lesbian-led families, was in fact completely unaffected by the reforms. Nevertheless the gay men who publically opposed the reforms did so in concert with, and using the language of, reactionary father's groups that are the acknowledged opponents of *every* form of lesbian – and gay – parenting.

Genetic/non-genetic

Divisions along the lines of genetic parenthood occur both within and across the groups under discussion. In intra-lesbian family law disputes, it is disturbingly common to find the genetic/gestational mother who had hitherto parented with the co-mother, claiming after separation that she is the only 'real' mother in rejecting the co-mother's claim to contact with or parental responsibility for a child that they jointly conceived and raised (Millbank 2008b).

It is also not uncommon to see non-normative families formed through assisted reproduction claiming or attempting to claim normative status by reference to other reproductive outsiders. So, for example, surrogacy families with a dual-genetic link to the child may claim a higher social status (or greater legal entitlement such as superior access to parentage transfer mechanisms) compared to surrogacy families with only one genetic parent, on the basis that it is 'really' their child.

Claims from, or about, families formed through reproductive assistance which contain a dual or single genetic link, may also privilege that link in a way that distances them from wholly non-genetic families – in particular those formed through adoption. While differences in experience between adoption and other methods of family formation are indeed important to acknowledge, there is a discernible trend in some recent literature to claim that the 'problems' of adoption do not occur in surrogacy (see e.g. Standing Committee on Law and Justice, NSW Parliament 2009: 3.151–3.152). Such claims may be quite sweeping (although some carefully note factors other than genetics such as the history of coercion and deception surrounding adoption practices in the past, or issues in the development of attachment in the adoption of older children: see e.g. Golombok 2006b). In doing so, these claims contribute to an understanding of adoptive families as inherently flawed or problematic, undermine the notion of caregiving as a fundamental aspect of parenthood, and make coalitions across groups far more difficult to achieve. In an equal and opposite drive, groups representing adopted adults have lobbied against third party contributions in ART and surrogacy on the basis that this replicates what they see as the harms of adoption. These arguments are sometimes framed as broad claims that it is inherently harmful for children to be raised by 'non-biological parents' or by other than 'natural' parents (see e.g. submissions from Tangled Webs and VANISH in a recent surrogacy inquiry: Standing Committee on Law and Justice, NSW Parliament 2009).

Conclusion

There may be many more areas of contest and conflict beyond those touched on above. Yet, even with this proviso, I still claim that it is productive in both a scholarly and a practical sense to begin to think about the common interests of reproductive outsiders. While unquestionably challenging, I contend that there is something transformative in the ideas of solidarity, and of coalition, in the area of family formation – a context so often regarded as private, inviolate and highly individualized. It is arguable that in the current era of genetic essentialism there is much to be gained by reproductive outsiders in acting together, and drawing upon both strength of numbers and their broad diversity of claims and experiences, in order to counteract dominant discourse around 'natural' family.

Acknowledgements

Many thanks to Robert Leckey, Isabel Karpin and Anita Stuhmcke for their comments on earlier drafts. Funding to attend the 'Queer/Empire' Symposium which gave rise to this collection was provided by the Social Sciences and Humanities Research Council of Canada and through Australian

Research Council Discovery Project funding for the 'Enhancing Reproductive Opportunity' research project conducted by Millbank, Stuhmcke and Karpin.

Notes

1 Compare Jeffrey Redding's call for another ostensibly alliance, in that case between religious and sexual minorities in the US.
2 Of course there are significant differences among these countries also, for example in the level of public funding available to support assisted reproduction services.
3 I use 'infertile' in this chapter, but acknowledge that this is a very loose term encompassing a wide range of social and clinical factors that may impair fertility (some of which may be overcome in time or with treatment), unexplained inability to conceive, as well as the experience of couples where in fact only one partner has impaired fertility.
4 Including, in Diane Blood's case, through her subsequent lobbying efforts to have the deceased genetic father listed on the birth certificates: see 'Diane Blood Registers Sons' *BBC News Online*, 1 December 2003. Blood had previously won litigation against the UK government regulator for the right to transfer her dead husband's sperm to Belgium so that she could attempt to conceive there, as the regulator would initially allow her neither to use nor export the sperm: *R v. Human Fertilisation and Embryology Agency, ex parte Blood* [1997] 2 All ER 687.
5 I am mindful that the scope of autonomy is variable depending upon social power and has been, for example, far less available to impoverished, indigenous and disabled women who have suffered reproductive abuses at the hands of government and welfare agencies including pressured and forced sterilisation. See Cossman 2007: ch. 3, on the continuing and racially biased intrusion of government policy in the US into women's familial choices when they are welfare dependent.
6 For example there have been several public inquiries into surrogacy laws in Australia in recent years, all of which were styled 'altruistic' such that any discussion of payment was completely excluded by the terms of reference.
7 See for example recent surrogacy reforms in Victoria, Australia, which require that in order to be eligible for ART treatment a surrogate must first be approved by a treatment panel and, among other things, not genetically connected to the child, over 25, have already given birth to a previous child, have received counselling and legal advice, not received any payment, and have no criminal conviction for a violent or sexual offence, nor any child removal proceeding under welfare provisions: *Assisted Reproductive Treatment Act 2008* (Vic) Part 4, ss 14, 42.
8 Compare Jon Binnie's concern, in this volume (Ch. 2), with the inscription of sexual minorities in relation to neoliberal discourses of consumerism.
9 These claims appeared in 2005 and 2006, but are no longer on the current AME website. The '19 Reasons' can be viewed through the 'WayBack Machine' web archive: <http://web.archive.org/web/20050404131641/australianmarriage equality.com/todo/index.htm> (accessed 2 June 2009)
10 Status of Children Act 1996 (NSW) s. 14 as amended 2008.

References

ABC News, 'Sperm Donor Shortage', 17 July 2008.
Appell, A. R. (2008) 'The Endurance of Biological Connection: Heteronormativity,

Same-Sex Parenting and the Lessons of Adoption', *Brigham Young University Journal of Public Law*, 22(2): 289–325.

Boyd, S. (2007) 'Gendering Legal Parenthood: Bio-Genetic Ties, Intentionality and Responsibility', *Windsor Yearbook of Access to Justice*, 25(1): 63–94.

Cahn, N. (2009) 'Necessary Subjects: The Need for a Mandatory National Donor Gamete Registry', *DePaul Journal of Health Care Law*, 12(1): 203–24.

Crabb, S. and Augoustinos, M. (2008) 'Genes and Families in the Media: Implications of Genetic Discourse for Constructions of "The Family" ', *Health Sociology Review*, 17(3): 303–12.

Cossman, B. (2007) *Sexual Citizens: The Legal and Cultural Regulation of Sex and Belonging*, Stanford, CA: Stanford University Press.

Daniels, K. (2007) 'Anonymity and Openness and the Recruitment of Gamete Donors. Part 1: Semen Donors', *Human Fertility*, 10(3): 151–8.

Dempsey, D. (2004) 'Donor, Father or Parent? Conceiving Paternity in the Australian Family Court', *International Journal of Law, Policy and the Family*, 18(1): 76–102.

Diduck, A. (2007) ' "If only we can find the appropriate term to use this issue will be solved": Law, identity and parenthood', *Child and Family Law Quarterly*, 19: 458–80.

Dolgin, J. (2000) 'Choice, Tradition, and the New Genetics: The Fragmentation of the Ideology of the Family', *Connecticut Law Review*, 32(2): 523–66.

—— (2008) 'Biological Evaluations: Blood, Genes and Family', *Akron Law Review*, 41(2): 347–98.

Donovan, C. (2006) 'Genetics, Fathers and Families: Exploring the Implications of Changing the Law in Favour of Identifying Sperm Donors', *Social and Legal Studies*, 15(4): 494–510.

Ettelbrick, P. (2001) 'Domestic Partnership, Civil Unions or Marriage: One Size Does Not Fit All', *Albany Law Review*, 64(3): 905–14.

Godman, K., Sanders, K., Rosenberg, M. and Burton, P. (2006) 'Potential Sperm Donors', Recipients' and their Partners' Opinions towards the Release of Indentifying Information in Western Australia', *Human Reproduction*, 21(11): 3022–6.

Golombok, S. et al. (1999) 'Social Versus Biological Parenting: Family Functioning and the Socioemotional Development of Children Conceived by Egg or Sperm Donation', *Journal of Child Psychology and Psychiatry*, 40(4): 519–27.

Golombok, S. et al. (2006a) 'Surrogacy Families: Parental functioning, Parent–child Relationships and Children's Psychological Development at Age 2', *Journal of Child Psychology and Psychiatry*, 47(2): 213–22.

—— (2006b) 'Non-Genetic and Non-Gestational Parenthood: Consequences for Parent–Child Relationships and the Psychological Well-Being of Mothers, Fathers and Children at Age 3', *Human Reproduction*, 21(7): 1918–24

Jadva, V. et al. (2003) 'Surrogacy: The Experiences of Surrogate Mothers', *Human Reproduction*, 18(10): 2196–204.

Kelly, F. (2002) 'Redefining Parenthood: Gay and Lesbian Families in the Family Court – the Case of *Re Patrick*', *Australian Journal of Family Law*, 16: 204–26.

Kelly, T. (2007) Second Reading Speech, *Assisted Reproductive Technology Act 2007*, NSW Legislative Council, *Hansard*, 27 November: 4383.

Laing, J. and Oderberg, D. (2005) 'Artificial Reproduction, the Welfare Principle, and the Common Good', *Medical Law Review*, 13(3): 328–56.

MacCallum, F. et al. (2003) 'Surrogacy: The Experience of Commissioning Couples', *Human Reproduction*, 18(6): 1134–342.

Millbank, J. (2006) 'The Recognition of Lesbian and Gay Families in Australian Law: Part 2 Children', *Federal Law Review*, 34(2): 205–59.

—— (2008a) 'Unlikely Fissures and Uneasy Resonances: Lesbian Co-mothers, Surrogate Parenthood and Fathers' Rights', *Feminist Legal Studies* 16(2): 141–67.

—— (2008b) 'The Limits of Functional Family: Lesbian Mother Litigation in the Era of the Eternal Biological Family', *International Journal of Law, Policy and the Family*, 22(2): 149–77.

Parkinson, P. (2009, 4th edn) *Australian Family Law in Context: Commentary and Materials*, Pyrmont, Australia: Thomson Reuters (Professional).

Polikoff, N. (1993) 'We Will Get What We Ask For: Why Legalizing Gay and Lesbian Marriage Will Not "dismantle the legal structure of gender in every marriage" ', *Virginia Law Review*, 79(7): 1535–50.

—— (2005) 'For the Sake of All Children: Opponents and Supporters of Same-Sex Marriage Both Miss the Mark', *New York City Law Review*, 8(2): 573–98.

Prohibition of Human Cloning Act 2002 (Cth) s. 21; (Human Cloning for Reproduction and other Prohibited Practices Act 2003 (NSW) s. 16.

Repromed (2008) 'Donor Information: Guidelines for Donors and Recipients'.

Reuters (2008) 'British Sperm Donor Shortage Critical' 12 November. Online: <http://in.reuters.com/article/lifestyleMolt/idINTRE4AB2P220081112> (accessed 2 July 2009).

Rhiannon, L. (2008) *Miscellaneous Acts Amendment Act 2008*, NSW Legislative Council Debates, *Hansard*, 3 June 7886.

Riggs, D. (2008) 'Lesbian Mothers, Gay Sperm Donors and Community: Ensuring the Well-Being of Children and Families', *Health Sociology Review*, 17(3): 226–34.

Ripper, M. (2008) 'Australian Sperm Donors: Public Image and Private Motives of Gay, Bi-sexual and Heterosexual Donors', *Health Sociology Review*, 17(3): 313–25.

Shanner, L. (2003) 'Legal Challenges to Donor Anonymity', *Health Law Review*, 11(3): 25–8.

Smith, I. D. (2007) 'Now They Want to Abolish Fatherhood', *Daily Mail* (UK) 17 November. Online: <http://www.dailymail.co.uk/news/article-494705/Now-want-abolish-fatherhood--changes-IVF-laws-erase-need-Dads.html> (accessed 3 July 2009).

Somerville, M. (2007) 'Children's Human Rights and Unlinking Child–Parent Biological Bonds with Adoption, Same-Sex Marriage and New Reproductive Technologies', *Journal of Family Studies*, 13(1): 179–201.

South, G. (2009) 'IVF – the Baby Business', *New Zealand Herald*, 16 February. Online: <www.nzherald.co.nz/business/news/article.cfm?c_id=3&objectid=10556535> (accessed 3 July 2009).

Standing Committee on Law and Justice, NSW Parliament Legislative Council (2009) *Legislation on Altruistic Surrogacy in NSW* (29 May).

Storrow, R. (2005) 'Quests for Conception: Fertility Tourists, Globalization and Feminist Legal Theory', *Hastings Law Journal*, 57(2): 295–330.

—— (2007) 'The Bioethics of Prospective Parenthood: In Pursuit of the Proper Standard for Gatekeeping in Infertility Clinics', *Cardozo Law Review*, 28(5): 2283–320.

Turkmendag, I. et al. (2008) 'The Removal of Donor Anonymity in the UK: The Silencing of Claims by Would-Be Parents', *International Journal of Law, Policy and the Family*, 22(3): 283–310.

van den Akker, O. (2001) 'The Acceptable Face of Parenthood: The Relative Status of Biological and Cultural Interpretations of Offspring in Infertility Treatment', *Psychology, Evolution and Gender*, 3(2): 137–53.

—— (2003) 'Genetic and Gestational Surrogate Mothers' Experience of Surrogacy', *Journal of Reproductive and Infant Psychology*, 21(2): 145–61.

—— (2005) 'A Longitudinal Pre Pregnancy to Post Delivery Comparison of Genetic and Gestational Surrogacy', *Journal of Psychosomatic Obstetrics and Gynaecology*, 26(4): 277–84.

—— (2007) 'Psychosocial Aspects of Surrogate Motherhood', *Human Reproduction*, 13(1): 53–62.

Chapter 8

Queer–religious potentials in US same-sex marriage debates

Jeffrey A. Redding

These are troubled times for relations between American queers and American religions. After many years of relatively successful efforts at prodding American religions into a less phobic stance on human sexuality, further progress seems to have hit a roadblock with the passage of Proposition 8 in California in 2008.[1] In reaction to this California ballot initiative, the streets of American cities have witnessed loud scenes of anger and protest, often directed at Mormons[2] and their temples.[3] More quietly, gays, lesbians, and also queers have renewed their fire on a traditional nemesis, the Catholic Church, and also newly discovered ones as well, namely African-American churches.[4]

In this chapter, I would like to suggest that these protests and the animosity fueling them have been counter-productive from an American queer perspective. Certainly, Proposition 8 was a troublesome legal and social development, and people should always have the freedom to criticize their adversaries. That being said, it is not clear who (if anyone) should be a queer adversary and the object of queer protest. Notwithstanding this uncertainty, in this chapter I argue that if queers are to protest anyone at this moment in time, those protests need to be directed at *everyone* making hegemonic claims about (gay and lesbian) identity and dignity – including LGBT same-sex marriage advocates. Moreover, beyond suggesting an unorthodox queer adversary in this chapter, I will simultaneously suggest an 'orthodox' ally, namely the religious opponents of contemporary LGBT same-sex marriage advocates.[5]

As is well known in both theoretical and political circles, there has been a long-standing tension between gay and lesbian (now commonly known as LGBT) activists and queer activists. Broadly speaking, queer theoreticians and activists have advocated less assimilationist and less 'normalizing' views about sexuality (and social order) than those which LGBT advocates have pushed. Nonetheless, in response to Proposition 8, and other religiously motivated efforts to restrict the availability of same-sex marriage, traditionally raucous queer perspectives and voices concerning the social regulation of sexuality have either quieted themselves or been quieted/shushed.[6]

In these times of immense political uncertainty, both within and without the US, I believe that this quiescence is understandable. Yet I also believe it is unfortunate, and that real opportunities to forge new kinds of political alliances between queers and others, and also real possibilities of generating uniquely queer-positive legal frameworks, are being lost in a largely silent queer retreat into a strictly secular sexuality politics.[7]

Mainstream LGBT politics, including same-sex marriage advocacy, can be firmly located in this kind of secular politics.[8] That being the case, I do not believe that queer politics has to or necessarily should locate itself similarly and, in this chapter, I argue not only that LGBT same-sex marriage advocates' jurispathic[9] efforts in support of legal uniformity are averse to queer interests, but that Proposition 8 and other religion-philic, non-strictly-secular family law agendas hold real promise for queer interests.

Indeed, while supporters of Proposition 8 have said many homophobic things, Proposition 8 itself opened up a unique opportunity for queers to engage in new legal thinking, activism, and legislation around queer norms concerning relationship-recognition and family law. Crucially, Proposition 8 returned California to a situation of radical non-legal uniformity, or legal pluralism, where same-sex couples are (again) governed by a domestic partnership regime, while mixed-sex couples are governed by the regime of marriage. In Proposition 8's reinvigoration of the same-sex domestic partnership regime, this controversial ballot initiative created an arena which one might call queer legal space. I believe this semi-sovereign[10] arena allows unprecedented potential – and protection – for future (domestic partner) legislation which can be not only more directly responsive to queer lives, queer relations, and queer families than majoritarian marriage ever will be, but also legislation which can be better than existing legal articulations and enforcements of majoritarian marriage.

In other words, one can see Proposition 8 as having created not a 'separate but equal' legal setup, but the real possibility of a 'separate and better' one for queers. Ultimately, as I discuss in more detail below, I believe one can see Proposition 8 – and its supporters – as having opened up new and meaningful vistas in queer *agency* and, as a consequence, queer *dignity*. And as mentioned above, this situation has come about through the mechanism of legal pluralism with respect to laws pertaining to relationship-recognition and the family.

In contrast, American same-sex marriage advocates have largely been advocating for legal uniformity, i.e. one-size-fits-all marriage for everyone. While hegemonic and dangerous in itself, this jurispathic position has also raised the ire of many (though certainly not all)[11] religious people. Moreover, the possibility of peaceful and productive relations between same-sex marriage advocates and their religious adversaries has not been advanced (to say the least) by tactics deployed at post-Proposition 8 rallies around the US. For example, a constant refrain at these protests has been the willful distortion and mocking disrespect of religious (and, most notably, Mormon) beliefs and practices.[12]

At this point in time, it seems clear that contemporary same-sex marriage advocates have largely turned their backs on the Church of Jesus Christ of Latter-day Saints, the Catholic Church, and other religious groupings (Christian evangelical, Muslim, Jewish, and otherwise) which have not been (allegedly) progressive enough to reinterpret and reform their religious texts, practices, and silences to allow for same-sex marriage. In response, my goal in this chapter will be to suggest that American queer activism needs to realign itself at this moment in time, deepening its traditional skepticism of contemporary same-sex marriage advocates, while initiating an embrace of the radically religious. Indeed, however tempting and self-satisfying (and occasionally witty) it might be to adopt the flippant stance towards Mormons and other religious folk that many LGBT same-sex marriage advocates have adopted, I believe that American queer thought and activism can and should adopt a substantially different approach.

American queer practice could more firmly distance itself from contemporary LGBT politics without embracing the radically religious. As the maxim goes, the enemy of one's enemy is not necessarily one's friend. However, in what follows, after first demonstrating the kind of ill-advised arguments for family law uniformity that contemporary (LGBT) same-sex marriage advocates are putting forward, I discuss how, in contrast, religious movements and groups have taken the lead in advocating for alternatives to majoritarian marriage, both in the US and elsewhere. This is not to say that religious people fall into line on the question of family law dis/uniformity, but it is to say that where one finds legislated alternatives to majoritarian marriage, it is often religious people who have successfully argued for and achieved these alternatives. This suggests that American queer practice not only can learn from religious political practice, but also that, to the extent that religious people are in the forefront of efforts to moderate norm-domineering states, queer politics can find a ready ally in the religious in efforts to escape majoritarian marital regimes.

In this chapter, I want to not only highlight a theoretically and politically important tension between American queer and LGBT agendas in the arena of marriage rights, but also suggest that this tension might have to grow in the future, especially to the extent that the designated-enemies of the LGBT same-sex marriage movement are very likely, in fact, queer allies. Admittedly, the terms 'enemy' and 'ally' are hyperbolic ones, especially to the extent that it is nearly impossible to find any entity which, in its entirety, and on all issues, can be simplistically characterized as either/or. That being said, I will use these terms in this chapter, provocative and misplaced as they may be, because I believe that only strong language can work to dislodge the present array of agendas and alliances out of its awkward and unproductive stasis. In sum, then, this chapter represents an attempt to encourage all participants in the American same-sex marriage debates to engage in new thinking, new alliances, and new tactics. Without changes in imagination and tactics, any winner of this particular battle will inherit a social and legal infrastructure which has been deeply and irreparably damaged.

LGBT advocacy on dignity and same-sex marriage

My quest for a new discourse and new alliances in the same-sex marriage debate begins with an exploration of the idea of dignity, and its simplistic appropriation by LGBT same-sex marriage advocates. Dignity is crucial to discuss given that both the California and Connecticut Supreme Courts, in line with LGBT advocacy strategies, have recently invoked this concept when characterizing what is at stake for gays and lesbians with respect to 'marriage', as opposed to 'domestic partnerships' or 'civil unions'. In this part, I will first outline these two high courts' positions on the issue of dignity, and also its relationship to the phenomena of legal non-uniformity/pluralism generally and same-sex marriage specifically. In the next part, I will then move from this explanatory exposition to a critical examination of these decidedly under-theorized (yet nonetheless important) US state court opinions, as well as the LGBT legal advocacy of which they are the direct result.

With respect to California, in *In re Marriage Cases*, the California Supreme Court was asked to decide whether California's relationship-recognition system was consistent with the California's state constitution's guarantees of the right to marry and the right to equality (*In re Marriage Cases* 2008: 701–2). Under this relationship-recognition system, 'marriage' was reserved for opposite-sex couples, while same-sex couples had access only to a parallel 'domestic partnership' regime. Like California, some other states had also created two parallel systems of family law within their borders, but California's regime of different laws for different sexual orientations was somewhat unusual in that it accorded domestic partners 'virtually all of the same legal benefits and privileges, and . . . legal obligations and duties . . . that California law affords to and imposes upon a married couple' (ibid. 698).[13] Accordingly, what the California Supreme Court had to decide in this case was whether California's 'separate but equal' family law system was constitutional under the California Constitution. Ultimately, the Court held that this system was not constitutional, and that same-sex couples had to be given 'marriage' licenses just like opposite-sex couples.

There were many groundbreaking and interesting aspects to this decision. For example, it represented the first instance of a state supreme court applying a 'strict scrutiny' standard to discrimination against gays and lesbians (ibid. 751).[14] The decision was also noteworthy in its contemplation of the possibility that the State of California might create a relationship-recognition regime – available to everyone – that would use a rubric other than 'marriage' (ibid. 764).[15] As important as these aspects of the decision were, I want to concentrate here on an aspect of the Court's decision which has remained under-examined, namely the Court's discussion of the concept of 'dignity' and its relationship to pluralistic family law systems. The Court's words as to dignity and family law pluralism are worth quoting at length here:

> One of the core elements of the right to establish an officially recognized family that is embodied in the California constitutional right to marry is a couple's right to have their family relationship accorded dignity and respect equal to that accorded other officially recognized families, and assigning a different designation for the family relationship of same-sex couples while reserving the historic designation of 'marriage' exclusively for opposite-sex couples poses at least a serious risk of denying the family relationship of same-sex couples such equal dignity and respect.
>
> (ibid. 701–2)

Like other parts of the Court's opinion, the Court's discussion of dignity was breathtaking, though this time in an unfortunate way. As the next part discusses, the Court's discussion of the *necessary* relationship between dignity, legal pluralism, and relationship recognition (e.g. marriage) was ahistorical and lacked empirical grounding. Indeed, as the next part discusses, the Court avoided any deep exploration of relevant family law realities and debates both in the US and around the globe, including those directly pertaining to family law pluralism, dignity, and minority rights.[16]

Less than six months after the California Supreme Court's decision, the Connecticut Supreme Court followed with its own path-breaking opinion on same-sex marriage. In *Kerrigan v. Commissioner of Public Health*, the Connecticut Supreme Court was asked to decide whether Connecticut's practice of 'segregat[ing] heterosexual and homosexual couples into [the] separate institutions' of (respectively) 'marriage' and 'civil union' violated the Connecticut Constitution's protections as to substantive due process and equality (*Kerrigan v. Commissioner of Public Health* 2008: 144).[17] Similar to California's system of parallel relationship recognition, Connecticut's civil union scheme 'conferred on [civil] unions all the rights and privileges that are granted to spouses in a marriage' (ibid. 143).

As with the California opinion which shortly preceded it, there were many aspects to the Connecticut opinion, other than its views on how best to protect gay and lesbian dignity, which are interesting and important. These include the Connecticut Court's finding that any sexual orientation classifications in law are quasi-suspect and deserve intermediate scrutiny (ibid. 141). Here, however, I concentrate on the Connecticut Supreme Court's finding that the denial of marriage to same-sex couples implicates the dignity interests of these couples, and also gay and lesbian individuals more generally.

Setting the stage for its eventual holding, the Connecticut Court observed in its opinion that, while superficially equal, neither marriage nor civil unions in Connecticut operated in a historical vacuum. According to the Court, '[a]lthough marriage and civil unions do embody the same legal rights under our law, they are by no means "equal" . . . [T]he former is an institution of transcendent historical, cultural and social significance, whereas the latter most surely is not' (ibid. 152). Moreover, the withholding of 'marriage' nomenclature to same-sex couplings is especially problematic for the Court given that 'historically [gays and lesbians have] been the object of scorn, intolerance, ridicule or worse' (ibid. 153). Given this history, the Court found it could not 'discount the plaintiffs' assertion that the [Connecticut] legislature, in establishing a statutory scheme consigning same sex couples to civil unions, has relegated them to an *inferior status*, in essence, declaring them to be *unworthy* of the institution of marriage' (ibid. 150, emphasis added).

Using an intermediate level of scrutiny, yet otherwise relying heavily on the California Supreme Court's reasoning and words, the Connecticut Court ultimately held that Connecticut's relationship-recognition scheme implicated the dignity interests of gays and lesbians, including their right to be treated with equal dignity under the law (ibid. 150–1).[18] With respect to equality, the Court stressed the 'overriding similarities' between opposite-sex and same-sex couples (ibid. 162). For the Court, gay and lesbian people 'share the same interest in a committed and loving relationship as heterosexual persons who wish to marry, and they share the same interest in having a family and raising their children in a loving and supportive environment' (ibid.). Given this posited fundamental equivalence between same-sex and opposite-sex couples, the Court held that 'firmly established equal protection principles lead[ ] inevitably to the conclusion that gay persons are entitled to marry the otherwise qualified same sex partner of their choice. . . . [S]ame sex couples cannot be denied the freedom to marry' (ibid. 262–3).

Both the California and Connecticut Supreme Courts clearly believe that the dignity and status of gays and lesbians is necessarily undercut by a relationship-recognition regime that does not treat their relationships in the same way as heterosexual relationships. In the next part, I want to cast doubt on this position. Let me be clear here: I believe that, with further elaboration and support, the California and Connecticut Supreme Courts *might* be right about the relationship between dignity, legal pluralism, and same-sex marriage, at least in the context of the contemporary US. However, I also believe that the existing dignity claims which are being articulated by LGBT same-sex marriage advocates, and judges sympathetic to their advocacy, demonstrate less than adequate regard to the complexity of non-straight communities in the US, and also rely on legal models and arguments which are shortsighted, outdated, and simplistic.

In the next part, I strip away the veneer of obviousness that attaches to presently popular (if unexamined and under-theorized) dignity claims. By doing so, I suggest that these dignity claims neither necessarily win the battle for same-sex marriage, nor necessarily result in the best legal situation for queer people specifically, with their potentially divergent needs, expectations, and desires with respect to family law. My project is a homo-philic one that is interested in queer (and LGBT) dignity, but finds it in places other than majoritarian marriage. With all this in mind, my project also suggests the need for new political alliances. In what follows, I discuss both these new goals and new alliances.

Potential queer–religious visions of dignity and family law: the importance of agency

The American LGBT rights movement's present and unyielding focus on same-sex marriage rights is both a historic and global anomaly.[19] *Why* many American LGBT people have come to see their dignity as intertwined with majoritarian, heterosexual understandings and implementations of family law is an important question to consider – and an important reality to acknowledge.[20] However, along with this 'why' question, one also has to ask *whether* queer (*qua* queer) political capital should, like LGBT political capital, also be invested in efforts to pry open the mausoleum of majoritarian marriage.

In this part, I argue that, while dignity is an important goal, it can be readily located in places other than majoritarian marriage. This is especially the case if one understands (queer) dignity to include a notion of (queer) *agency*. Moreover, to the extent that this agency is facilitated and enhanced by the creation and elaboration of 'queer legal spaces' – such as non-marital, domestic partnership relationship-recognition regimes – these 'separate and better' alternatives should be advocated for with the participation and assistance of groups and organizations, often religiously affiliated, which have had experience in developing alternatives to majoritarian marriage.

One such alternative available in a handful of American states, is that of 'covenant marriage'. Covenant marriages are different from 'regular' marriages, in that:

> covenant spouses agree to restrict their pursuit of a 'no-fault' divorce, and by virtue of the premarital counseling, do so knowingly and deliberately … Thus, the covenant marriage law permits an immediate divorce for proof of fault by the other spouse in more circumstances than the law applicable to 'standard' marriages. In contrast, in the absence of fault, the covenant marriage law requires significantly more time living separate and apart.[21]
>
> (Spaht 1999: 1097–8)

Covenant marriages are more difficult both to enter (required pre-marital counseling) and to exit (restrictions on no-fault divorce). While there are many non-religion-specific reasons that have been given in support of creating this family law option, it is clear that covenant marriages have the support of many of the religious people and organizations which are opposed to same-sex marriage.[22] I believe queer persons and organizations should initiate an embrace of these individuals and groups.

Covenant marriages are but one example of what Joel Nichols refers to as 'multi-tiered' family law systems (2007). Also within this genus of family law systems are 'personal law' systems, found in numerous countries around the world. Personal law systems legislate and otherwise legally enforce different family law norms for different religious communities.[23] Both religiously – and secularly – motivated countries possess personal law systems, with one of the most-discussed such systems being found in modern-day, secular India.

For example, in India's pluralistic system of family law, one finds a 'Hindu Marriage Act' (which also governs divorces between Hindu marital parties), and one also finds the 'Indian Christian Marriage Act'. Furthermore, the 'Indian Divorce Act' governs Christian divorces, while the 'Dissolution of Muslim Marriages Act' governs some kinds of Muslim divorces. There are many other examples of these kinds of statutes in India, as well as a large body of religion-specific, judicially-developed common law that relates to the family.[24]

While the motivations behind India's personal law system are complex, contested, and dynamic over the course of history,[25] today the preservation of this system can be thought of as 'intended to help [. . .] religious minorities express their cultural particularity and pride' (Kymlicka 1995: 31). Indeed, looking at personal law systems in India and elsewhere, what is interesting to note is that 'second class' citizens – for example, Christians and Muslims in the case of Hindu-majority India – often (though not always) oppose efforts to amalgamate them into a common, unitary family law system.

In other words, in these systems, many people view family law pluralism as not only coexisting with the dignity of minorities, but actually as somewhat of a *prerequisite* for that dignity. Of course, there are intense disagreements between different members of any given minority group about the proper content of the family law which applies to the group. Furthermore, these disagreements are often resolved at the expense of minority women. These (fortunate) debates and (unfortunate) abuses aside, the legal and political situation in many personal law systems nonetheless presents a very different read on the relationship between dignity and family law pluralism than that found in the California and Connecticut Supreme Courts' recent opinions. In these systems with religiously-based family laws, and also the contemporary American one with its religiously-motivated covenant marriages, both refuge and dignity can be found outside of the confines of majoritarian marriage.

As the California and Connecticut Supreme Courts see it, however, gay and lesbian dignity is inextricably wound up in formal equality and access to the heterosexual institution of majoritarian marriage. This account of dignity is not entirely wrong, but it also, to its detriment, ignores the need of people to have *agency* with respect to their own lives, as a prerequisite to them feeling like they have dignity. Religious people both inside and outside of the

US have exerted agency – and, hence, experienced dignity – with respect to family law. They have done so being active authors of that law, demonstrating noteworthy authority over and responsibility for it.[26]

In this respect, I worry about what will happen to queer agency – and queer dignity – if queers get subsumed into an institution of marriage which has been built (however awkwardly) for and by heterosexuals. It was disturbing, for example, when the Connecticut Supreme Court approvingly cited from the amicus brief filed by the Connecticut Catholic Conference in that state's same-sex marriage case. Wrote the Court:

> [T]he following observation of Connecticut Catholic Conference, Inc . . . is relevant. 'In *our culture*, there has been a *consensus* on . . . [the] unique ethical foundations [of marriage]: that the union should be for life (permanency), that the union should be exclusive (fidelity), and that the love that sustains and nurtures the union should be characterized by mutual support and self-sacrifice (selflessness).' These ideals apply equally to committed same sex and committed opposite sex couples who wish to marry.
> (*Kerrigan v. Commissioner of Public Health* 2008: 248, n. 76)

In its 'progressive' move to enhance gays and lesbians' dignity, the Connecticut Supreme Court ends up incorporating gays and lesbians into an antiquated vision of marriage which holds many heterosexuals hostage every day.

Moreover, if anything, the reinvigoration of right-wing politics surrounding marriage in the US cautions against queer people vesting dignity in an institution which very likely could come under the control of conservative forces. This is not just something to worry about with respect to 'red' states like Louisiana or Utah. Even in 'blue' redoubts such as New York, one finds antiquated – yet now revived – arguments about the institution of marriage increasingly *en vogue*. For example, the State of New York's highest court recently argued the existence of a persisting connection between marriage and heterosex. Explaining its decision to uphold the traditional legal definition of marriage in that state, the New York court emphasized in its recent opinion that marriage was for heterosexuals – and heterosexuals only – because '[h]eterosexual intercourse has a natural tendency to lead to the birth of children . . . [Same-sex] couples can become parents by adoption or . . . other technological marvels, but they do not become parents as a result of accident or impulse' (*Hernandez v. Robles* 2006: 359). In other words, marriage is important as a social prophylactic when the condom breaks.

While there may be some upfront dignity cost that comes with being denied access to the institution of marriage, it is not at all clear that – in the long run – queer dignity will be enhanced by being subsumed in a family regulation regime whose central concern is how to handle the situation which arises when the condom breaks. Larger gains as to dignity very likely might be had with the development of a body of family law which is *for* and *by* queer people. A version of civil unions or domestic partnership may very likely be the way to go. Queers will arguably have a much greater voice in the future legislation and elaboration of these relationship-recognition and relationship-regulation regimes than they ever will in a majoritarian marriage system.

That being said, there are legitimate reasons to not like the existing 'alternative' civil union and domestic partnership systems. For one, they clearly need sexier, updated monikers. Nomenclature is a very important issue, and getting 'civilized' or 'domesticated' may not be attractive to many queer people. While I doubt it, it may be the case that only getting 'married' will satisfy people's need for rite-of-passage oratorical fireworks. However, even in that case, a separate (non-majoritarian) 'queer marriage' regime would create more opportunity for queer agency surrounding 'queer marriages'. Without a separate regime and the possibilities it presents for experimentations and alternatives in both the form and substance of family law, queer votes will likely fall on deaf ears. This cannot be what dignity absolutely requires.

Conclusion

In the contemporary American political lexicon, 'fundamentally' religious people – whether orthodox, evangelical, Mormon, Taliban, or otherwise – are often depicted and treated as queerly as any gay or lesbian person is. In the eyes of the state and mainstream society, religious people who do not behave are just as dangerous as sexually queer people and their uncooperative desires.

In this environment, it would seem that queer sexuality and queer religiosity have much to gain by working with each other to moderate the pernicious effects of a power-jealous and norm-domineering state. In this chapter, I have argued the worth of exploring future political alignment between the two, and have argued one agenda item – namely the adoption of a more pluralistic administration of family law – with which to initiate this mutual exploration. Of course, who would join this alliance remains to be seen, and it is not the suggestion of this chapter that all queers and all religious people will always and forever be able to work together. Both queer and religious interests are fissiparous and always evolving, and one can never assume alignment either within or between these groupings.[27] That being said, the assumption *has been* that queer folk and non-mainstream religious folk (e.g. Mormons, the overly-orthodox, etc.) are always-already enemies. In this chapter, I have worked to suggest that this assumption is facile, especially in the current context.

In some respects, this chapter presents a revolutionary argument, especially to the extent that the queer–religious alliance that it suggests can only work to deepen an existing tension between contemporary queer and LGBT activisms. In other respects, however, the argument is conservative and conciliatory – though certainly not unprincipled or un-theorized – especially to the extent that it suggests that the dual-track (or pluralist) family law which has emerged in California and other states, and which is commonplace in countries all over the world, is something that holds real promise. Whether revolutionary or conservative, my hope is that this chapter will cause some people to consider real alternatives to the destructive and corrosive politics surrounding same-sex marriage presently.

Acknowledgements

Portions of this chapter were presented previously at the American Society of Comparative Law's 2008 Annual Meeting, two symposia on California's Proposition 8 at Chapman University School of Law during the 2008–9 academic year, a faculty workshop at Saint Louis University School of Law, and the Queer/Empire conference at McGill University's Faculty of Law which led to this volume. I thank participants at each of these fora for their questions and comments, and also Kim Brooks, Mary Anne Case, Glenn Cohen, Katherine Darmer, Adrienne Davis, Roger Goldman, Menaka Guruswamy, Holning Lau, Robert Leckey, Chantal Nadeau, Doug Nejaime, Karen Petroski, Kerry Ryan, Pete Salsich, Kendall Thomas, Molly Wilson, and Kenji Yoshino for very helpful individual comments and conversations. Kate Mortensen and Jonathan Keiser provided very helpful research assistance in the writing of this chapter, and Yale's Fund for Lesbian and Gay Studies (FLAGS) provided generous research support. Rajeev Dhavan provided a very comfortable place to work in the last days of writing this chapter. Of course, all errors of fact and judgment remain mine alone.

Notes

1 Proposition 8 is also known as the California Marriage Protection Act, and it was approved by voter-ballot initiative and enacted into law by Californians on 4 November 2008. Proposition 8 inserted the following provision into the State of California's constitution: 'Only marriage between a man and a woman is valid or recognized in California.' For more information on Proposition 8, see California Secretary of State 2008. Compare discussions of these developments by Margaret Denike and Ruthann Robson, both in this volume (Chs. 9 and 12 respectively).
2 I will be referring to members of the Church of Jesus Christ of Latter-day Saints as 'Mormons' in this chapter. See Church of Jesus Christ of Latter-Day Saints 2000a.
3 See, e.g., Rovzar 13 November 2008; Associated Press 13 November 2008; Towle 9 November 2008.
4 For commentary relating to same-sex marriage supporters' blaming of African-American churches for the Proposition 8 vote outcome, see, e.g., Morrison 10 November 2008; Williams 14 November 2008.
5 Contrast Jenni Millbank's effort to presage an alliance combining heterosexual and queer subjects seeking to overcome obstacles to parenting, in this volume (Ch. 7).

6 For one important pre-Proposition 8 queer statement of principles pertaining to family, see The April Working Group 2006.

7 Indeed, see the queer statement *supra* note 5 for a queer declaration of support for the idea that there should be '[s]eparation of church and state in all matters, including regulation and recognition of relationships, households, and families'.

8 I realize that this is a controversial claim, but I believe it is more than defensible, and supported by a recent report by the influential US-based National Gay and Lesbian Task Force. See National Gay and Lesbian Task Force 2009. See also Janet Jakobsen's observation that 'gay politics has all too often bought into the idea that because the problem of sexual regulation seems based in religion, the answer is to defend secular freedom' (2005: 288).

9 I am, of course, using this term in the Coverian sense. See Cover 1983.

10 See below note 25 for further discussion of what I intend by the use of this term, especially in relation to the idea of 'agency'.

11 See, e.g., *Varnum v. Brien* 2009 for the Iowa Supreme Court's observations in this respect, as well as the numerous amicus briefs filed by religious organizations in favour of same-sex marriage in that case and other same-sex marriage litigation.

12 Some signs at these protests contained the following slogans and statements: 'You want three wives, I want one husband', 'I Don't Need 5 Wives, Just 1 Husband' and 'Keep Your Magic Undies off My Civil Rights'. For photos of signs at Proposition 8 protests outside of Mormon temple and elsewhere, see NBC Los Angeles 2008, Gonzalez 2008, Huston 2008. For a statement from the Mormon religion's leadership firmly disavowing polygamy, see Church of Jesus Christ of Latter-Day Saints 2009b.

13 According to the Court, nine differences remain between domestic partnerships and marriages in California (see *In re Marriage Cases* 2008: 720, fn 24). Some of these differences are arguably to the benefit of people entering into a domestic partnership, while others arguably impose burdens that people entering marriage do not face. An example of an advantage would be that domestic partnerships are easier to dissolve than marriages in California. An example of a burden placed solely on people wishing to enter a domestic partnerships is the requirement that such people have a common residence; there is no such common-residence requirement for people marrying. See ibid.

14 See also Yoshino 15 May 2008 (discussing uniqueness of California Supreme Court opinion with respect to applying strict scrutiny standard to sexual orientation discrimination), available at <http://www.slate.com/id/2191530/>.

15 See also Murray 2008 (discussing the California Supreme Court's opening the door to the possibility that the State of California may create a new type of officially recognized relationship, equally available to all people, which is not called 'marriage').

16 The reality of family law around the globe does not completely escape the Court's notice in this opinion. Indeed, when discussing the California Attorney-General's arguments pertaining to the historical definition of marriage, the Court does observe that 'until recently, there has been widespread societal disapproval and disparagement of homosexuality in many cultures' and that, as a result, 'the designation of marriage continues to apply only to a relationship between opposite-sex couples in the overwhelming majority of jurisdictions in the United States and around the world' (*In re Marriage Cases* 2008: 761–2). Furthermore, the Court ably makes use of a Canadian Supreme Court opinion when describing how the history of discrimination against gay people cautions against thinking that any separate and parallel family law system for them can be anything but discriminatory (756, quoting *M. v. H.* [1999]: 54–55 [68]).

17 The Connecticut Supreme Court decided to focus its analysis and holding on the equal protection issues which were raised in this case. See, e.g., *Kerrigan v. Commissioner of Public Health* 2008: 157–227.

18 Also 244–6 and 248–50 for discussion indicating the strong influence of the prior California Supreme Court opinion.

19 See generally Polikoff 2008 (discussing the history and global context of the current push for same-sex marriage rights in the US).

20 For one thoughtful effort at explaining contemporary LGBT interest in majoritarian marriage, see Chauncey 2004.

21 For more information on a specific covenant marriage law, including details of its passage and legal and other objections to the law, see Nichols 1998.

22 See Feld 2002. For more recent covenant marriage activism, see Sprigg 14 February 2008, for testimony to the State of Maryland's Senate, by the Family Research Council's Vice President for Policy, Peter Sprigg, in favor of a covenant marriage bill proposed in that state.

23 For a more detailed discussion of personal law systems, see Redding 2008.

24 There is also family law (for example, the recently-enacted Protection of Women from Domestic Violence Act) which is not administered along communitarian lines.

25 India's present personal law system can be traced back at least to the 1772 decision by Warren Hastings, the British viceroy for India at the time, to 'in all Suits regarding Marriage, Inheritance, Cast, and other religious Usages or Institutions, [apply] the Laws of the Koran with respect to [Muslims], and those of the Shaster with respect to [Hindus]'. A Plan for the Administration of Justice (1772). For a discussion of this British policy, see Galanter 2000. See also Hooker 1975. After independence, and after much debate, the post-colonial Indian state decided to keep its colonial-era personal law system.

26 What constitutes agency is, obviously, a difficult question, and one that requires more discussion than that which can be gone into here. Briefly, however, and following Perveez Mody, I am using the term to mean a 'careful and deliberate calculus of action' which takes into account existing social context and consideration of real possibilities. See Mody 2008: 193. Following others' sophisticated treatment of this term (see, e.g., Mahmood 2005), I am not using 'agency' as a synonym for 'autonomy' or any simplistic notion of 'sovereignty'. Indeed, the 'separate' regime of queer law that I argue for in this chapter will, under existing governmental structures, have to come into force through legislation passed by heterosexually dominated state legislatures. This situation would parallel the setup in India, where Parliament is responsible for legislating or otherwise enabling (the bulk of) religious minorities' personal law. The thought here is that, with domestic partnerships, etc. being thought of as queer ventures, that queers will have unmatched political influence with respect to how any given state legislature shapes and legislates queer law. Indeed, minorities in India exercise this sort of 'control' over – or 'agency' with respect to – their different personal laws.

27 I am mindful here of Nayan Shah's related caution that '[i]ncommensurate lives, acts, politics, and ways of knowing are frequently subsumed into a unitary category, such as "lesbian," "gay," "homosexual," and transgender" ' (2005: 282).

References

April Working Group, The (2006) 'Beyond Same-Sex Marriage: A New Strategic Vision for All Our Families and Relationships', Beyondmarriage.org. Online: <www.beyondmarriage.org> (accessed 22 June 2009).

Associated Press (13 Nov. 2008) 'Rally for gay marriage held in New York City', Online: <http://abclocal.go.com/wabc/story?section=news/local&id=6502751> (accessed 22 June 2009).

California Secretary of State (2008) 'Official Voter Information Guide'. Online: <http://voterguide.sos.ca.gov/past/2008/general/title-sum/prop8-title-sum.htm> (accessed 22 June 2009).

Chauncey, G. (2004) *Why Marriage?*, Cambridge: Basic Books.

Church of Jesus Christ of Latter-Day Saints (2009a) 'Style Guide – The Name of the Church'. Online: <http://newsroom.lds.org/ldsnewsroom/v/index.jsp?vgnextoid= ca07ae4af9c7e010VgnVCM1000004e94610aRCRD> (accessed 22 June 2009).

—— (2009b) 'Latter-Day Saints and the Practice of Plural Marriage'. Online: <www.newsroom.lds.org/ldsnewsroom/eng/background-information/polygamy-latter-day-saints-and-the-practice-of-plural-marriage> (accessed 22 June 2009).

Cover, R. (1983) 'Nomos and Narrative', *Harvard Law Review*, 97(1): 4–68.

Feld, S., Rosier, K. and Manning, A. (2002) 'Christian Right as a Civil Right: Covenant Marriage and a Kinder, Gentler, Moral Conservatism', *Review of Religious Research*, 44: 173–83.

Galanter, M. and Krishnan, J. (2000) 'Personal Law and Human Rights in India and Israel', *Israel Law Review*, 34: 101–33.

Gonzalez, R. (2008) 'I Don't Need 5 Wives, Just 1 Husband'. Online: <http://lh6.ggpht. com/_780ZZpC_ZNU/SRgdL1yCBwI/AAAAAAAAAJs/nIvwa8j4u4w/s400/Not5 WivesCropx390.jpg> (accessed 22 June 2009).

Hernandez v. Robles (2006) 7 N.Y.3d 338.

Hooker, M. B. (1975) *Legal Pluralism: An Introduction to Colonial and Neo-Colonial Laws*, New York, NY: Oxford University Press.

Huston, K. (2008) 'You Want Three Wives, I Want One Husband', *Utne Reader*. Online: <ww.utne.com/uploadedImages/utne/blogs/Spirituality/Prop8protest.jpg> (accessed 22 June 2009).

In re Marriage Cases (2008) 76 Cal. Rptr. 3d 683.

Jakobsen, J. (2005) 'Sex + Freedom = Regulation: Why?', *Social Text*, 84–5: 285–308.

Kerrigan v. Commissioner of Public Health (2008) 289 Conn. 135.

Kymlicka, W. (1995) *Multicultural Citizenship: A Liberal Theory of Minority Rights*, New York, NY: Oxford University Press.

M. v. H. [1999] 2 S.C.R. 3.

Mahmood, S. (2003) *Politics of Piety: The Islamic Revival and the Feminist Subject*, Princeton, NJ: Princeton University Press.

Mody, P. (2008) *The Intimate State: Love–Marriage and the Law in Delhi*, New Delhi: Routledge.

Morrison, T. (2008) 'Debunking the Black Blame', *The Advocate*, November 10. Online: <http://advocate.com/exclusive_detail_ektid65518.asp> (accessed 22 June 2009).

Murray, M. (2008) 'Equal Rites and Equal Rights', *California Law Review*, 96: 1395–1404.

National Gay and Lesbian Task Force (2009) *A Time to Build Up: Analysis of the No on Proposition 8 Campaign and Its Implications for Future Pro-LGBTQQIA Religious Organizing*, National Gay and Lesbian Task Force. Online: <www.thetaskforce.org/reports_and_research/time_to_build_up> (accessed 22 June 2009).

NBC Los Angeles (2008) 'Keep Your Magic Undies Off My Civil Rights', *NBC*. Online: <ww.nbclosangeles.com/news/local/Prop_8_Protestors_March_LA_Streets.html> (accessed 22 June 2009).

Nichols, J. (1998) 'Louisiana's Covenant Marriage Law: A First Step toward a More Robust Pluralism in Marriage and Divorce Law?', *Emory Law Journal*, 47: 929–1001.

—— (2007) 'Multi-tiered Marriage: Ideas and Influences from New York and Louisiana to the International Community', *Vanderbilt Journal of Transnational Law*, 40: 135–96.

Polikoff, N. (2008) *Beyond (Straight and Gay) Marriage: Valuing All Families under the Law*, Boston, MA: Beacon Press.

Redding, J. (2008) 'Slicing the American Pie: Federalism and Personal Law', *New York University Journal of International Law and Politics*, 40: 941–1018.

Rovzar, C. (2008) 'Gays Turn Anger, Snappy Sarcasm toward Mormon Church', *New York Magazine*, November 13. Online: <http://nymag.com/daily/intel/2008/11/gays_turn_anger_snappy_sarcasm.html> (accessed 22 June 2009).

Shah, N. (2005) 'Policing Privacy, Migrants, and the Limits of Freedom', *Social Text*, 84–5: 275–84.

Spaht, K. and Symeonides, S. (1999) 'Covenant Marriage and the Law of Conflicts of Laws', *Creighton Law Review*, 32: 1085–120.

Sprigg, P. (14 February 2008) 'In Support of Senate Bill 186 – Covenant Marriage', testimony before the Judicial Proceedings Committee of the Maryland State Senate. Online: <www.frc.org/get.cfm?i=TS08B01> (accessed 22 June 2009).

Towle, A. (2008) *Prop 8 Protest in New York City*, November 9. Online: <www.towleroad.com/2008/11/prop-8-protes-1.html> (accessed 22 June 2009).

Varnum v. Brien (2009) 763 N.W.2d 862 (Iowa).

Williams, B. (2008) 'Blaming the African American Community Oversimplifies Prop 8 Results', *Huffington Post*, 14 November. Online: <www.huffingtonpost.com/byron-williams/blaming-the-african-ameri_b_143892.html> (accessed 22 June 2009).

Yoshino, K. (2008) 'Magisterial Conviction: Why the California Supreme Court Did More Than Legalize Gay Marriage', *Slate*, 15 May. Online: <www.slate.com/id/2191530/> (accessed 22 June 2009).

Chapter 9

What's queer about polygamy?

Margaret Denike

Introduction: riding the slippery slope

After a generation of living openly and relatively undisturbed in the polygamous community of Bountiful in British Columbia, Canada, two leaders of a Fundamentalist sect of the Mormon Church of Latterday Saints (FLDS) – Winston Blackmore and James Oler – were charged with violating the archaic Canadian Criminal Code provisions on polygamy.[1] These highly publicized arrests occurred within a year of a similar spectacle in the US, when state authorities raided a Texas FLDS compound, 'Yearning for Zion', and apprehended over 400 children. Spectacular as these arrests appear, they come as no real surprise: in Canada, polygamy has been readied for public scrutiny and state intervention for some time now after police investigations in the early 1990s were followed by a number of government commissioned reports.[2] At the same time, across the border in the US, while the self-styled 'prophet' Warren Jeffs became the subject of a national manhunt, the first polygamy trial in Utah in almost 50 years was held in 2001. Tom Green, the outspoken FLDS patriarch who was comfortable enough about coming out as a polygynist to trumpet the cause and his life with six wives in a British-made documentary,[3] and as a vocal guest on the US talk show circuit, was convicted of bigamy. Polygamists' day of reckoning has arrived. Again. Returned to the fray of state intervention, at once spectacularized, fictionally normalized,[4] and morally catastrophized.

At the same time, through the past decade, though not without persistent and vociferous resistance, the civil rights claims of gays and lesbians have stretched the bounds of the legal regimes of relationship recognition. Gay marriage has been legalized in Canada, and incremental legislative reform and litigation are ongoing in the US. Throughout these movements, religious and social conservatives who have opposed extending rights to gays and lesbians, and who have sought to, as they put it, 'defend' marriage, have pointed again and again at polygamy as the fate of 'letting' gays marry.[5] Polygamy is conjured and constituted as queer in these instances, defined *by way of* sexual orientation as a threat to proper social, political, religious, cultural, and moral order.[6]

Immediately after Winston Blackmore's arrest, his lawyer Blair Suffredine announced in an interview with CBC News that his strategy would rely on the recent legalization of same-sex marriage and the proliferation of cohabitation agreements. He would claim that, among other things, 'the legality of same-sex marriage makes it difficult to argue that it's a criminal offence to enter into conjugal relationships with more than one person at the same time if all adults are consenting.' After all, Suffredine added, 'many people across the country live in communal relationships without breaching any laws, and that it is only once someone undertakes a ceremonialized promise to look after the other person, that such relationships are rendered a criminal act' (CBC News). He promised to ride the slippery slope, and to make real what might otherwise seem like the classic myth-making and fear-mongering of conservative opposition to same-sex marriage: that the groundwork for defending polygamy has been laid both by the legalization of gay and lesbian marriage and by the supportive advocacy that has sought to expand the terms by which the state recognizes relationships of interdependency and care. The viability of this strategy turned on what was at once self-evident yet unspeakable in many contexts: that there are very few differences between these forms of relationships, or for that matter, between them and 'normal' heterosexuality, despite how keen folks are to make them incommensurable.

Countless commentators, legal scholars, and equality advocates have responded to the fear-mongering and slippery slope arguments by emphasizing that there are fundamental differences between these marital arrangements, generally casting polygamy as hyper-patriarchal, perverse, and inherently inequitable, and monogamous same-sex unions as 'normal', 'democratic' and illustrative of sex and gender equality. This distinction between sexual perversity and sexual equality, proffered through discourses that defend the rights of gays and lesbians while dismissing those of polygamists, is often underwritten by – and substantiated through – racial and colonial assumptions about the social and cultural conditions and practices of polygamy (Calhoun 2005: 1042). Attending to the rhetoric that analogizes and differentiates same-sex marriage to and from polygamy, this paper tracks the homonormative[7] and homonationalist (Puar 2007) currents in these assumptions, sketching moments of the incorporation of homosexuality into mainstream, nationalist frameworks, and their contingency on orientalist, xenophobic formations. In other words, I treat the recent spectacle of the state's crackdown on polygamy, and all of the hype in the media, scholarly literature and investigative reports that has spurred it on, as a site through which the relationships and desires legitimized by contemporary Canadian and US national identities, and their colonial and normative proclivities, are consolidated into a relatively narrow, traditionally Christian form of monogamous conjugality. It is a site where sexuality can be seen to collude with nationhood through religious imperatives, where the 'state's desire', as Judith Butler describes it, circumscribes 'the field of intelligible and speakable sexuality', legitimizing and 'sanctifying' monogamy and its kinship as the condition of recognition, entitlement, and obligation, while rendering other forms unintelligible, or at least scandalous, at this contemporary historical moment (Butler 2004). In this context, invariably abstracted through cultural stereotypes of sexual perversity and political tyranny, polygamy in general – and polygynists in particular – serve as a negative figuration against which monogamous same-sex relations are secured as coherent, morally intelligible and consistent with the (white) ethos of the nation's colonial present. Through a certain collusion of gay and lesbian equality advocacy, polygamy has been a backdrop to the moral and political staging of certain gay relations as *not* queer, as proper to the nation's citizenship, all the while marking the limit of its toleration and conditions of inclusion.

The race of polygynists

One of the notable features of the Bountiful arrests is that they mark the first time in a century that criminal action has been taken against polygynists in Canada, and the first time this rather obscure white man's law has been used against the specific religious minority that the law is commonly presumed to have been drafted to target: fundamentalist Mormons who emigrated from the US to Western Canada in the 1880s and 1890s to escape the sweeping state action against them across the border. Until now, the only two convictions under the polygamy provisions of Canada's Criminal Code were against Aboriginal men, in 1899 and 1906,[8] for living with two 'wives', the absence of a solemnizing ceremony aside. In sentencing Bear's Shin Bone to a five-year prison term for what the judge acknowledged was one of the customs of the Blood Indians, Rouleau J. had little else to say other than that these very customs (of living non-monogamously in a conjugal relationship of some sort with two women) – were exactly what the criminal law had contemplated. The Criminal Code, s. 278(a) made criminal *anything* – 'any form of polygamy' that was entered into by:

> practices, or, by the rites, ceremonies, forms, rules or customs of any denomination, sect or society, religious or secular, or by any form of contract, or by mere mutual consent, or by any other method whatsoever, and whether in a manner recognized by law as a binding form of marriage or not, agrees or consents to practise . . .
>
> (*R. v. Bear's Shin Bone*)

From the outset, these provisions were used specifically to target marital practices that were different from the *one* form that is, as the English court put it in the notorious precedent of *Hyde*, 'understood in Christendom', – i.e., the one between 'one man and one woman'.[9] The new criminal law was instrumental in consolidating the religious persuasion and customs of the new nation, against the Jewish, Muslim, Asian, Indian, and Aboriginal customs with which polygamy was associated. Among other things, polygamy thus stood for the different religious customs that threatened the political and cultural unity and moral authority of a Christian colony, marked on the homeland and its borders through the lives of Aboriginals and immigrants.[10]

The presumption of the normative superiority of European 'civilization', or more generally of 'Christendom', pervades the reasoning in these and the few other cases where polygamy has been on trial (namely in the areas of immigration family law). In Canada, all but one of these has concerned Asian and East Asian immigrants and refugees.[11] Among these, in the 1948 case of *Lim v. Lim*,[12] the B.C. Supreme Court judge acknowledged the injustice of his own decision in finding no support in Canadian or British law to compel him to recognize the marriage between Mr. and Mrs. Lim. This finding had severe material consequences for Mrs. Lim in her pursuit of alimony after the dissolution of her 30-year marriage, and for all other immigrants whose marriages were contracted in China. Though the judge found it 'repellent to one's sense of justice', he reasoned in accordance with *Hyde* that because the marriage had been contracted in a country where polygamy was legal, it was 'potentially polygamous' and thus exempt from the legal entitlements provided under Canadian family law.

This racial context of anti-polygamy initiatives in Canada is a critical trajectory for considering the links that have been frequently forged between queer and polygamous relationships. As Sarah Carter (2008) has shown with Canada, Nancy Cott (2000) and Martha Ertman (2008) with the United States, and Nan Seuffert (2003) with New Zealand, there is plenty of historical evidence to suggest what really troubles the western imagination and moral sentiment about polygamy has had less to do with ensuring that the state promotes personal relations of gender equality than with ensuring that these relations are not tarred with the brush of barbarism or with the cultural practices of the foreigners that the emergent state was keen to actively exclude. While so much of the noise about polygamy in North America these days appears to carry concerns about a predominantly white religious minority, and casts the contentious questions of current debates in terms of gender equality, the very framing of such questions is conditioned by the xenophobia that riddles the history and application of this law, and particularly by the ethnocentric notion that the (mis)treatment of women is a measure of the backwardness and incivility of *other* cultures.

Building the slippery slope

Throughout the 1990s, as courts and legislatures in Canada and the US were pressed to address the question of extending civil marriage to gays and lesbians – with all of the benefits and burdens attached to its recognition and regulation by the state – the subject of polygamy found occasion to enter almost every political exchange. Polygamy has been invoked less as a set of material practices that characterize tens of thousands of existing relationships among predominately white FLDS communities in North America than as a spectre of moral outrage. It was, at least as far as the opposition was concerned, the inevitable prospect or vanishing point of gay and lesbian marriage campaigns. Polygamy was – and continues to be – the dominant frame of the so-called 'same-sex marriage debates': it is typically held out as the next destination on the slippery slope that begins by 'tinkering' with marriage, or rather, with 'changing its definition' – as if it ever had only *one* – and the types of relationships it might include.

The refrain of conservatives who have opposed the recognition of gay and lesbian relationships is all too familiar: if the state were to open the door of the institution and 'sacrament' of marriage to include same-sex unions, it would be just a brief matter of time before practitioners of polygamy, pedophilia, incest, and bestiality would be pounding to get in, forcing the state to recognize and support them as well. Indeed, as an increasingly popular topic in the media, polygamy has entered public discourse through a queer context – including through daily barrages of peculiar public opinion polls, such as that which appeared in the CBC report that announced the arrest of Bishop Blackmore, inviting readers to vote on a simple but incoherent question: 'If same-sex marriages are legal, should polygamist marriages be legal?' (CBC News).

The conservatively reiterated analogies between same-sex and polygamous marriages play on an assumption that what is politically intolerable and socially repulsive about gay relationships is their proximity to polygamous ones, including to their racial conditioning, however much the latter is stereotypically familiarized as predominately white and exclusively heterosexual. So too is the disdain toward polygamy fostered by its queer affiliation, postulated as the dire consequence of the state's tolerance, as that which, on the trajectory of queer claims, must remain beyond acceptance and recognition *because* of its cultural otherness. These assumptions are facilitated by the western fantasy of polygamy as an exotic and cultish phenomena that can and should be eradicated, despite the fact that it is common enough to be practised in the majority – about 83 percent – of societies worldwide (Gher 2008: 561; Myers 2006: 1460), including by an estimated 30,000 to 100,000 people in Canada and the US alone (Duncan 2008). These plural marriages resemble the countless second and third marriages that have spawned the mixed and extended families that characterize the growing majority of the other adult relationships that *are* recognized by the state in Canada and the US. But however common, and however much plural marriages echo newly typical family structures, there is overwhelming public opposition to entertaining such similarities.[13]

Speaking of slippery slopes

In the US, the spectre of polygamy was a regular feature of the legislative debates and public hearings before the Senate Judiciary Committee that led to the federal Defense of Marriage Act (DOMA) in 1996. Many commentators warned that same-sex marriage would lead to the legalization of polygamy, incest, pedophilia, 'or anything' for that matter.[14] This Act was designed to enable states to refuse to recognize same-sex marriages that were legal in other states. The prospect of gays marrying was often represented by opponents as an act of war, not just against the institution of heterosexual marriage, but against the nation and civilization (Chambers 1997: 55–9). At these hearings, in language reminiscent of *Hyde*, Gary Bauer, the President of the Family Research Council, characterized monogamous heterosexual marriage as 'the core of civilization'; and as Jesse Helms put it, Congress has the responsibility to protect 'the moral and spiritual survival of this nation', *by* 'protecting and preserving monogamous heterosexual marriage' from gay threats (quoted in ibid. 56).[15] The analogy between same-sex marriage and polygamy was instrumental in casting the gay marriage question as a risk to the very civility of America; guarding against the spectre of polygamy was what differentiated this nation from the dark and distant backward cultures of elsewhere. It is reminiscent of the reasoning of the prominent nineteenth century political philosopher, Francis Lieber, whose arguments were included in Chancellor James Kent's *Commentaries on American Law*[16] and cited by US Supreme Court in its first ruling on the polygamy:[17] in a popular magazine article addressing Utah's petition for statehood, Lieber claimed that monogamy was 'one of the pre-exisitng conditions of our existence as white men'. To accept anything else in its place was 'to destroy our very beings . . . and when we say *our* we mean our race – a race which has its great and broad destiny, a solemn aim in the great career of civilization' (Lieber 1855: 11; Cott 2000: 114–5). As was the case with the historical racialization of white man's polygamy, the slippery slope that leads from same-sex to polygamous relations inevitably arrives at the end of western and northern civilization as we know it. The responsibility of the state, by this view, is to protect 'us' from heading there.

Similarly, the compulsion to invoke polygamy as the fate of ceding to gay rights claims also characterizes legal reasoning issued by courts in response to queer claims. In the 1996 case of *Romer v. Evans*, where the US Supreme Court ruled against an amendment to Colorado's constitution that would have prevented local governments from banning discrimination based on sexual orientation, Justice Scalia's notorious dissent chastised the Court for providing gays with 'special treatment', remarking that homosexuality was no different from polygamy when it came to the social harms that it produced.[18] Polygamy also featured prominently in the debates surrounding the 1999 Vermont Supreme Court decision in *Baker v. State* (the exclusion of same-sex couples from the Common Benefits Clause of the state's constitution); the 2003 decision of the Massachusetts Supreme Judicial Court in *Goodridge v. Department of Public Health* (on the extension of benefits and obligations conferred by civil marriage to same-sex couples) (Emens 2004: 279); and the 2003 case of *Lawrence v. Texas*,[19] which resulted in the decriminalization of sodomy (Myers 2006: 1454; Emens 2004: 278). In the discussions of these cases, the spectre of polygamy stands in where the nation's sexual morality is poised to collapse. On this queer trajectory, polygamy marks the absence of value – the end of the state's desire as we know it.

Homonormative formations: distinguishing polygamy and same-sex marriage

Of particular note is how the proliferation of analogies between same-sex marriage and polygamy has informed the responses of feminist legal theorists, GLBT advocates, and equality activists to questions of whether the state should expand its recognition of existing, diverse relationships of interdependency and care beyond those marked by 'conjugal' monogamous unions. The gravitational force of the slippery slope has prompted various attempts to emphasize the differences between the two, more often than not, coming to the defence of same-sex unions and extolling the virtues of monogamy, while at the same time repudiating polygamy in order to rationalize the differences in ways that highlight the comparatively 'normal' qualities of same-sex unions. In other words, it has given rise to homonormative responses that insist on how gay unions are 'virtually normal' (Sullivan 1995), 'indistinguishable' (Strassberg 1997) from heterosexual ones; and indeed, so 'perfectly opposed' to polygamy, as E. J. Graff put in a book widely celebrated by advocates of same-sex marriage, that 'the same social system could not stretch to admit both' (2004: 176). As Graff claims, 'Those who fear that same-sex marriage will lead to incest and polygamy aren't looking at the facts. Tribal and despotic societies put kin first, allowing in-marriage and polygamy', as well as the subordination and exploitation of women. Such regimes bear little resemblance to 'democratic egalitarianism', which gives rise to same-sex marriage and 'treats women and men as equals in morals, politics, sex and marriage' (ibid.).

As we see here, it's not uncommon to find racist tropes invoked to mark the normative superiority of same-sex (monogamous) relations, and their consistency with the 'higher' forms of social and political governance. Consider, as well, the discussion developed in Maura Strassberg's frequently cited essay, 'Distinctions in Form and Substance', written in the wake of DOMA debates in the US, and coming to the defence of gay marriage. To emphasize the fundamental differences between these relationships, Strassberg turns to Hegel's distinction between (European) monogamous and (Asian) polygamous marriages, arguing how only the former serves a critical function in nurturing the values of individuality, autonomy and liberty in a cohesive society, and the creation of a singular ethical bond between individuals as well as with the community.[20] In contrast, due to its inherent gender inequality and patriarchal religious doctrine, which, for 'Fundamentalist Mormons' dictates that godhead is restricted only to men through the acquisition of wives, polygamy is thus 'antithetical to the modern state' (Strassberg 1997: 1593). Based on the fulfilment of an emotional and ethical connection to one other person, the doctrinal underpinnings of monogamous marriage, she holds, are 'totally incompatible with those of polygamy'. Same-sex marriage, as she sees it and lives it, is 'founded on respect for individual difference, autonomy, and equality, as well as social unity'; it 'does not pose the kind of threat to the foundation of the modern liberal state that polygamy may have posed' (ibid. 1618). The same holds true for interracial marriages, monogamous ones at least.

Similarly, Ruth Khalsa argues that 'dyadic' relationships, which marriage-prone same-sex couples enjoy, not unlike heterosexuals, are superior to plural ones, as they better enable the fulfilment of the normative 'purposes' of marriage in 'Western' societies that have embraced social and economic equality and values of individuality and autonomy. Echoing Strassberg, polygamy, she adds, is 'fundamentally antithetical' to these principles, as it is based on a less 'advanced' model of economic-dependency in marriage (2005: 1668–9). The normative suggestion here is that same-sex marriage is more consistent with the 'underlying values' of progressive 'democratic' societies, which, unlike those of authoritarian regimes, include individuality, autonomy, and mutuality. Consider as well the approach of William Eskridge in his book, *The Case for Same-Sex Marriage*, published at the height of the DOMA debates. Eskridge extols the virtues of marriage in advancing a formal equality argument for extending civil marriage to gays and lesbians, largely because they, too, enjoy the proper values of monogamy's 'companionate' emotional bonds. Polygamy, on the other hand, he surmises, is based on male authoritarianism and undermines women's equality, fostering tension and jealousy among sister wives and exacerbating hierarchical structures within the marriage (1996: 149). According to Richard Posner, on whose authority Eskridge relies, such types of relationships are 'common' in 'non-Western societies and contrary to the interests of civil society' (1992: 69).[21]

Philosophers and legal theorists engaged with this question appear to maintain a conviction that same-sex marriages and polygamous marriages are 'substantially disanalogous', especially when it comes to gender hierarchy and women's equality. However, it may well be in part *because* of the pervasive social hostility toward polygamy that they have emphasized the difference and remained silent on advocacy for removing the bar to plural marriages (Calhoun 2005). We see this, for instance, in Jaime Gher's consideration of how the association with polygamy has undermined same-sex marriage campaigns and given queer relations a bad name. She calls upon human rights activists and scholars to continue to distance same-sex marriage from plural marriage 'to avoid relinquishing the movement's hard-earned cultural capital and societal support', however much, as she acknowledges, in maligning polygamy, advocates have been 'playing into the cultural narrative that plural marriage is resoundingly barbaric and misogynistic' (2008: 560). Ideally, the struggle for relational equality would include the respect for diversity, and not be performed at the expense of those whose relationships and communities are decimated by the initiatives to enforce criminal bans on polygamy (ibid. 561).

A more productive response to the fear-mongering of homophobes – and the *reductio* arguments of opponents to same-sex marriage, as Calhoun suggests, may instead be, 'And indeed, why not also polygamy?' (2005: 1027). Rather than ceding to the normative and nationalist logic that animates slippery slope arguments, we need to attend to the assumptions that pervade these discussions: i.e., that the legal recognition of polygamous marriage is inconsistent with a liberal, democratic and egalitarian society. To the extent that we care about the state's recognition of diverse family forms and equality in relationships of interdependency that are lived so widely, domestically and globally, equality advocates have been too quick to justify, monogamous conjugality as the state's desire and the condition for legal intelligibility and recognition. Rather than distance ourselves from certain restrictions on familial marriages, as Ruthann Robson advises, we'd be better to examine the way we participate in these prohibitions, especially through our quests for assimilation into institutions like marriage. A more expansive notion of equality, she adds, requires that when we advocate for relationship law reform, we measure the success of our efforts 'in terms of who and what we are excluding'. After all, 'equality with all disfavoured groups is as important as our equality with heterosexuals' (2002: 777). And as we know, it is those who are most disparaged and socially marginalized, those whom the heteronormative imperative commands of its loyal subjects to publically disavow, that are the objects and abject of discrimination and that are particularly and invariably in need of the consideration, advocacy and equality provisions that a tolerant and inclusive, substantive democracy might pride itself upon.

Viewing the slopes through an orientalist lens

The colonial context is crucial to understanding such social and legal responses to polygamy in North America.

If we look 'sideways' from this legal and political spectacle surrounding polygamy, currently and historically, as Siobhan Somerville (2005: 237) suggests we do to see concurrences of race and sexual orientation during the US civil rights movement, we might be more able to see how heavily racism and homophobia are imbricated in the anti-polygamy initiatives and their discourses of complicity. We might also see, concurrently, how the fears that polygamy invokes are deeply intertwined with those based on racial, sexual, cultural and religious difference. The temporal and causal framing (i.e., if same-sex marriage *then* polygamy) of slippery slope arguments – and the normativizing responses to them – restricts our view and curtails our critical analyses of these interrelations and their effects.

Perhaps the most notorious and frequently cited lines from the first case in the US to address the constitutionality of the criminal provisions on polygamy – *Reynolds v. US* (1878) – articulated the distinction between the ethos of 'western nations' and that of those that are defined and debased by practices of polygamy. Upholding these provisions, the US Supreme Court remarked that:

> [p]olygamy has always been odious among the northern and western nations of Europe, and, until the establishment of the Mormon Church, was almost exclusively a feature of the life of Asiatic and of African people . . . [F]rom the earliest history of England polygamy has been treated as an offence against society.
>
> (*Reynolds* 1878: 164)

Unlike monogamy, polygamy gives expression to a certain principle of patriarchy that, when applied to large communities, 'fetters the people in stationary despotism' (ibid. 166). Seen through what Martha Ertman calls an 'orientalist lens', the suggestion here is that polygamy is, of course, *natural* to the 'Asiatic and African people' in a way that differentiates the odium of the *other* from the superiority of the colonizing west. Attachment to this distinction has long sustained the interdependency of nationalism on xenophobia, and it continues to inform the crusades of (Christian monogamous) marriage and their repudiation of 'Mohammedan' polygamy.

Ertman further argues that what makes polygamy so repulsive for the western nations is this very association with the racial others against which it defines its social, moral and political superiority. In her remarkable paper on the subject, she elucidates the extent to which the consistently negative response to polygamy in Mormon communities relates to the thought that their *white* members would stoop to the level of other races, that they would commit what she calls 'race treason' and engage in practices that were 'unnatural' for them, 'even as it was "natural" for purportedly backward, lascivious people of Asia and Africa' (2008: 28). This is evident in the specific expressions of racism that permeate nineteenth century representations of polygamists, and particularly cartoons that satirized Mormons in printed pamphlets and newspapers. Through these representations, Ertman points to how racial treachery is read through, and interwoven with, tropes of political treason: Mormons were seen to be an imminent threat to the political order of an emergent Christian republic, well on their way to establishing a separatist theocracy.

These associations have persisted since *Reynolds* – and continue to colour the discourses that forge parallels and insist on distinctions between polygamy and same-sex relations. The suggestion that polygamy poses a threat to civilization, and to the structures of higher forms of government, has become a predictable feature of gay and lesbian equality rights jurisprudence, even though the topic is tangential and typically irrelevant to the court decisions. Consider, for example, *In re Marriage Cases* (2008), the judgment in which the Supreme Court of California ruled that the exclusion of gays from civil marriage was unconstitutional.[22] Through slippery slope logic that draws on the colonial assumptions inherited from *Reynolds*, the decision explicitly clarified the limits of its decision to extend marriage to same-sex couples in these terms: recognizing the right of gay couples to marry:

> does not mean that this constitutional right similarly must be understood to extend to polygamous or incestuous relationships. Past judicial decisions explain why our nation's culture has considered the latter types of relationships inimical to the mutually supportive and healthy family relationships promoted by the constitutional right to marry.
>
> (*In re Marriage Cases* 2008: n. 52)[23]

The court added that that while discrimination against gays and lesbians is 'no longer constitutionally permissible, the state continues to have a strong and adequate justification for refusing to officially sanction polygamous or incestuous relationships because of their potentially detrimental effect on a sound family environment' (ibid.).[24] More recently, as New Hampshire became the fourth state in the US to legalize same-sex marriage, the Senate bill included an amendment explicitly prohibiting 'polygamy and marriage of family members' (Manuse 2009).

Conclusion

In the recent past, homosexuality has been socially and symbolically 'endlessly cathected with death' (Puar 2007: xiii) – as figures of HIV/AIDS (Bersani 1989; Sontag 1989; Butler 1992; Weeks 1992) and threats to social and moral order, parcelled out from the livelihoods of nationalism. With its decriminalization, however, there has been a substantial shift, as Jasbir Puar describes it, a 'biopolitical re-orientation' of queerness in relation to life and the regulatory mechanisms that foster and support it. This shift is marked by the entry of gays and lesbians into the heteronormative institutions of 'the nation', into the markets of the production, proliferation, regulation, and management of life, into the familial legitimacies of state recognition. As Eng, Halberstam and Muñoz entertain in 'What's Queer about Queer Studies Now?', this neo-liberal moment is characterized by a particular convergence of economic and political spheres that find queer critiques of family abandoned in favour of demands for access to the 'nuclear family' and other 'privileges of the state' (2005: 10–11). This shift is characterized as much by patterns of inclusion and assimilation as by distinction, repudiation and expulsion: only *some* queer relationships are brought into the folds of the body and life of the nation – a convergence that Puar calls 'homonationalism' and that is contingent on orientalist and xenophobic formations. Invariably racially marked *others* are parcelled out, 'disidentified' with the state (Butler 1992; Muñoz 1999), readied for eradication and extinction. For the purpose of her project, Puar looks to how constructs of terrorists and 'terrorist populations' are rendered expendable through tropes of excessive, perverse sexuality, through imputed 'fundamentalist' death-driven demonic designs, and through depictions of masculinities that are 'metonymically tied to all sorts of pathologies of the mind and body – homosexuality, incest, pedophilia, madness, and disease' (2007: xxiv).

The point goes to the collusion of nationalism, religious sexual morality, and gay rights campaigns: it is against this racially and sexually perverse masculinity – and its 'queerly racialized terrorist population' – that are set the 'properly queer' subjects of the nation, assimilatable *in* their transgression, embraced by a nationalist ethos that prides itself on the liberal democratic values of tolerance, acceptance, freedom, and equality. Queerness, in Puar's project, is an 'operative technology' by which gay subjects are disciplined through national belonging, while concurrently constituting 'perverse populations' that are 'called into nominalization and control', 'unnationalized' (ibid. 10) and readied for detention, deportation and death. These processes can be tracked through the trajectories of the media, scholarship, public policies and jurisprudence that contextualize human rights campaigns.

As the above discussion attempts to elucidate, such a framework and purview can also assist in clarifying some of the stakes in the slippery and *reductio* arguments that characterize same-sex marriage debates and the catastrophizing claims of those who oppose gay unions, as well as the responses to which they have given rise. Not unlike those of terror and security, the discourses that both connect and distinguish polygamous and same-sex unions, preoccupied as they are with what should or should not count among the state's legitimate sex, make frequent recourse to the perverse relations that the state can't tolerate or must eradicate. This is done in part through tactics and tropes of racialization and colonization, through a constitutive demonization of others as politically and morally treasonous 'cults', secretive, incestuous networks, fundamentalist 'runaway sects', and shameful unshakable tyrannies of illegitimate, patriarchal regimes. It is against this spectre of 'polygamy' – this moral outrage in all of its mythic abstraction, in its manifest inequality, male tyranny, subjugation of women, sexual exploitation of children – that the civility of gay and lesbian monogamy is taking shape and seeking home in the heartland of national tolerance. The ascendency of homonormativity is contingent on what Puar calls the 'ascendency of whiteness' (ibid. 31–2), which, in this instance of a public reckoning with white man's polygamy, can be seen to collude with the reassertion of 'Christendom's' matrimonial, conjugal monogamy – and the proliferation of stories of its relatively superior relational equality, the very hierarchy of which is organized and substantiated through xenophobia.

The question remains: how do we, as feminist and queer social and legal theorists and advocates, engage with the reality and the spectacle of current criminal interventions in the FLDS polygynous communities, where the blunt tools of criminal law – and the rationale used to justify using them – promise to mark the end of a slippery slope, and to enforce a law of monogamous conjugality, however socially and politically problematic these models may be? How do we work with and against the racially framed representations of sexually exploited and subjugated women and children in polygamous communities – representations that have been instrumental in justifying these interventions, even if only at times as an alibi? In addressing such questions for public policy purposes, and in considering the prospect of extending the state recognition and support of a broader range and diversity of family forms, we need to be cognizant of the machinations and tactics of *othering* – and our complicity within them – that are at work in defences against the crude arguments of those who oppose same-sex marriage and in the responses to them. We need to bring into view the less visible racist and imperial frameworks of these debates, which lend themselves to re-entrenching monogamous conjugality as the only measure worthy of relationship recognition.

Acknowledgements

I am grateful to Robert Leckey, Ruthann Robson and Nan Seuffert for their resourcefulness and helpful comments on an earlier version of this chapter.

Notes

1 In September 2009, after the drafting of this chapter, these charges were quashed by the Supreme Court of British Columbia, on account of the overly aggressive approach of the Attorney General of B.C. in pursuing the prosecution of Blackmore and Oler. As this chapter goes to print, the Court is now conducting Reference hearings on the constitutionality of polygamy laws, and over a dozen interest groups are slated to intervene.
2 See Status of Women Canada (2005), and reports of the Attorney-General.
3 The British-made documentary, on Tom Green, entitled *One Man, Six Wives, and Twenty-Nine Children* was released in 2000 at the New York International Documentary Film Festival.
4 Consider the increasingly popular HBO television series, *Big Love*, which throws the political intrigues and daily dramas of a fictional polygamous trio out of the closet and into the living rooms of millions of North Americans, a majority of whom would applaud such arrests and support criminal sanctions against

polygamy, however much their own lives and relationships may differ little from them. For a reflection on the resonances between this series and the same-sex marriage question, see Cossman (2008).

5 Compare Jeffrey Redding's reading of potential alliances between sexual and religious minorities, in this volume (Ch. 8).

6 Compare Nan Seuffert's analysis, in this volume (Ch. 11), of the connections between national progress and containment of deviant sexualities.

7 Lisa Duggan uses the term 'new homonormativity' to describe the mainstreaming of gay politics that is characterized, for example, by the Independent Gay Forum (IGF) in the US – a neoliberal organization that positions itself against both anti-gay conservativism and 'radical' left-wing queer politics, that upholds and sustains dominant heteronormative assumptions and institutions, and that promises the possibility of 'a privatized depoliticized gay culture anchored in domesticity and consumption'.

8 *R. v. Bear's Shin Bone* (1899), 4 Terr. LR 173 (NWT SC) and *R. v. Harris* (1906), 11 CCC 254 (Qc. Sup. Ct.). See Kelly (2007) and Carter (2008) for a discussion of these cases. Sarah Carter's book, *The Importance of Being Monogamous*, provides a thoughtful analysis of how the political and judicial approach to non-mono-gamous unions such as these are imbricated in nation-building. See Kaufman (2005) and Kelly (2007) for discussions of early polygamy cases in Canada.

9 Such is the term used by Judge Penzance in *Hyde v. Hyde*, the language of which has since been used throughout Britain's colonies as the authoritative source of *the* so-called 'definition of marriage'. He dismissed the petition to dissolve a polygamous marriage that had been contracted in Salt Lake City in 1856 on the grounds that a marriage contracted in a place where polygamy was illegal was not a legal marriage in the first instance: 'I conceive that marriage, as understood in Christendom, may for this purpose be defined as the voluntary union for life of one man and one woman, to the exclusion of all others' *Hyde v. Hyde* (1866), LR. 1 P & D 130. It's worth noting that the peculiar declaration of this judge has served for over a century in common law as the authority for denying *both* polyg-amous and same-sex relationships.

10 Nancy Cott addresses the exclusion of 'actual polygamists', and 'persons who admit their belief in the practice of polygamy' from US immigration as a feature of nation building that was steeped in prejudice against the 'Mongolian race'. Between July 1908 and February 1910 alone, 131 would-be immigrants were denied entry 'because they were polygamists' (2000: 139).

11 *Re Lee Cheong* (1923), 33 BCR 109; *Yew v. Attorney-General of British Columbia* (1924), 33 BCR 109 (BCCA); *Lim v. Lim*, [1948] 2 DLR 353 (BCSC); *Sara v. Sara* (1962), 31 DLR (2d) 566; *Re Hassan and Hassan* (1976), 12 OR (2d) 432 (HC); *Ali v. Canada (Minister of Citizenship & Immigration)* (1998), 154 FTR 285.

12 *Lim v. Lim*, [1948] 2 DLR 353 (BC SC).

13 Current popular opinion polls find 85 percent of Canadians opposing the legaliza-tion of polygamy (COMPAS 2009), and 90 percent of Americans considering it to to be 'morally wrong' (Gallup 2007). Nonetheless there is wide social and legal support for second marriages, as long as they are marked 'legitimately', temporally and ceremonially. Over half of 'normal' marriages in the US end in divorce, with the majority of divorced people eventually remarrying.

14 Defense of Marriage Act: Hearing on s. 1740 before the Senate Comm. on the Judiciary, 1996 WL 387295 (11 July 1996). David Chambers (1997: 58 n. 25) and Elizabeth Emens (2004: 279 n. 11) point to several examples among the submis-sions to this committee that explicitly relate the legalization of same-sex marriage to the sanctioning of polygamy and pedophilia.

15 142 Cong. Rec. S10,068 (daily ed. 9 September 1996), cited in Chambers (1997: 56).
16 A treatise of the 1820s, which, as Nancy Cott notes, 'was used by generations of American law students, lawyers and judges' (2000: 114).
17 *Reynolds v. United States.*
18 *Romer v. Evans* 517 U.S. 620 (1996) at 648; cited in Sigman (2006: 105).
19 123 S.Ct. 2472 (2003).
20 Commenting on Strassberg's reliance on Hegel, Ruthann Robson reminds us that underlying Hegel's distinctions between monogamy and polygamy is a notion that is fundamental to the teleology of his major work, *Phenomenology of Mind*: that 'Oriental religions', associated with polygamy, are illustrative of the early, 'primitive' stages (of mind/spirit's progress), which ultimately aspired to the highest, 'Revealed Religion' – Christianity (2002: 772).
21 See Chambers (1997 n. 31) for a comment of the substantial role of Posner's assumptions in Eskridge's argument.
22 For a discussion on the California marriage litigation, including the May 2009 opinion, see Ruthann Robson, in this volume (Ch. 12).
23 To substantiate this claim, the Court cites *Reynolds v. United States* (1878) 98 US 145, 165–6, 25 L.Ed. 244; *Davis v. Beason* (1890) 133 US 333, 341, 10 S.Ct. 299, 33 L.Ed. 637; *People v. Scott* (2007) 157 Cal.App. 4th 189, 192–4, 68 Cal.Rptr.3d 592; *State v. Freeman* (2003) 155 Ohio App. 3d 492, 801 N.E.2d 906, 909; *Smith v. State* (Tenn.Crim.App. 1999) 6 S.W.3d 512, 518–20).
24 Citing *Potter v. Murray City* (C.D.Utah 1984) 585 F.Supp. 1126, 1137–40, affd. (10th Cir.1985) 760 F.2d 1065, 1068–71, cert. den. (1985) 474 U.S. 849, 106 S.Ct. 145, 88 L.Ed.2d 120; *People v. Scott, supra*, 157 Cal.App. 4th 189, 193–4, 68 Cal.Rptr.3d 592.)

References

Bala, N. (23 November 2007) 'Is polygamy next after same-sex marriage?', *Lawyers Weekly*, 27: 28.
Bala, N., Duval-Antonacopoulos, K., MacRae, L. and Paetsch, J. J. (2005) 'An International Review of Polygamy: Legal and Policy Implications for Canada', in *Polygamy in Canada: Legal and Social Implications for Women and Children: A Collection of Policy Research Papers*, Ottawa: Status of Women Canada.
Bersani, L. (1987) 'Is the Rectum a Grave?', *October* 43 (winter): 197–222.
Butler, J. (1992) 'Sexual Inversions', in D. M. Stanton (ed.) *Discourses of Sexuality: From Aristotle to AIDS*, Ann Arbor, MI: University of Michigan Press.
—— (2004) 'Is Kinship Always Already Heterosexual?', in *Undoing Gender*, New York, NY: Routledge.
Calhoun, C. (2005) 'Who's Afraid of Polygamous Marriage: Lessons for Same-Sex Marriage Advocacy from the History of Polygamy', *San Diego Law Review*, 42(3): 1023–43.
Campbell, A. (2005) 'How Have Policy Approaches to Polygamy Responded to Women's Experiences and Rights? An International, Comparative Analysis', in *Polygamy in Canada: Legal and Social Implications for Women and Children: A Collection of Policy Research Papers*, Ottawa: Status of Women Canada.
—— (2009) 'In the Name of Mothers', *Globe and Mail*, 10 January, A17.
Carter, S. (2008) *The Importance of Being Monogamous: Marriage and Nation Building in Western Canada*, Athabasca: Athabasca University Press.

CBC News (2009) 'Polygamy Leader Makes Court Appearance', 21 January. Online: <http://news.aol.ca/article/polygamy-leader-makes-court-appearance/493803/> (accessed 25 January 2009).

Chambers, D. L. (1997) 'Polygamy and Same-Sex Marriage', *Hofstra Law Review*, 26: 53–83.

COMPAS Inc. Public Opinion and Public Research. (2009) 'Public Opinion on Polygamy: First of Two National Polling Reports to the Institute of Canadian Values'. Online: <www.familyaction.org/Articles/issues/family/marriage/poly-compaspoll. pdf> (accessed 27 August 2009).

Cossman, B. (2008) 'Betwixt and Between Recognition: Migrating Same-Sex Marriages and the Turn toward the Private', *Law and Contemporary Problems*, 71(3): 153–68.

Cott, N. F. (2000) *Public Vows: A History of Marriage and Nation*, Cambridge, MA: Harvard University Press.

Drummond, S. (2009) 'A Marriage of Fear and Xenophobia: Our Criminalization of Polygamy Isn't about Protecting Women', *Globe and Mail*, 6 April.

Duggan, L. (2003) *The Twilight of Equality? Neoliberalism, Cultural Politics and the Attack on Democracy*, Boston, MA: Beacon Press.

Duncan, E. J. (2008) 'The Positive Effects of Legalizing Polygamy: "Love is a Many Splendored Thing" ', *Duke Journal of Gender Law and Policy*, 15: 315–38.

Emens, E. (2004) 'Monogamy's Law: Compulsory Monogamy and Polyamorous Existence', *New York University School of Law Review of Law and Social Change*, 29: 277–376.

Eng, D. L. with Halberstam, J. and Muñoz, J. E. (2005) 'What's Queer about Queer Studies Now?', *Social Text*, 23(3 & 4): 1–17.

Ertman, M. M. (2008) ' "They Ain't Whites, They're Mormons": An Illustrated History of Polygamy as Race Treason', University of Maryland School of Law Legal Studies Research Paper No. 2008–37. Online: <http://ssrn.com/abstact=1270023> (accessed 27 August 2009).

Eskridge, W. N. Jr. (1995) *The Case for Same-Sex Marriage: From Sexual Liberty to Civilized Commitment*, New York, NY: Free Press.

Frei, D. (2006) 'Polygamy, Gays and TV', *Advocate*, issue 964, June 6, page 4.

Gallup (2007) 'Tolerance for Gay Rights at High Water Mark'. Online: <www.gallup.com/poll/27694/tolerance-gay-rights-highwater-mark.aspx> (accessed 29 August 2009).

Gautier, A. (2005) 'Legal Regulation of Marital Relations: An Historical and Comparative Approach', *International Journal of Law, Policy, and Family*, 19(1): 47–72.

Gher, J. M. (2008) 'Polygamy and Same-Sex Marriage: Allies or Adversaries within the Same-Sex Marriage Movement', *William and Mary Journal of Women and the Law*, 14: 559–604.

Graff, E. J. (1999) *What Is Marriage For?*, Boston, MA: Beacon Press.

In re Marriage Cases (2008) 43 Cal.4th 757, 76 Cal.Rptr.3d 683, 183 P. 3d 384.

Kaufman, A. (2005) 'Polygamous Marriages in Canada', *Canadian Journal of Family Law*, 21: 315–43.

Kelly, L. M. (2007) 'Bringing International Human Rights Law Home: An Evaluation of Canada's Family Law on Polygamy', *University of Toronto Faculty of Law Review*, 65(1): 1–38.

Khalsa, R. K. (2005) 'Polygamy as a Red Herring in the Same-Sex Marriage Debate', *Duke Law Journal*, 54: 1665–94.

Lieber, F. (1855) 'The Mormons: Shall Utah Be Admitted into the Union?', *Putnam's Monthly*, 5(27): 2–13.

Manuse, A. (2009) 'New Hampshire Senate Passes Gay Marriage Bill', *Reuters*, April 29. Online: <www.reuters.com/article/domesticNews/idUSTRE53S72J20090429> (accessed 29 August 2009).

Muñoz, J. E. (1999) *Disidentifications: Queers of Color and the Performance of Politics*. Minneapolis, MN: University of Minnesota Press.

Myers, M. G. (2006) 'Polygamist Eye for the Monogamist Guy: Homosexual Sodomy . . . Gay Marriage . . . Is Polygamy Next?', *Houston Law Review*, 46: 1451–86.

Puar, J. (2007) *Terrorist Assemblages: Homonationalism in Queer Times*. Durham, NC: Duke University Press.

Razack, S. (2005) 'How is White Supremacy Embodied? Sexualized Racial Violence at Abu Ghraib', *Canadian Journal of Women and the Law*, 17: 341–63.

Robson, R. (2002) 'Assimilation, Marriage and Lesbian Liberation', *Temple Law Review* 75(4): 709–819.

Seuffert, N. (2003) 'Shaping the Modern Nation: Colonial Marriage Law, Polygamy, and Concubinage in Aotearoa New Zealand', *Law Text Culture*, 7: 186–220.

Sigman, S. M. (2006) 'Everything Lawyers Know about Polygamy is Wrong', *Cornell Journal of Law and Public Policy*, 16: 101–86.

Somerville, S. (2005) 'Queer Loving', *GLQ: A Journal of Lesbian and Gay Studies*, 11(3): 335–70.

Sontag, S. (1989) *AIDS and its Metaphors*, London: Allen Lane.

Status of Women Canada (2005) *Polygamy in Canada: Legal and Social Implications for Women and Children: A Collection of Policy Research Reports*, Ottawa.

Strassberg, M. I. (1997) 'Distinctions of Form and Substance: Monogamy, Polygamy and Same-Sex Marriage', *North Carolina Law Review*, 75: 1501–624.

Sullivan, A. (1995) *Virtually Normal: An Argument about Homosexuality*, New York, NY: Knopf.

Todd, D. (2009) 'Polygamy Case May Test Limits of Canadian Same-Sex Marriage', *The Pew Forum on Religion and Public Life*, January 23. Online: <http://pewforum.org/news/display.php?NewsID=17395> (accessed 29 August 2009).

Weeks, J. (1992) 'Values in an Age of Uncertainty', in D. M. Stanton (ed.) *Discourses of Sexuality: From Aristotle to AIDS*, Ann Arbor, MI: University of Michigan Press.

Part 4

Exclusion

Chapter 10

An 'imperial' strategy?

The use of comparative and international law in arguments about LGBT rights

Nicholas Bamforth

It is now common to see comparative or international law arguments used before legislatures and courts when they consider the legal treatment of LGBT rights issues. Conservative jurists have responded to this practice with hostility. A particularly vocal criticism is Justice Scalia's dissent in *Lawrence v. Texas* (2003). Critics from the left, for their part, have suggested that such international comparisons may involve a 'we-know-best' style sub-version of local conceptions of justice, perhaps amounting to a form of im-perialism: a criticism which brings to mind Leonard Woolf's contention that under nineteenth- and early twentieth-century European imperialism, 'the Government' of colonised which territories 'was a European government and the inhabitants were subjected to European laws' (1928: 12). Given the global availability of information, debate about the use of comparative and inter-national material is likely to be ongoing. When thinking about LGBT issues and ideas of 'empire' and the 'imperial', we might therefore ask whether LGBT litigants, or their opponents, or both, are acting in an imperialistic style in using – or rebutting the use of – comparative and international law arguments. Behind this lies a broader question, namely whether the use of legal or moral arguments on a trans-cultural basis is undesirable precisely because of an association with the 'imperial'.[1]

With these questions in mind, the first section of the chapter will explore some arguments surrounding *Lawrence*. I will suggest that when the term 'imperialistic' is fully considered, the tangibly 'imperial' approach was in fact Justice Scalia's in his denunciation of 'foreign' law. Since argument about *Lawrence* quickly shifts into the normative realm, the second section will consider whether it is appropriate to argue about the law's treatment of sexu-ality on a universalist or a relativist/localised basis. I will argue that hard-line universalist and relativist approaches raise problems of justice and efficacy, and that an intermediate position or strategy, which can avoid the 'imperial' or 'empire-related' problems associated with universalism, is preferable. Further-more, the use of comparative authority is not always 'imperialistic': whether it is appropriate to so describe it depends, rather, on the extent to which the actors involved occupy socially empowered or disempowered positions.

Use of comparative and international law

Two key dimensions are apparent in discussions about the appropriate reach of arguments concerning the law's regulation of sexuality. The first, which is more 'technical' or 'practical', concerns the extent to which it is workable or useful for legislatures, lobbyists, courts and litigants to employ comparative or international law when arguing about or determining the content or correct interpretation of national law. The second, more 'normative' or 'abstract' dimension, concerns how far arguments about the proper content or interpretation of the law is (or should be seen as) applicable across cultures or presumptively universal rather than rooted in the values of and confined to the culture in which they are advanced. Neither dimension is confined to the regulation of sexuality, although the first is highly visible in this context, and the second is influenced by our understanding of sex, gender and sexual orientation (and the approach taken to the second can influence that taken to the first). Both might be associated with the theme of 'empire' to the extent that the use of arguments on a trans-cultural or universal basis is seen as an 'imperialistic' manoeuvre.

The first dimension is illustrated by the debate about the US Supreme Court's use of comparative law to help justify its conclusion, in *Lawrence*, that a state anti-sodomy statute was incompatible with the Due Process Clause of the Fourteenth Amendment and that the earlier, contrasting decision in *Bowers v. Hardwick*[2] should be overruled. William Eskridge categorises *Lawrence* as 'the first time that the Supreme Court has cited foreign case law in the process of overruling an American constitutional precedent' (2004: 555), although non-US authority had been cited in other contexts. In his judgment, Justice Kennedy noted that the 'sweeping references' made in *Bowers* to 'the history of western civilization and to Judaeo-Christian moral and ethical standards' as a factor supporting anti-sodomy legislation 'did not take account' of contradictory authorities (*Lawrence* 2003: 572). 'Of even more importance' was the decision of the European Court of Human Rights in *Dudgeon v. United Kingdom*,[3] decided almost five years before *Bowers*, that the criminal prohibition of private consensual gay sex contravened the European Convention on Human Rights (*Lawrence* 2003: 573). Furthermore, '[t]o the extent *Bowers* relied on values we share with a wider civilization . . . [its] reasoning and holding . . . have been rejected elsewhere': the Court of Human Rights followed *Dudgeon* in later cases, and '[o]ther nations . . . have taken action consistent with an affirmation of the protected right of homosexual adults to engage in intimate, consensual conduct . . . [which] has been accepted as an integral part of human freedom' (ibid. 576–7). Justice Scalia, dissenting, challenged this use of comparative authority:

> Constitutional entitlements do not spring into existence because some [US] States choose to lessen or eliminate criminal sanctions on certain

behaviour. Much less do they spring into existence . . . because foreign nations decriminalize conduct. The *Bowers* majority . . . rejected the claimed right to sodomy on the ground that such a right was not 'deeply rooted in this Nation's history and tradition'.

(ibid. 598)

He also emphasised that it was dangerous to use such *dicta*, since – citing Justice Thomas from *Foster v. Florida* – 'this Court . . . should not impose foreign moods, fads, or fashions, on Americans' (ibid. 598).[4]

At first sight, Kennedy might appear to be treating *Bowers'* lack of fit with values the US shared 'with a wider civilisation' as a matter of empirical difference, in so far as he was measuring the prevailing opinion and showing that analogous constitutional provisions to those in *Bowers* had been interpreted differently elsewhere: most obviously, in *Dudgeon*. Eskridge thus suggests that 'the fact that *Bowers* had received a hostile reaction among judges in Europe' and in some 'traditionalist' US states 'provided a neutral reason' for the *Lawrence* majority 'to believe there was an emerging consensus' and that this precedent had misread the 'libertarian traditions' of America and fellow democracies (2004: 557). Eskridge notes, however, that Kennedy must also have been engaged in a normative exercise:

The foreign precedents were both normative focal points, helping an American judge to evaluate the consistency of sodomy laws with fundamental and shared constitutional principles, and normative feedback, deepening concerns . . . about the harmfulness as well as the incorrectness of *Bowers*.

(ibid.)

Meanwhile, Scalia's comment about '*this Nation's* history and tradition' might at first look like an observation of fact, but the context and subject matter suggest that it was playing a normative role. The normative dimension is made explicit through Scalia's *openly* normative assertion that it was 'dangerous' to use non-US *dicta* which imposed 'foreign moods, fads or fashions' on Americans, something which might be summed up as 'Americans know best about American values and the constitution'. *Lawrence* might therefore be thought to demonstrate how rapidly the 'technical' dimension collapses into its 'normative' counterpart.

A similar point can be made about the arguments of academic opponents of *Lawrence*. Steven G. Calabresi, for example, suggests that '[i]f one agrees with Justices Scalia and Thomas, as I do, that most of what the Court does involves interpretation and not policy-making, then one will think foreign court decisions are usually not relevant' (2004: 1106). By using the word 'relevant', Calabresi is apparently trying hard to avoid an argument about whether it is *desirable* to use comparative authority, instead shifting the focus to the 'practical' issue of how helpful it is. However, once one questions whether it is possible (or always possible) cleanly to separate 'interpretation' from 'policy-making', the focus on 'practicality' may seem too thin, especially when Calabresi makes clear his preference for an explicitly (normative) 'originalist' approach. Later, Calabresi suggests that while it may be relevant that the European Convention prohibits sexual orientation discrimination, 'it is a long leap' from that statement to 'the proposition that the United States Supreme Court should take sides in the culture war looming in this country over gay rights by outlawing discrimination against gays' (ibid. 1122). He also states that there is 'a big difference between supporting the decriminalization of something and making it into a new national right' (ibid. 1123). Such throw-away assertions – which many would dispute and which considerably exaggerate what was decided in *Lawrence* – must undermine any impression that Calabresi's arguments are merely empirical or 'technical'. A slightly different running together of the 'technical' and 'normative' may be associated with assertions that overestimate the extent to which non-US authority was decisive. Joan L. Larsen, for example, associates *Lawrence* with an approach whereby judges 'looked to the judgments and practices of foreign nations and international agreements to determine what the content of the domestic constitutional rule should be' (2004: 1295). Yet as Cass Sunstein notes, the *Lawrence* Court 'did not simply announce that the Constitution protects sexual conduct as such . . . Instead, the Court stressed an "emerging recognition," which it located in a number of places' (2004: 1061), including the US Model Penal Code and the legislative histories of the US states.[5] It is not difficult to speculate that such overestimations may be influenced by discomfort, in normative terms, with the substance of the decision.

It is quite possible to understand in a relatively 'neutral', 'technical' sense arguments about the unhelpfulness or inapplicability in national litigation or law-drafting of concepts drawn from comparative or international law. However, it seems extremely difficult to confine arguments about *Lawrence* to this 'neutral', 'technical' sense, as highlighted by Scalia's emotive language about 'danger', and by the other points considered above. If it is not possible to separate the 'technical' from the 'normative', how might normative opposition to *Lawrence* be understood in terms of ideas of 'empire' or 'imperialism'? Conservative opponents are not claiming that the use of comparative precedent is itself 'imperialistic'. To do so would be bizarre when the United States is so much more powerful than any signatory to the European Convention and, traditionally, more legally isolationist. Rather, conservative opposition might itself be seen as 'imperialistic' in a different sense: that is, as an assertion that the political, social and moral power of the United States is such that its laws must be interpreted according to American values only and should in no sense be 'degraded' by reinterpretation in the light of non-American precedent (a position not far removed from Justice Scalia's comment about the 'danger' of using non-American precedent). This would fit logically with Woolf's description of imperialism as involving the imposition of a (stronger) imperial power's laws on (weaker) colonies: for a self-conceived imperial power would see no reason to take account of the laws of weaker nations, whether colonies or allies, when considering its own laws. An 'imperial' interpretation of Scalia's position draws support from Eskridge's reading of *Lawrence*. Eskridge notes that 'country after country has recognized rights for gay people . . . without negative consequences for the body politic' and suggests that Kennedy 'implicitly recognized' that this 'political experience' is 'instructive for the United States' because, '[o]nce other countries have accorded gay people . . . equal treatment without wrenching their pluralist systems, the price of denying gay people the same rights in the United States goes up and the arguments against equality grow shakier' (2004: 559). This, in turn, helped 'signal other countries that the Court is attentive to their norms and is a cooperative court' (ibid. 558). On this view, the Supreme Court's acknowledgement of the *power* of lessons from overseas was the very opposite of 'imperialist'.

A deeper normative question

Underlying the debate about comparative authority is a deeper and more clearly normative question: namely, what is right or wrong about using arguments from abroad when urging a change to or reinterpretation of the law in a given jurisdiction. There are strongly contrasting philosophical views about whether arguments for (or against) the use of law in particular ways or to particular ends may be used with equal validity across time and across cultures (what might be termed a 'universalist' position) or whether arguments of justice must be more localised (a 'relativist' position). This forces us to consider whether it is appropriate to condemn *all* societies whose laws (whether about sexuality or other issues) fail to match up to the standards demanded by our own theories of justice, or whether our theories may only properly be used to assess the laws of the society or societies in which they evolved: in other words, whether our arguments may be of 'universal' or purely 'local' application. If a country invokes 'local cultural and religious values' to justify the passage of legislation which explicitly discriminates against particular groups, for example, can people from outside the country legitimately condemn this by reference to their own theories of justice, or must any arguments be based only on the values of the local culture?

I will argue that absolute universalism and pure moral relativism are undesirable and inadequate approaches. Before doing so, I should stress that the debate is of direct relevance to the issue of 'empire' or 'imperialism', in so far as the imposition (actual or perceived) of the values of one country on another could be seen, depending on perspective, *either* as an exercise in imperialism *or* as an attempt properly to empower an unjustly disadvantaged minority or promote freedom more generally. A good example is offered by

President Robert Mugabe's persistent use of government (including legal) authority to persecute lesbians and gay men in Zimbabwe. In August 1995, when Mugabe first launched his campaign against what he categorised as the threat of moral corruption 'posed' to the country by male homosexuality, his government responded to protests from European, North American and South African human rights groups by suggesting that it was inappropriate for people from Europe or North America to use *their* moral standards rather than prevailing local values to evaluate the legitimacy of his campaign, which merely reinforced 'traditional' African values. On this view, it was tantamount to moral imperialism for nations with different moral standards to judge Zimbabwe by those standards. For the human rights groups, by contrast, there was a moral imperative to do something to help those persecuted by the Mugabe regime.[6]

Starting with relativist approaches, Michael Walzer has argued that ideas about human rights do not emerge from any conception of a common, universal humanity: rather, rights and rights-claims are 'local and particular in character' (1983: xv). It is therefore a mistake to search for a single underlying sense of justice that all societies can rightfully embrace: instead, different societies will have their own varying notions. 'History', Walzer suggests, 'reveals no single good and no naturally dominant good' (ibid. 11); and, since social meanings are historical in character, what counts as a just or unjust distribution of goods will change over time. Theorists should not, therefore, be seeking to devise ideal and universally applicable notions of justice (and hence universally applicable arguments about law and rights): instead, they should be searching for theories that are appropriate to the society from which they are drawn, and whose common life they reflect. In matters of morality, argument is no more than an appeal to the common meanings which prevail in a given political community, and therefore vary according to the community in question. For Walzer, 'Justice is rooted in [a community's own] distinct understandings of places, honours, jobs, things of all sorts that constitute a shared way of life. To override these understandings is (always) to act unjustly' (ibid. 314).

On this view, any struggle against the existing social (or legal) order of a given society should take place from within that society, and cannot – if it is to count as just – be based upon some claim that the society fails to meet an externally determined standard (Plant 1991: 346–7). Sexual minorities would therefore presumably need, in order to defend themselves, to base their arguments on a sufficiently 'authentic' interpretation of the 'traditional values' of their society. Given the moral relativism inherent in Walzer's position, any other argument could presumably be met by the rebuttal that 'this is the way we've always done things here'.

As Ernest Gellner notes, pure relativism of this type must 'allow illiberal values their place in the sun' and 'deprives us of the means – indeed of the right – to express deep revulsion' at such values (1995: 59). By what means,

Gellner asks rhetorically, could a relativist condemn a society which con-
doned, as part of its *own* deep-rooted moral code, slavery, gulags, female
circumcision or gas chambers? If marginalised groups can only appeal to the
values internal to their culture in order to build arguments to change the law
– that is, to the values of the culture which is *already* oppressing them – they
would appear to be in an almost hopeless position (Kymlicka 1989: 65–6).
Moral relativism may also make it difficult to assess whether a group can even
properly be described as unfairly oppressed. To quote the convinced universalist Richard Mohr, 'Without culturally-neutral values, we cannot know that
certain groups aren't simply being put in their proper place' when they are
harshly treated by a society: 'we are unable to tell when ill-treatment and
ill-will is warranted and when they constitute oppression' (1995: 12–3). This
point is echoed by Gellner, who suggests that '[m]odern liberty differs from
its ancient predecessor not merely because it stresses individual freedom
over collective self-rule: it also includes the notion of trans-ethnic or trans-
political truth, which is not simply engendered by a culture and its practices'
(ibid. 61).

A related argument has been developed by Ronald Dworkin, who suggests
that if anything can be seen as a traditional social practice of a given community, it is worrying about what justice really is. We presume, in other words,
that justice is a critic of the community's practices rather than their mirror,
implying that justice is a matter of general, transcultural standards by which
a society can be evaluated and criticised. Ultimately, Dworkin claims:

> political theory can make no contribution to how we govern ourselves
> except by struggling, against all the impulses that drag us back into our
> own culture, toward generality and some reflective basis for deciding
> which of our traditional distinctions and discriminations are genuine and
> which spurious, which contribute to the flourishing of the ideals we want,
> after reflection, to embrace, and which serve only to protect us from the
> personal costs of that demanding process. We cannot leave justice to
> convention and anecdote.
>
> (1986: 219–20)

The practical deficiencies of relativism are particularly evident in relation to
the law's regulation of sexuality. If we adopt a purely relativist approach,
litigants in a case like *Lawrence* would be unable to draw support from standards prevailing outside the US, for Justice Scalia's approach would surely
capture American relativist opposition to the use of anything 'non-American'.
We would also have to condemn the High Court of Delhi's use of European,
South African, US and Canadian precedents in its ruling in *Naz Foundation v.
Government of NCT of Delhi* (*Naz* 2009) that the Indian Penal Code's criminalisation of consensual gay sex violated the Indian Constitution. Relativism
would be acting to *exclude* arguments which are intended to help members of

a locally disempowered group (i.e., a group which is subject to general or prevailing social and/or legal hostility,[7] whose members are stigmatised as unworthy of full consideration as human beings because of a characteristic they are assumed to possess, provided always that there is no conclusive argument of justice which explains and justifies why they are so treated).

In this context, *relativism* would be playing an 'imperial' role by saying 'Our society already knows best when it discriminates against LGBT persons and that's our business and nothing to do with anyone else: we stand alone.' This takes us to the nub of the 'imperial' issue. When we characterise conduct, assertions or attitudes as 'imperialistic' or 'reminiscent of empire', we tend to assume that the 'imperial' actor is (and probably perceives itself to be) extremely powerful and perhaps in some sense special, deriving some notion of entitlement from this. It follows that it is simplistic to characterise the normative use of precedent or argument from outside a society as 'imperial' *in and of itself*: rather, such a characterisation depends on the relative power of the society (or its power relative to the other actor) and perhaps on the motivation of the stronger society (if there is more than one) or actor. On this view, it could well seem like imperialism for the United States government or Supreme Court to tell the authorities of other, weaker countries that those countries will be penalised if they refuse to apply US legal precedent as part of their own law. But it is hardly imperialism for litigants from a socially disempowered group – in *Lawrence*, gay men from the state of Texas who were arrested for having consensual sex in their own home – to seek to advance their cause by employing overseas precedent. If 'imperialistic' is, at root, a relativistic categorisation, the visibly 'imperial' manoeuvre seems, in this context, to be Justice Scalia's refusal to give credence to 'dangerous' non-American case law.

A purely relativist condemnation of comparative precedent also looks slightly absurd if applied to the *Naz Foundation* decision, for the Indian Penal Code was itself a product of British imperial rule. The gay sex provisions – which *imposed* Judaeo-Christian moral standards on Indians (*Naz* 2009: paras. [3], [7]) – were held to violate India's *post-independence* Constitution, Indian judicial interpretations of which had intentionally made use of foreign precedents even from the time of 'early' post-independence cases (Thiruvengadam 2008: 69).[8]

If relativism is thought to be practically damaging to the position of socially disempowered groups and to be normatively undesirable, theories of justice which lay claim to universal application might begin to seem attractive, for they would enable us to employ similar criteria for moral assessment in all circumstances (offering clear lines of defence to disempowered sexual minorities in repressive jurisdictions) and might – as Dworkin suggests – fit with our intuitions about justice as something standing above localised, day-to-day life. However, when applied with too much enthusiasm, universalist approaches generate practical and normative problems of their own. Given the sheer variety of ways in which human understanding and behaviour varies across cultures, it seems facile not to acknowledge that moral assessments *also vary*, to an extent, according to the society and period in question. It also seems presumptuous to assert, without more, that a particular theory of justice must apply regardless of the circumstances. The criticism here is that highly universalist approaches are arrogant: the charge of moral presumptuousness, if not imperialism, could be thought to carry weight where a theory characterises itself, without more, as automatically applicable in assessing the laws of all societies. A further concern is that such theories are prone to fail as defences of human rights. Given the differences between cultures, arguments which are expressed in *unduly* general terms run the risk of not making their point with real effect at the local level where it needs to be made most powerfully.

This second concern has been developed by Richard Rorty, who suggests that universalist arguments may be unhelpful if we are concerned to guarantee effective day-to-day protection against ill treatment. Rorty argues that declarations of universally valid human rights are empty if they mean nothing to the people whose behaviour they are supposed to constrain. Many people, Rorty suggests, live in a world in which their sense of moral community extends no further than their family, clan or tribe. If they have never conceived that they may owe moral commitments to members of other groups, or that those groups deserve moral respect, then abstract demands to respect them are likely to seem nonsensical. According to Rorty:

> To get whites to be nicer to Blacks, males to females, Serbs to Muslims, or straights to gays, to help our species link up into ... a 'planetary community' dominated by a culture of human rights, it is of no use whatever to say, with Kant: Notice that what you have in common, your humanity, is more important than these trivial differences. For the people we are trying to convince will rejoin that they notice nothing of the sort.
>
> (1993: 125)

The implication of Rorty's view is that arguments can only hope to provide an *effective* basis for better legal or social treatment for sexual minorities where they make sense according to local understandings: abstract, universal theories which say nothing about day-to-day life will have little resonance and little ability to afford effective protection.[9]

This concern about efficacy may be particularly important when dealing with sexuality given the debate between essentialist and constructionist approaches to gender, sex and sexual orientation. Essentialism is, according to Diana Fuss, 'most commonly understood as a belief in the real, true essence of things, the invariable and fixed properties [of] which define the "whatness" of a given entity' (1990: xi. See also Weeks 1991: 95; Stein 1990:

325–6). An essentialist theory of gender might therefore distinguish humans as 'male' and 'female' according to what are categorised as eternal, transhistorical and immutable characteristics. Constructionists argue, by contrast, that social categories are, to varying degrees, culture specific: they are the product of social dialogues and assumptions which vary between societies and eras. In Fuss's words, 'Constructionism . . . insists that essence is itself a[n] historical construction' (ibid. 2). Essentialist and constructionist analyses of sexual orientation and sexuality can produce radically different conclusions. Steven Epstein suggests that:

> [w]here essentialism took for granted that all societies consist of people who are either heterosexuals or homosexuals . . . constructionists demonstrated that the notion of 'the homosexual' is a sociohistorical product, not universally applicable . . . and where essentialism would treat the self-attribution of a 'homosexual identity' as unproblematic – as simply the conscious recognition of a true, underlying 'orientation' – constructionism focused attention on identity as a complex developmental outcome, the consequence of an interactive process of social labelling and self-identification.
>
> (1990: 250–1)

To the extent that we veer in a constructionist direction (and it is fair to say that most theorists do to some extent), we need to acknowledge – if our arguments about sexuality are to seem realistic – the existence of differences between cultures and time periods. Logically, this might suggest that it is unrealistic to expect that the same theories of justice can be applied in *exactly* the same ways across all such cultures, given that their *subject matters* are likely to differ or to appear to do so.

This point may appear to count, to some extent, in favour of relativism, but an important question is the extent to which it is, in practice, ever possible to be *wholly* relativist. Analytically, this question arises when considering theories of justice in general. Despite the moral relativism of much of his work, Michael Walzer acknowledges the existence of 'a kind of minimal and universal moral code' (1987: 24) which operates on a transcultural basis in the sense that nearly all societies have prohibitions on murder, cruelty, deception and betrayal. Equally, Bernard Williams draws attention, as part of his critique of moral relativism, to a universalist aspect. Williams suggests that '[i]n its vulgar and unregenerate form . . . [relativism] . . . consists of three propositions: that "right" means (can only be coherently understood as meaning) "right for a given society"; that "right for a given society" is to be understood in a functionalist sense; and that (therefore) it is wrong for people in one society to condemn, interfere with, etc., the values of another society' (1993: 20). As Williams points out, the third proposition is clearly *nonrelative*: for moral relativists appear to be claiming that it is *always* wrong to condemn the moral values of another society from the outside, a claim which is itself of a universal, transcultural nature.

The previous argument implies that in logic, relativism and universalism must to an extent overlap. Judith Butler's use of *both* local and universalist understandings in her (constructionist) account of gender and sex suggests, in addition, that overlap or convergence may arise in more *strategic or political terms* when thinking about sexuality. Butler's performative account of gender (1999: esp. xxv–xxviii, 183–93), tied to the argument that the notion of sex is itself a construction (ibid. esp. 8–46, 192–3, 199–203), has often been associated with anti-universalism. Moya Lloyd suggests that '[t]hroughout her work, Butler has been at pains to challenge the assumption that a principle, law or substance exists outside of culture and language that forms the basis for understanding either sex or sexuality or subversion' (Lloyd 2007: 101). Butler repeatedly condemns universalism in her book *Gender Trouble*, stressing that the power of feminist analysis can be:

> undercut precisely by its globalizing reach . . . Feminist critique ought to explore the totalizing claims of a masculinist signifying economy, but also remain self-critical with respect to the totalizing gestures of feminism. The effort to identify the enemy as singular in form is a reverse-discourse that uncritically mimics the strategy of the oppressor instead of offering a different set of terms.
>
> (1999: 18)

Furthermore:

> [u]niversalistic claims are based on a common or shared epistemological standpoint . . . this globalizing gesture has spawned a number of criticisms from women who claim that the category of 'women' is normative and exclusionary and is invoked with the unmarked dimensions of class and racial privilege intact . . . the insistence upon the coherence and unity of the category . . . has effectively refused the multiplicity of cultural, social, and political intersections in which the concrete array of 'women' are constructed.
>
> (ibid. 19)

However, Butler later acknowledged that in practical LGBT rights activism, claims of universality could have 'important strategic use', so that 'the assertion of universality can be proleptic and performative, conjuring a reality that does not yet exist, and holding out the possibility for a convergence of cultural horizons that have not yet met' (ibid. xviii). Butler seems, in other words, to be endorsing the use of universalist arguments by socially disempowered groups as a mechanism for working towards a position of empowerment. She confronted the point head on when stating that:

[a] reductive relativism would say that we cannot speak of the human or of international human rights, since there are only and always local and provisional understandings of these terms, and that the generalizations themselves do violence to the specificity of the meanings in question. This is not my view ... I think we are compelled to speak of the human, and of the international, and to find out in particular how 'human rights' do and do not work.

(2005: 75)

Butler sought to tie this to her account of gender. While speaking of the human as a category, she argues, 'we must also be part of a critical demo-cratic project' which acknowledges the limitations and intermediate nature of existing social categories (ibid.). In consequence, 'we must follow a double-path in politics: we must use' the language of international human rights:

to assert an entitlement to conditions of life in ways that affirm the constitutive role of sexuality and gender in political life, and we must also subject our very categories to critical scrutiny, find out the limits of their inclusivity and translatability, the presuppositions they include, the ways in which they must be expanded, destroyed, or reworked.

(ibid. 76)

More specifically, 'local conceptions of what is "human" ... must be sub-jected to reinterpretation, since there are historical and cultural circum-stances in which the "human" is defined differently' (ibid. 75). Taken in the round, Butler's comments seem to herald the possibility of an intermediate position or strategy which seeks to avoid the pitfalls of pure relativism or absolute universalism.

Without specifically co-opting Butler's model, the possibility of such a position or strategy deserves serious consideration given that it might avoid many of the problems associated with 'empire' or 'imperialism', while still allowing us to make comparative judgments where this is appropriate. Since this is an intermediate position or strategy, aspects of relevant universalist and moral relativist approaches can, where appropriate, be borrowed or developed. Comments offered by Stephen Sedley, an English judge, offer a useful starting point. Sedley argues that we can accept that statements about human rights are rooted in a particular time and culture *without* consigning them 'to the bin of relativism' (1995: 386–7). A society's views about the content of fundamental human rights will vary with the times and any list of currently accepted human rights will itself be a product of a particular time and place. Claims about 'universal' human rights can only properly be understood when set against their distinctive historical backdrop.

These aspects of Sedley's argument are clearly relativist. However, he also suggests that:

there are moral and practical continuities – of which the democratic principle is one – which can be powerfully represented as fundamental values, at least within the temporal and social horizons of each society. This relatively modest foundation for the legitimacy of human rights has perhaps the virtue that, without reducing all discourse to incoherent subjectivity, it recognises that a single 'right' outcome to every issue is attainable, if at all, only locally and temporarily.

(ibid. 390)

This is still largely relativist, but the idea of 'continuities' seemingly implies that each society has a *bedrock* of fundamental values which can be interpreted and developed to provide a satisfactory answer at any given time. The interpretation and the answer may vary, but the outline values to which they pay lip-service are more permanent. A later part of Sedley's argument clearly distinguishes it from pure moral relativism. He claims:

If . . . we are to escape the cold wind of history which blows sooner or later on [universal] higher-order laws and self-evident truths, it is to our present epoch's consensus about society's ground rules that we should turn. To admit this is to admit . . . that different societies will agree on different ground rules, and to accept accordingly that we have both a right to review and recast our standards and an obligation to make the case for the adoption of them by others rather than continue to assert loftily that ours, being self-evident, are the only acceptable ones.

(ibid. 396)

While denying that there are universally valid notions of human rights, Sedley nonetheless rejects the view that it is impermissible to use our own standards to measure or criticise other societies. While it may be wrong to work from the unrealistic universalist assumption that our standards are the only valid ones – i.e., to prejudge situations on the basis that our standards *automatically* apply – it is acceptable to press other people to adopt our standards on their merits if, at the same time, we are willing to listen to their arguments.[10] This must imply that we *can* properly rank certain values as superior on their merits, if only for our own benefit, the notion of justice used to do this being (to some extent) general and transcultural in nature. Sedley's argument thus allows us to reject what could be described as the moral imperialism of universalist theories – their assumption that a theory of justice can automatically apply to all societies at all times – while preserving the ability to criticise, according to our own theory of justice, the values of other societies. We can believe that our own theory is better than any alternative, but acknowledge that it is necessary to convince members of other societies of this point rather than just asserting, imperialistically, that our theory applies to them.

An intermediate position or strategy could thus refuse to opt for moral relativism *while endorsing* Rorty's view that presumptively universal theories are likely to be ineffective. Indeed, it could go beyond Sedley's argument by accepting that people can properly believe that their theory or justification *should* be regarded as universally applicable. But however framed, such a position or strategy would depart from the universalist outlook in its scepticism about the ability of presumptively universal standards to enhance the position of disempowered social minorities in societies whose values are radically different from the theorist's own. It would therefore refuse to talk about automatically applicable standards, and by doing so seek to avoid moral imperialism in practice. By invoking such a strategy, the pitfalls of pure moral relativism – for example, the inability to condemn other societies for their treatment of sexual minorities – can be avoided, as can the arrogance of universalism given the strategy's acceptance of the need to engage in dialogue with others, a process which will involve give as well as take.

Conclusion

If it is right to say that the arguments about the use of comparative authority in *Lawrence* tend ultimately to be normative, and if an intermediate position or strategy concerning the reach of arguments of justice provides the best way to deal with debate about the law's regulation of sexuality, then such a position or strategy might be able to stand behind and underpin Kennedy's approach in *Lawrence*. An intermediate position or strategy – while allowing us to avoid the problems associated with pure relativist or universalist approaches – can seem somewhat pragmatic in its operation. It places considerable weight on the importance of efficacy and on the relative positions of countries and actors, and on questions of empowerment and disempowerment. Nonetheless, it has much to commend it. If a pure relativist approach were correct, very considerable obstacles would be placed in the way of anyone from outside Zimbabwe who sought to assist those persecuted by the Mugabe government. If an absolute universalist approach were right, intervention would be likely to fall foul of the charge of 'imperialism'. If the legal entitlements of LGBT individuals are to be protected in a world where hostility exists on a grand scale and it is easy (and sometimes justifiable) to raise concerns about 'empire' and 'imperialism', an intermediate way forward has considerable potential.

Notes

1 Compare the concerns of Ratna Kapur, in this volume (Ch. 3), with queer theory as a Western export.
2 (1986) 478 US 186.
3 [1981] 4 EHRR 149.

4 *Foster v. Florida* (2002) 537 US 990.
5 Sunstein's interpretation is reinforced by the distance between Justice Kennedy's statement that 'When our precedent has been ... weakened ... criticism from other sources is of greater significance' (*Lawrence* 2003: 576) and claims that overseas precedent is 'determinative'.
6 E.g., *The Pink Paper*, 11 August, 18 August and 1 September 1995, *Guardian*, 3 August 1996, p. 15.
7 In the case of LGBT individuals, see Amnesty International (2001), *Crimes of Hate, Conspiracy of Silence: Torture and Ill-treatment Based on Sexual Identity*, London: Amnesty International.
8 See the contribution by Ratna Kapur in this volume (Ch. 3).
9 Compare Jon Binnie's account, in this volume (Ch. 2), of the specificities of LGBTQ politics in Central and Eastern Europe relative to Western European discourses.
10 There are analogies here to Leckey's (2009) 'thick instrumentalist' approach.

References

Butler, J. (1999, originally 1990) *Gender Trouble*, New York: Routledge.
—— (2005) 'On Being Beside Oneself: On the Limits of Sexual Autonomy', in N. Bamforth (ed.) *Sex Rights: The Oxford Amnesty Lectures 2002*, Oxford: Oxford University Press.
Calabresi, S. G. (2004) '*Lawrence*, the Fourteenth Amendment, and the Supreme Court's Reliance on Foreign Constitutional Law: An Originalist Reappraisal', *Ohio State Law Journal*, 65: 1097–132.
Dworkin, R. (1986) *A Matter of Principle*, Oxford: Oxford University Press.
Epstein, S. (1990) 'Gay Politics, Ethnic Identity: The Limits of Social Constructionism', in E. Stein (ed.) *Forms of Desire: Sexual Orientation and the Social Constructionist Controversy*, New York, NY: Garland.
Eskridge, W. (2004) '*Lawrence v. Texas* and the imperative of comparative constitutionalism', *International Journal of Constitutional Law*, 2(3): 555–60.
Fuss, D. (1990) *Essentially Speaking: Feminism, Nature and Difference*, New York, NY: Routledge.
Gellner, E. (1995) 'Sauce for the Liberal Goose', *Prospect*, November: 56–61.
Kymlicka, W. (1989) *Liberalism, Community and Culture*, Oxford: Clarendon Press.
Larsen, J. L. (2004) 'Importing Constitutional Norms from a "Wider Civilization": *Lawrence* and the Rehnquist Court's Use of Foreign and International Law in Domestic Constitutional Interpretation', *Ohio State Law Journal*, 65: 1283–328.
Lawrence v. Texas (2003) 539 US 558.
Leckey, R. (2009) 'Thick Instrumentalism and Comparative Constitutionalism: The Case of Gay Rights', *Columbia Human Rights Law Review*, 40(2): 425–78.
Lloyd, M. (2007) *Judith Butler*, Cambridge: Polity.
Mohr, R. (1995) 'The perils of postmodernity for gay rights', *Canadian Journal of Law and Jurisprudence*, 8(1): 5–18.
Naz Foundation v. Government of NCT of Delhi (2009), High Court of Delhi, July 2.
Plant, R. (1991) *Modern Political Thought*, Oxford: Basil Blackwell.
Rorty, R. (1993) 'Human Rights, Rationality, and Sentimentality', in S. Shute and S. Hurley (eds.) *On Human Rights*, New York, NY: Basic Books.
Sedley, Sir S. (1995) 'Human Rights: A Twenty-First Century Agenda', *Public Law*, 1995: 386–400.

Stein, E. (1990) 'The Essentials of Constructionism and the Construction of Essentialism', in E. Stein (ed.) *Forms of Desire: Sexual Orientation and the Social Constructionist Controversy*, New York, NY: Garland.

Sunstein, C. (2004) 'Liberty after *Lawrence*', *Ohio State Law Journal*, 65: 1059–80.

Thiruvengadam, A. K. (2008) 'In Pursuit of "The Common Illumination of Our House": Trans-Judicial Influence and the Origins of PIL Jurisprudence in South Asia', *Indian Journal of Constitutional Law*, 2: 67–103.

Walzer, M. (1983) *Spheres of Justice: A Defence of Pluralism and Equality*, Oxford: Blackwell.

—— (1987) *Interpretation and Social Criticism*, Cambridge, MA: Harvard University Press.

Weeks J. (1991) *Against Nature: Essays on History, Sexuality and Identity*, London: Rivers Oram.

Williams, B. (1993) *Morality: An Introduction to Ethics*, Cambridge: Cambridge University Press.

Woolf, L. (1928) *Imperialism and Civilization*, London: Hogarth Press.

Chapter 11

Reproducing empire in same-sex relationship recognition and immigration law reform

Nan Seuffert

Lesbian and gay activists favouring equal legal recognition of same-sex relationships can point to a host of successes in a number of countries over the last decade. Between 2004 and 2006 New Zealand passed its Civil Union Act, Canada passed the Civil Marriage Act, the UK passed the Civil Partnership Act and South Africa passed its Civil Union Act. Immigration law and policy applying to same-sex couples has also been liberalized in all of these countries in recent years. This groundswell of recognition has been somewhat of a phenomenon; in Canada for example, it has been noted that once courts recognized discrimination on the basis of sexual orientation, legal recognition of same-sex relationships, and provision of the right to marry, occurred with 'startling rapidity' (Young and Boyd 2006: 216). At the same time, opponents of marriage and other recognition for lesbians and gay men continue to decry the threat to civilization, marriage and the family – the cornerstones of society – supposedly posed by these developments.[1] This threat is often framed in terms of a counter-evolutionary decay or degeneration of society. Some lesbian and gay scholars warn of the regulatory and domesticating potential of these reforms. Other scholars, including myself, have argued that these types of reforms have shifted the terrain of legally and socially acceptable relationships from a simple dichotomy between heterosexual and gay and lesbian to acceptance of those same-sex couples who are willing to conform to heteronormative relationship models. This chapter continues this project by further unpacking a type of raced, gendered and classed normativity in the reforms: relationships of domination integral to empire. It traces ideas of decay, degeneration and domesticity in the production of sexuality in empire, in same-sex relationship recognition, and in the liberalization of same-sex immigration, all focusing on New Zealand. It highlights some of the raced and gendered configurations of empire embedded in the language of the reforms, arguing that the reforms operate in part to reproduce and re-embed, rather than disrupt, patterns of imperial domination.

Empire and sexuality

A rich body of scholarship maps ways in which imperialism and colonization have been integral to the production of the modern nation. Concepts such as 'progress', 'modernity', 'evolution' and 'development' emerged with the invention of 'race'; the latter was inseparable from the dynamics of domination built into these concepts (McClintock 1995: 1–5; Spoonley 1993: 1–11). Further, the categories of 'race' and 'gender' came into being in relation to each other, and are co-constitutive with relations of power, the modern industrial nation, colonization and imperialism.

Studies of sexuality and empire have also emerged relatively recently. Foucault's *History of Sexuality* refuted the 'repressive' thesis of Victorian sexuality and argued that sexuality was instead constructed and produced through regimes of regulation, patterns of surveillance, and stimulations of self-disciplinary regimes that penetrated into the most intimate domains of modern life (Foucault 1990; Stoler 2000: 3). Foucault argued that homosexuality emerged first as a species and then as an identity as part of a regulatory process of producing sexualities:

> The nineteenth-century homosexual became a personage, a past, a case history and a childhood, in addition to being a type of life, a life form, and morphology, with an indiscreet anatomy and possibly a mysterious physiology.
>
> (1990: 43)

Homosexuality defined the whole person as deviant: it 'was everywhere present in him: at the root of all his actions because it was their insidious and indefinitely active principle; written immodestly on his face and body because it was a secret that always gave itself away' (ibid.). The date of birth of this approach was 1870, the height of colonization in New Zealand.

Foucault has been called 'scrupulously ethnocentric' (Stoler 2000: 14, citing Spivak 1988; Clifford 1988: 265). He did not consider the emergence of categories such as sexuality in the context of empire; his was a self-contained version of sexuality, apparently only about the West. He ignored the ways in which the category of sexuality emerged with the modern nation and concepts such as race and gender, and failed to consider the nation-making and imperial process integral to the history of sexuality that he traces (Stoler 2000). Rudi Bleys' work partially filled the gap left by Foucault in mapping the production of sexuality in empire. Bleys also noted that what Foucault had subsumed under a linear trajectory from a pre-modern emphasis on sodomy, or acts, to a modern identity of homosexuality was actually a more complicated phenomenon (Bleys 1995: 7). He studied shifts in the construction of homosexuality in 'European ethnographic discourse about male-to-male sexual behavior outside the West' in part in order to contribute to the project of understanding the construction of racial, ethnic and cultural otherness (ibid. 9). As scholars such as Bleys, McClintock and Stoler have demonstrated so well, the production of sexuality, and its relations to race and gender, are integral to the shapes and forms of empire.

Sexual excess and domestication

Recent legal scholarship, including that of Ruthann Robson (1992) and Katherine Franke (2004), has discussed the domestication of lesbians and gay men through the law and through law reform. Domestication and the cult of domesticity were 'central to British imperial identity' (McClintock 1995: 36), and were integral to producing properly sexualized subjects. The act of domesticating may be closely linked with dominating, and also historically carried the meaning of civilizing (ibid. 35). It may be a process of taming and policing categories of gender, race and sexuality.

The cult of domesticity in England in the eighteenth and nineteenth centuries involved the domestication and regulation of women and women's bodies. 'Woman' was perceived as driven by uncontrolled sexual appetite and 'governed, not by reason, like men, but by . . . her maternal instinct . . . [or] her sexuality' (Poovey 1989: 9–11). Gradually during the eighteenth century there was a transformation of constructions of 'woman' from those involving sexual excess to the embodiment of domesticity (ibid. 9–10). Domestication was a continual process of taming the sexual urges of women, particularly middle class women, through properly positioning them in the heterosexual, monogamous household.

Domestication in the process of empire included the production of domestic space as a haven in the wildness or as a 'home' in the 'foreign' and alienating landscape or culture; this production was one of the roles of white women in colonization (Mohanran 1999: 147–74). As McClintock argues, 'Controlling women's sexuality, exalting maternity and breeding a virile race of empire-builders' was crucial to empire (1995: 47). The private domestic sphere was the proper site for the performance of heterosexual patriarchal masculinity.

Domestication as the taming of sexual licentiousness also provided justifications for the colonization of peoples outside of Europe. Indigenous and colonized peoples were often constructed as having primitive, unregulated sexualities, and were perceived as engaging in promiscuity that included same-sex behaviours (Bleys 1995: 65; Wiesner-Hanks 2001: 221). Gender, race and sexuality coalesced in conceptualizations of sodomy as associated with cross dressing, effeminacy and passivity (Bleys 1995: 71, 81–96, 115). The feminization of colonized peoples contributed to their construction as suitable targets for civilizing through domestication.

Rituals of domesticity inducted colonized peoples, through a narrative of domestic progress that was raced and gendered, into a hierarchical relationship to white men (McClintock 1995: 35). Creating empire required the 'construction of domestic space and retraining the colonised in techniques of motherhood, cleanliness, and domestic duty' (Merry 2000: 15). Education was a prime tool for both civilizing the colonized peoples and 'domesticating' the 'savage' races. In New Zealand, for example, British women acted (and reacted) as 'civilisers' teaching the indigenous Maori girls to be proper 'wives' and 'domestic servants' (Laing and Coleman 1998: 4; Smith 1992: 44; Merry 2000: 15).

Same-sex sexual practices were 'nonproductive' and opposed to domesticity, reproduction and empire building. Gendered domesticity involved not only taming and regulating the sexuality of women, but regulating the sexuality of both colonizing and colonized men. The effeminacy and penetrability of the colonized male could result in a crisis in masculinity in some situations (Chari 2001: 281); white women perceived the homo-eroticized bonding of colonizing and colonized men as a threat of sexual competition (ibid., citing Nandy 1988: 9–10). The regulatory power of rituals of domesticity placed the sexuality of both men and women appropriately in the raced and gendered heterosexual household. Most New Zealand historical accounts confirm that during at least the Victorian period, '[s]ex and sexual desire were meant to occur only between married adults, within the home. Anything else was deviant and therefore undesirable', although it has also been suggested that the forbidden was eroticized (Daley 2005: 48, 52–62).

Evolution and degeneration

Evolutionary theory and its foil of degeneration emerged as a potent political force in the making of race and in justifying colonization and empire in the late nineteenth century. The idea that human evolution involved moving away from a 'polymorph perversity' that included same-sex sexual behavior and was associated with primitive peoples, to a more civilized, monogamous heterosexuality circulated, particularly in the late nineteenth century (Bleys 1995: 155). In one version degeneration was the result of the biblical fall of man from a perfect state, which was followed by deterioration of the human body in an unhealthy environment (ibid. 152). Ideas of degeneration also figured in constructions of same-sex sexual behaviour as a crisis of modernity, a 'symptom of transition to a new historical era'; modernity was associated with decadence, degeneration and relapse into primitiveness (ibid. 155). Degeneration was also often associated with social crises and contagion, figured as particularly reflected in the criminal classes and perceived as a threat to white male potency (McClintock 1995: 46–7).

The historical record of sexuality among Maori in New Zealand is itself a product of colonization. Its interpretations are full of inconsistencies and contradiction in which circulated ideas of evolution, degeneration and sexual licentiousness. It has been argued that at least some European colonizers viewed Maori through the lens of hard primitivism as dark savages who displayed masculine independence in contrast to other Pacific indigenous people who were seen as timid and feeble (Moloney 2005: 41). They were not seen as subject to long term degeneration or effeminacy; instead their primitiveness was figured, at least in some of the historical record, as violent hyper-masculinity in need of further evolution. Maori were sometimes positioned as in an adolescent stage of development with the potential for maturation and improvement, in need of parental discipline to subdue their violence and control their sexuality. Such 'parental' discipline was to be supplied by the colonizers, justifying colonization as an aid to evolution towards civilization (Moloney 2005: 41; Kapur 2007: 542).

Consistent with the idea that masculinity includes the domestication of women through marriage, 'married' Maori women were generally seen as sexually modest and as maintaining 'marital fidelity'. However, there was a perception that Maori women who were not 'married' engaged in sexual licentiousness, particularly commercial sex with the crews of European vessels (Moloney 2005: 42–5). This was figured as contamination from contact with degenerate European classes (ibid. 42–4). It was a symptom of the 'crisis of modernity', the dark side of evolution and progress, in the colonies. The idea of sexual licentiousness resulting from contamination fits in to broader discourses of empire and degeneration as a symptom of transition to modernity (McClintock 1995: 46–8).

There is apparently a relative dearth of colonial records of same-sex sexual conduct among Maori. This results in arguments that same-sex sexual practices did not exist in Maori culture, that such practices were obscured by missionaries, and that they were invisible to others due to the lens of hard primitivism and masculinity through which Maori society was viewed (Moloney 2005: 42–6; Te Awekotuku 2001: 1–11). Rudi Bleys (1995) suggests another interpretation. Although he does not explicitly mention New Zealand, he argues that in Australia and the Pacific the late nineteenth century concept of homosexuality as a lifelong identity may have obscured from the colonizers' view individual acts of same-sex conduct that were not accompanied by cross dressing or effeminacy.

Domesticity, degeneration and marriage

Foucault recognized that the law of marriage was one of two great systems in the West for governing sex (1990: 39–40). More recent scholarship has traced the ways in which marriage has operated as a regulatory regime in the dynamics of empire building, race, gender and sexuality and in the production of the modern nation (Franke 1999; Merry 2000: 256–7; Cott 2000: 3–8; Seuffert 2003; Stoler 2000: 130–6; McClintock 1995: 284–9, 323–6). In England the project of modernity included attempts to regularize sexual and marital behavior and punish the newly categorized 'deviants', in part in order to clarify what constituted a valid marriage. This project included minimizing recognition for informal marriage practices, the results of which were labeled 'concubinage' (Stone 1992: 17; Seuffert 2003: 209).[2] These informal practices included 'broomstick weddings' (where a couple jumps over a broom in the presence of witnesses) and continued into the nineteenth century (Parker 1989: 139–40; Seuffert 2003: 209). Monogamous marriage represented the apex of the evolution of sexual practices; polygamy was also positioned as pre-modern:

> England's toying with and ultimate rejection of polygamy near the end of the eighteenth century is part of the nation's defining itself both as distinct from and morally superior to the polygamous Other. Monogamy is instituted as part of England's national definition, and whatever practices its explorers might find to tempt them in other worlds, England asserts its public stance that marriage means one man, one wife, at least in law.
>
> (Nussbaum 1994: 149)

Monogamous heterosexual marriage was integral to England's definition of itself as superior, and facilitated justifications for empire.

As Katherine Franke has so thoroughly and convincingly argued, in the US, marriage of former slaves was a project of nineteenth-century social reformers that focused on lifting 'uncivilized people up from a natural savage state . . . into proper citizens' and 'provided these reformers with a domesticating technology or lever that could pry the uncivilized apart from their savage ways' (1999: 251–2). Franke's careful historical analysis reveals a variety of forms of slave relationships in addition to monogamous marriage (ibid. 272–4). After the civil war these relationships were regularized through various state mechanisms in manners that were sometimes harsh and violent, with the result that a decade later African-Americans were performing within Victorian cultural institutions and norms in relation to sexuality, 'evidencing their own successful domestication' (ibid. 292). Domestication included setting up a free man as the head of a household responsible for the support of a wife and children, producing masculinity and patriarchy with an emphasis on duties and responsibilities (ibid. 295–304). The parallel marital reform movement more generally, which attacked common law marriage, also had the goal of 'taming wanton licentiousness and civilising uncontrollable desire' (ibid. 295).

Historically, as part of the project of empire building, indigenous peoples were encouraged to marry and to adopt European family structures in order to civilize and regularize their relationships. 'Civilizing' or domesticating sexuality through Christian rituals such as marriage, medicalization and socio-legal regulation were often major concerns of colonization (see Merry 2000: 221–57). As Franke notes in relation to African-Americans, this process required making former slaves into husbands and wives – domestication required a heterosexual male at the head of the household (with economic and legal responsibilities emphasized as a priority), comprised of one man and one woman (Franke 1999: 300–304). At the same time, white masculinity and supremacy was maintained in part through a process of new laws criminalizing previously legal behaviour and statuses, such as poverty, which perpetuated the idea of black male sexuality as threatening (ibid. 304–6).

Monogamous heterosexual marriage as the apex of evolution and civilization, as well as ideas about evolution as progress and degeneration as slippage backwards into a primitive past, are reflected in this quote from an 1897 New Zealand newspaper:

> According to the rationalistic view ... marriage is simply an outcome of something inherent in human nature, and is subject to development as other institutions are, such as the family and the State. It is the result of a process of evolution from tribal promiscuity and 'marriage by capture,' through polyandry and polygamy, to the very imperfect form of monogamy now prevailing.
>
> (MacGregor 1897)

Marriage, the family and the state are all identified here as institutions that evolve from primitive savagery through various stages of civilization. These institutions will continue to evolve indefinitely into the future. The idea of the family as a heterosexual ordering of sexuality, with same-sex practices as degenerate, was also referenced in New Zealand at this time: Wilde's 'degeneracy' had to be protected against (Brickell 2005: 65–6).

Domestication, degeneration, same-sex relationship recognition and immigration

In this part I want to consider the re-embedding of imperial ideas of evolution, degeneration and domestication in the recent recognition of same-sex relationships and the extension of that recognition to immigration law and policy in New Zealand.

Progress and degeneration in same-sex relationship recognition

The tropes of domesticity and degeneration are prominent in the parliamentary debates on the Civil Union Bill in New Zealand, shaping the terrain and the positions on each side of the debate.[3] For example, the Civil Union Bill was introduced to Parliament with the statement:

> [C]ivil union will be a new legal entity, designed to reflect the diversity of New Zealand society and people's personal choices about their

> relationships in the 21st century. This bill is appropriate to the time, which recognises the reality of relationships instead of attempting to deny their existence.[4]

This quote resonates with the idea that the evolution of relationship recognition reflects the progress of civilization, a progressive modernity. It embraces the idea that marriage evolves, and that the twenty-first century witnesses another step in its evolution, recognition of same-sex relationships.

The leading opposition party to the bill stated, 'This is not a civil union; this is a civil disgrace . . . this bill will tear the social and moral fabric of New Zealand society asunder.'[5] The idea of disgrace suggests a loss of grace, or degeneration away from biblical perfection. The emphasis on a civil disgrace plays on the term civil union and evokes notions of civilization; combined with the image of rending the social and moral fabric of society, it evokes ideas of degeneration as loss of civilization and backwards slippage into primitiveness.

Decay and degeneration also feature explicitly in these quotes opposing the bill:

> If the bill passes it will undermine a stability that has been the foundation of this country. Moral fibre and virtue seem to be irrelevant, and this bill will certainly erode, disrupt, and create a decay in the family structure as we see it today, which has always been the hallmark of this nation.[6]
>
> When will this Parliament realise that in this bill the beginning of a very deep decaying process is being set in place for future generations?[7]

Here the reference to 'decay' explicitly evokes ideas of degeneration and loss of civilization for the nation. Consistent with the ideas of degeneration, contagion and contamination that I discussed above, homosexuality is positioned as a negative symbol of the crisis of modernity, contrasted to a ' "traditional" way of life based on heterosexual marriage and strict gender roles that existed before the perversion of the colonial encounter' (Stychin 1998: 194). While the quote introducing the bill positions it as evolutionary movement forward, this quote associates it with negativity and as decay and perversion of the traditional heterosexual family.[8]

The idea of the family as crucial to the structure of nation in both of these quotes, either as a hallmark or a cornerstone, also invokes and links to colonial concepts of domesticity. The domestic as a site is also integral to the performance of heterosexuality, situating the white male at the head of the household in a position of gender dominance and at the head of the colony in a position of racial dominance, with a '[f]amily of black children ruled over by a white father' (McClintock 1995: 358).

The idea in the 1897 quote from New Zealand reproduced above, namely, that heterosexual monogamous marriage, coupled with proper Victorian domesticity, may be imperfect but is nevertheless the apex of evolution, retains currency in contemporary debates. It is reflected in the last lines of this quote:

> What this bill is doing is casualise relationships. This trend has been happening in this country for 30 years, and we can see the damage it has done to families. . . . I am not suggesting that marriage is perfect, but as Winston Churchill simply responded when asked whether there was a better system than democracy: 'It's not perfect but I can't think of a better one.' I cannot think of a better institution than marriage. I cannot think of a better role model for our young kids than to see mum and dad with two or three kids as the cornerstone of our society.[9]

Here the idea that this imperfect form of heterosexual monogamy has resulted from a process of evolution is clarified by reference to the current trend of the 'casualization' of relationships, positioned as a backwards, degenerative move by reference to the resulting damage to families. The term evokes the pre-modern practice of informal marriages or relationships, labeled concubinage, which had necessitated regularization and formalization as part of the project of modernity and empire. The reference to Winston Churchill evokes a period of traditional values in the midst of a crisis of modernity; marriage is positioned as a venerated institution under attack to be saved from degeneration, akin to democracy in importance and in the constituting and sustaining of the modern nation. The Churchill quote as applied to marriage and the 1897 newspaper quote discussed above are strikingly similar.

Perhaps not surprisingly, those supporting the Civil Union Bill did not argue for it on the basis that it provided an opportunity to configure more equitably the moral fabric of society which, woven in projects of empire and processes of domination, reflected historically entrenched racial, gender and sexual hierarchies and power differentials. Instead, lawmakers supported the Bill on the basis that it would not significantly change the current order of society. In particular, support focused on maintaining and strengthening the institution of the family as the cornerstone of society and of long term monogamous exclusive intimate relationships. References to exclusive relationships counter assumptions of same-sex sexual licentiousness and promiscuity deeply embedded in empire:

> Those who argue that stable and committed relationships form the fundamental basis of a good society should welcome this bill as supporting and identifying in law an even greater number of stable, committed, and exclusive relationships with legal rights and responsibilities. It is miraculous that there are so many stable, committed, same-sex relationships when our law provides such little support for them.[10]

We finally have in the House legislation that enables couples who are in a committed, stable, and exclusive relationship to have a choice as to the means by which they solemnize their relationship, so that they can have access to the law. It is a mark of a mature and tolerant community.[11]

Both of these quotes mention exclusivity as an integral part of same-sex relationships, reassuringly alongside commitment and stability. The first quote couples these ideas with rights and responsibilities, and both refer to the law. The law is positioned as crucial to the production of stable and exclusive relationships in the first quote. In the second the reference to a 'mature' community suggests that evolution has resulted in progress to the point where a mature society widens recognition of relationships to include same-sex relationships that fit the criteria of commitment and exclusivity. At the same time, the creation of the category of 'civil union' separate from marriage has been argued to be a relegation to second class status (see Seuffert 2006b: 287–8) and, as such, to reinscribe same-sex desire as inferior to a more evolved heterosexual desire. Traces of empire, ideas of evolution and progress to a higher level of civilization – one opposed to degeneration backwards into primitiveness – underlie and shape all of these ideas.

We are family: domestication in and through immigration law and policy

Immigration law and policy has historically both literally and figuratively shaped empire and modern nations. It involves the production of subjects at the boundary of the nation through regulation; identity is produced through the performance of meeting the criteria to the satisfaction of the officials (Seuffert 2009; Butler 2004: 41). The process includes the production of sexuality (Luibheid 2002). New Zealand's recent liberalization of immigration law and policy, which make it a relatively 'gay friendly' country for immigration (Seuffert 2009), requires the production of a properly domesticated subject at the boundary of the nation. Here I first outline the reforms, including the criteria for partnership immigration, and then analyze the criteria through the lens of domestication. I argue that conformation to the criteria requires properly domesticated gay and lesbian couples, reproducing the imperial dynamic of taming and policing perceptions of sexual licentiousness.

The process of liberalization of immigration criteria began in the early 1990s with the treatment of heterosexual and same-sex *de facto* partners under the same criteria except that same-sex partners had to be living together for four years rather than two (Chauvel 1994). In 2003 a 'partnership policy' was implemented that aimed to treat those in marriages and those in an 'interdependent partnership akin to marriage', whether opposite or same-sex couples, the same (Seuffert 2009).[12] With the passage of the Civil Union Act 2004 and the accompanying Relationships (Statutory References) Act 2005 the Immigration Act 1987 and Immigration Regulations 1999 were further amended to implement the current 'partnership policy' aligning civil unions with marriages, whether of the same or opposite sex couples.[13] The process of aligning the treatment of those heterosexual couples who were married with same-sex couples in a civil union also involved aligning the treatment of *de facto* couples, so that all three categories must meet the same criteria (ibid.). Therefore all of those who wish to enter the country as partners of permanent residents, citizens or immigrants must provide evidence to satisfy an immigration officer that they have been living together for 12 months or more in a partnership that is genuine and stable.[14] The 'traditional privilege' of married couples, which most recently in New Zealand meant that they had to prove only that they were currently living together in a genuine and stable relationship, without a requirement for a particular time period, has been abolished (see New Zealand Immigration Service 1997: 14). A brief outline and discussion of the criteria for a genuine and stable relationship are necessary to the consideration of domestication.

A partnership is considered to be genuine and stable if it has been entered into with the intention of being maintained on a long-term exclusive basis and is likely to endure.[15] *Factors* that have a bearing on whether the two people are living together in a partnership that is *genuine and stable* include the duration of the relationship; the existence, nature and extent of the partners' common residence; the degree of financial dependence or interdependence; the common ownership, use and acquisition of property; the degree of commitment of the partners to a shared life, children, the performance of common household duties by the partners; and the reputation and public aspects of the relationship.[16] *Evidence* that the partners are *living together* may include documents showing shared accommodation, such as joint ownership of residential property, joint tenancy agreements, and correspondence addressed to both of the partners at the same address.[17] *Evidence* that the partnership is *genuine and stable* may include a marriage certificate; a civil union certificate; birth certificates of children; evidence of communication between the partners; evidence of financial interdependency such as joint bank accounts; photographs of the parties together; documents indicating public recognition of the partnership; and other evidence that the parties are committed to each other emotionally and exclusively.[18] This final type of evidence of exclusive emotional commitment may include evidence of joint decision making and plans together, sharing of parental obligations, sharing of household activities, companionship and spare time, leisure and social activities and presentation to outsiders as a couple.

The immigration criteria embrace concepts of domesticity in a number of forms. Most obviously, factors such as the performance of household duties and evidence such as sharing parental obligations, household activities and joint decision making evoke images of domesticity as home, as the realm gendered female. The criteria require the production of evidence of Victorian notions of domestic harmony, embedded in empire building, and reflected in communications between the partners, joint decision making and shared plans, photos, public recognition, and emotional and exclusive commitment. The focus on economic criteria and ownership of property, as well as the reference to evidence of shared spare time and engagement in leisure and social activities, privileges those with money and middle class domestic aspirations, also consistent with Victorian class concepts of domesticity. The requirements for long term duration and exclusivity and evidence of interdependency represent proof of the taming of sexual licentiousness, and conformation to notions of monogamy necessary to empire.

As I, and others, have argued elsewhere, these criteria embrace heteronormativity and tend to require the production of homonormativized lesbian and gay couples who are depoliticized and willing to privatize their relationships into the domestic sphere (Seuffert 2009; Duggan 2002; Holt 2004). A similar argument, that immigration criteria make homosexuality 'intelligible through its domestication by the heteronormative institutions of intimacy', has been made in Australia (Yue 2008: 246–7). Carl Stychin has argued that queer migrants are incorporated into the nation through self-cultivation and disciplinary regulation, and are encouraged to mimic marriage as a prerequisite for immigration approval (2003: 105). The production of domesticated (same sex) relationships is as necessary to inclusion in the current project of nation building through immigration as it was at the height of the British Empire; configurations of empire are reproduced with the difference that the couples may be same sex.

The extent to which this very specific, Victorian, imperial domesticity masquerades as 'normality' and requires the production of homonormativized relationships, is highlighted by considering the criteria in light of the experiences of lesbians and gay men with 'home' and domesticity. These experiences suggest that Victorian notions of domesticity, and the regulation of sexuality through the performance of domesticity in the private household, are still policed and regulated, with stigma and punishment associated with transgression. Research in England, Australia and New Zealand has shown that gays and lesbians may experience ambivalence in relation to domesticity, 'home' and the related ideas of safety and comfort (Moran 2002). The household may be a 'heterofamilial' space (Lefebvre 1991). The parental home may have been sexualized as straight, and experienced as a place of exclusion, surveillance and judgment (Moran 2002: 281), where queer youths had to conceal their sexuality from their families (Johnston and Valentine 1995: 100–3). Gay hate crimes, including homicide, may be most likely to occur in the privacy of the gay victim's home, and are likely to be significantly more violent than other crimes; '[f]ar from being a location and effect associated with safety and security from sexualized violence, "home" is the place where we might be most likely to experience violence and experience it in its extreme forms' (Moran 2002: 275; Mouzos and Thompson 2000: 3). Lesbians are more likely to be subjected to violence by family members rejecting their sexuality in the home (Johnston and Valentine 1995: 103). Lesbians may be harassed or placed under surveillance by their children or their neighbours, the latter sometimes with resulting property damage (ibid. 109–10). For lesbian mothers, the household may also be a place of surveillance by school or welfare state officials, children's friends and neighbours (Moran 2002: 281). Gay men may maintain separate bedrooms to convince visitors that there is no sexual relationship (Kirby and Hay 1997: 296–8). Lesbians may feel compelled to 'dedyke' the household for homophobic visitors (Johnston and Valentine 1995: 106–7).

A simple dichotomy between public and private, with associations between a private sphere and domesticity, is also brought into question by research with lesbians and gay men. The household for lesbians may be a quasi-public, but lesbian-friendly space entertaining wider lesbian social networks, or providing affordable space for group meetings (Moran 2002: 291). Queers may use their homes to create gay and lesbian communities within domestic settings (Elwood 2000). The public/private dichotomy is also troubled by the finding that for some gays and lesbians in urban areas, feeling at 'home' may be more likely to be experienced in queer venues that allow for socializing in relative safety (Moran 2002). The traditional, Victorian-based notions of domesticity reflected in the immigration criteria ignore many of these aspects and experiences of 'home' for gays and lesbians, instead requiring for the purposes of recognition the reproduction of tropes of empire in the 'private' lives of gay and lesbian couples.

The criteria are likely to privilege white middle class lesbians and gay men who are happy to conform to heteronormative models of domesticity. Research in Australia with white, educated middle class gay and lesbian participants who have cohabited for between four and twenty years in urban areas drew attention to the significance of homes as private spaces where the participants could be themselves, feel safe and secure, and express sexual affection uncensored (Gorman-Murray 2006).

To the extent that the adoption of heteronormative, Victorian notions of domesticity is premised on 'coming out' as lesbian or gay, those from countries where 'coming out' is problematic will be disadvantaged (Seuffert 2009). Further, the process of 'coming out', and privileging lesbian or gay aspects of one's identity, may involve culturally specific notions of 'gay identity'. Ideas about gay identity and its performance, it might be argued, may be traced back to the Western construction of homosexuality as an identity, analyzed by Foucault. Debates about the possibility and cultural specificity of global gay identity have recently emerged and intensified (Stychin 2003: 97; see Binnie 2004: 32–49, 67–85). Adoption of homonormative domestic relationships may be premised on adopting Western forms of gay identity. Criteria embracing these forms of domesticity may in turn privilege those emigrating from Western, predominately white countries. For example, recent research in

New Zealand suggests that a small sample of lesbian and gay immigrants from 'Asia'[19] were less likely than other immigrants in the study to have disclosed their sexuality to other people and that they rated their ethnic culture as significantly more important than did other immigrants (Henrickson 2006: 72–3). Other research suggests that adoption of 'gay' identity may be perceived to be linked to adoption of 'white' values, or may mean the rejection of an ethnic identity (Santioso 1999). If 'coming out' is a culturally specific and Western phenomenon, and the immigration criteria of domesticity are premised on living together and being out to family, friends and others, then the criteria may reproduce the trope of empire by privileging those properly domesticated along racial lines, and excluding along the same racial lines entrenched in processes of imperialism.

Conclusion

Legal recognition of same-sex couples is often presented as an evolutionary step in the progress of civilization and the promise of progressive modernity. New Zealand's recognition of same-sex relationships and relatively gay-friendly immigration criteria privilege imperial values such as domesticity (i.e. gay-friendly) and the idea that civilizations evolve and that some civilizations are more evolved than others. As a result, these law reforms participate in reproducing relationships of empire, including power differentials figured by race, class and sexuality.

Acknowledgements

I would like to thank Prof Kim Brooks and Prof Robert Leckey for organizing the Queer/Empire Workshop, for successfully obtaining funding for the workshop from the Canadian Humanities and Social Sciences Research Council, for inviting me to the workshop, for setting a particularly collegial and friendly tone, for a great restaurant guide to Montreal, and for thoughtful comments on this chapter. Thanks also to the other participants in the workshop for wonderful presentations and stimulating comments and discussion. Finally, many thanks to Sarah Jeffs for efficient and thorough research assistance.

Notes

1 Compare Margaret Denike's analysis of such fearmongering, in this volume (Ch. 9).
2 I have argued that nineteenth-century New Zealand cases addressing the marriage laws and customs of the indigenous Maori people increasingly associated those laws and practices with pre-modern concepts such as concubinage and polygamy and opposed them to raced and gendered notions of civilization and progress associated with the modern nation-state (Seuffert 2003). On polygamy, see the chapter by Margaret Denike in this volume (Ch. 9).

3 I have analyzed these parliamentary debates for current stories of New Zealand as a nation or an imagined political community (Seuffert 2006b).
4 Hon David Benson-Pope MP, Associate Minister of Justice, Labour (24 June 2004) 618 NZPD 13927.
5 Brian Connell, National (24 June 2004) 618 NZPD 13929.
6 Bill Gudgeon, NZ First (7 December 2004) 622 NZPD 17447.
7 Bill Gudgeon, NZ First (24 June 2004) 618 NZPD 13933.
8 Compare, in this volume (Ch. 5), Jaco Barnard-Naudé's analysis of the legal path to recognition of same-sex relationships in South Africa.
9 Brian Connell, National (24 June 2004) 618 NZPD 13930.
10 Matiria Turei, Green (24 June 2004) 618 NZPD 13935.
11 Ibid.
12 Immigration Amendment Regulations (No. 3) 2003 (NZ), amending Regulation 20 of the Immigration Regulations 1999 (NZ), effective 29 September 2003 to 7 April 2005.
13 Relationships (Statutory References) Act 2005 (NZ), s. 7, Sch. 1; s. 12, Sch. 4. The *Immigration Act* 2009, passed in October 2009, replaced the *Immigration Act* 1987. Several of the core elements of the 1987 Act remain, and the criteria and rules for residence and temporary entry, as well as the partnership policy, with which this analysis is primarily concerned, were not under review. Department of Labour, 'Immigration Act Review: Discussion Paper' (April 2006), 6.
14 Immigration New Zealand (2009) R2.1.10, R2.1.15, R2.1.20, F2.10.1, F2.15.
15 Ibid. R2.1.20; F2.10.1. If a partnership is found to be genuine and stable but a couple have not been living together for 12 months or more, the final decision may be deferred and a temporary work visa or permit may be granted. Immigration New Zealand (2009) R2.1.15.5; F2.10.1; Ryken 2004: 3–4.
16 Immigration New Zealand (2009) F2.20b.
17 Ibid. F2.20.15a.
18 Ibid. F2.20.15c.
19 The study stated that all Asian-born participant responses were grouped together and that this group might be justified 'since cross-cultural research shows that, despite differences in specific experiences associated with countries of origin, factors which relate to cultural ideologies tend to be similar among Southeast and East Asian countries and collectively differ markedly from countries commonly referred to as "western" nations' (Santioso 1999: 70).

References

Armstrong, N. (1987) *Desire and Domestic Fiction: A Political History of the Novel*, New York, NY and Oxford: Oxford University Press.
Binnie, J. (2004) *The Globalization of Sexuality*, London: Sage.
Bleys, R. (1995) *The Geography of Perversion: Male-to-male Sexual Behaviour outside the West and the Ethnographic Imagination, 1750–1918*, New York, NY: New York University Press.
Booth, M. Z. (2002) 'Education for Liberation or Domestication? Female Education in Colonial Swaziland', in T. L. Hunt and M. R. Lessard (eds.) *Women and the Colonial Gaze*, New York, NY: New York University Press.
Brickell, C. (2005) 'The Emergence of a Gay Identity', in A. Kirkman and P. Moloney (eds.) *Sexuality Down Under: Social and Historical Perspectives*, Dunedin: University of Otago Press.
Butler, J. (2004) *Undoing Gender*, New York, NY: Routledge.

Chari, H. (2001) 'Colonial Fantasies and Postcolonial Identities: Elaboration of Post-colonial Masculinity and Homoerotic Desire', in J. C. Hawley (ed.) *Postcolonial, Queer: Theoretical Intersections*, Albany, NY: SUNY Press.

Chauvel, C. (1994) 'New Zealand's Unlawful Immigration Policy', *Australasian Gay and Lesbian Law Journal*, 4: 73–84.

Clifford, J. (1988) *The Predicament of Culture*, Cambridge, MA: Harvard University Press.

Cott, N. (2000) *Public Vows: A History of Marriage and the Nation*, Cambridge, MA: Harvard University Press.

Daley, C. (2005) 'Puritans and Pleasure Seekers', in A. Kirkman and P. Moloney (eds.) *Sexuality Down Under: Social and Historical Perspectives*, Dunedin: University of Otago Press.

Duggan, L. (2002) 'The New Homonormativity: The Sexual Politics of Neo-Liberalism', in R. Castronovo and D. D. Nelson (eds.) *Materializing Democracy: Toward a Revitalized Cultural Politics*, Durham, NC: Duke University Press

Elwood, S. (2000) 'Lesbian Living Spaces: Multiple Meanings of Home', in G. Valentine (ed.) *From Nowhere to Everywhere: Lesbian Geographies*, New York, NY: Haworth.

Foucault, M. (1990) *The History of Sexuality: Volume 1: An Introduction*, New York, NY: Vintage Books.

Franke, K. M. (1999) 'Becoming a Citizen: Reconstruction Era Regulation of African American Marriages', *Yale Journal of Law and the Humanities*, 11(2): 251–309.

—— (2004) 'The Domesticated Liberty of *Lawrence v. Texas*', *Columbia Law Review* 104(5): 1399–1426.

Gorman-Murray, A. (2006) 'Gay and Lesbian Couples at Home: Identity Work in Domestic Space', *Home Cultures*, 3(2): 145–67.

Henrickson, M. (2006) 'Lavender Immigration to New Zealand: Comparative Descriptions of Overseas-Born Sexual Minorities', *Social Work Review*, 18(3): 69–78

Holt, M. (2004) ' "Marriage-like" or Married? Lesbian and Gay Marriage, Partnership and Migration', *Feminism and Psychology*, 14(1): 30–35.

Immigration New Zealand (2 March 2009) 'Immigration New Zealand Operational Manual: Residence', Wellington: Department of Labour. Online: <www.immigration.govt.nz/nzis> (accessed 1 April 2009).

Johnston, L. and Valentine, G. (1995) 'Wherever I Lay My Girlfriend, That's My Home: The Performance and Surveillance of Lesbian Identities in Domestic Environments', in D. Bell and G. Valentine (eds.) *Mapping Desire*, London: Routledge.

Kapur, R. (2007) 'The Citizen and the Migrant: Postcolonial Anxieties, Law and the Politics of Inclusion/Exclusion', *Theoretical Inquiries in Law*, 8(2): 537.

Kirby, S. and Hay, I. (1997) '(Hetero)sexing Space: Gay Men and "Straight" Space in Adelaide, South Australia', *Professional Geographer*, 49(3): 295.

Laing, T. and Coleman, J. (1998) 'A Crack in the Imperial Text: Constructions of "White Women" at the Intersections of Feminisms and Colonialisms', in R. du Plessis and L. Alice (eds.) *Feminist Thought in Aotearoa New Zealand: Connections and Differences*, Auckland: Oxford

Lefebvre, H. (1991) *The Production of Space* (trans.), D. Nicholson-Smith, Oxford: Blackwell.

Luibheid, E. (2002) *Entry Denied: Controlling Sexuality at the Border*, Minneapolis, MN: University of Minnesota Press.

MacGregor, J. (7 October 1897) 'Marriage and Divorce: The Ecclesiastical and the Rationalistic Conceptions of Marriage Contrasted', *Otago Daily Times*.

McClintock, A. (1995) *Imperial Leather: Race, Gender and Sexuality in the Colonial Contest*, New York, NY: Routledge.

Merry, S. E. (2000) *Colonizing Hawaii: The Cultural Power of Law*, Princeton, NJ: Princeton University Press.

Mohanran, R. (1999) *Black Body: Women, colonialism and space*, St Leonards: Allen & Unwin.

Moloney, P. (2005) 'Shameless Tahitians and Modest Maori: Constructing the Sexuality of Pacific Peoples', in A. Kirkman and P. Moloney (eds.) *Sexuality Down Under: Social and Historical Perspectives*, Dunedin: University of Otago Press.

Moran, L. J. (2002) 'The Poetics of Safety: Lesbians, Gay Men and Home', in A. Crawford (ed.) *Crime, Insecurity, Safety in the New Governance*, Cullompton: Wilans Publishing.

Mouzos, J. and Thompson, S. (June 2000) 'Gay-Hate Related Homicides: An Overview of Major Findings in New South Wales', in *Australian Institute of Criminology: trends and issues*. Online: <www.aic.gov.au> (accessed 1 April 2009).

Nandy, A. (1988) *The Intimate Enemy: Loss and Recovery of the Self Under Colonialism*, Delhi: Oxford University Press.

New Zealand Immigration Service (1997) 'New Zealand Immigration Policy and Trends, Produced for The Population Conference', Wellington: Department of Labour, 13–14 November 1997.

Nussbaum, F. (1994) 'The Other Woman: Polygamy, *Pamela* and the Prerogative of Empire', in M. Hendricks and P. Parker (eds.) *Women, 'Race' and Writing in the Early Modern Period*, London: Routledge.

Parker, S. (1989) *The Marriage Act 1753: A Case Study in Family Law Making*, Oxford: Oxford University Press.

Poovey, M. (1989) *Uneven Developments: the Ideological Work of Gender in Mid-Victorian England*, London: Virago.

Robson, R. (1992) 'Mother: The Legal Domestication of Lesbian Existence', *Hypatia*, 7(4): 172–85.

Ryken, D. (2004) 'Immigration Rights for Cohabitees in New Zealand', *International Family Law Journal*, 18: 1–4.

Santioso, R. (1999) 'A social psychological perspective on HIV/AIDS and gay or homosexually active Asian men', *Journal of Homosexuality*, 36 (4/3): 69–85.

Seuffert, N. (2003) 'Shaping the Modern Nation: Colonial Marriage Law, Polygamy and Concubinage in Aotearoa New Zealand', *Law Text Culture*, 7: 186–220.

—— (2006a) *Jurisprudence of National Identity*, Aldershot: Ashgate.

—— (2006b) 'Sexual Citizenship and the Civil Union Act 2004', *Victoria University of Wellington Law Review*, 37: 281–306.

—— (2009) 'Same Sex Immigration: Domestication and Homonormativity', in S. Wong and A. Bottomley (eds.), *Changing Contours of Domestic Life, Family and Law: Caring and Sharing*, Oxford: Hart Publishing.

Smart, C. (1992) 'Disruptive Bodies and Unruly Sex: The Regulation of Reproduction and Sexuality in the Nineteenth Century', in C. Smart (ed.) *Regulating Womanhood: Historical Essays on Marriage, Motherhood and Sexuality*, London: Routledge.

Spivak, G. (1988) 'Can the Subaltern Speak?', in C. Nelson and L. Grossberg (eds.) *Marxism and the Interpretation of Culture*, Urbana, IL: University of Illinois Press.

Spoonley, P. (1988; 2nd edn 1993) *Racism and Ethnicity*, Auckland: Oxford University Press.

—— (1995) 'Constructing Ourselves: The Post-Colonial Politics of Pakeha', in A. Yeatman and M. Wilson (eds.) *Justice and Identity: Antipodean Practices*, Wellington: Bridget William Books.

Stoler, A. L. (2000) *Race and the Education of Desire*, Durham, NC: Duke University Press.

Stone, L. (1992) *Uncertain Unions: Marriage in England 1660–1753*, Oxford: Oxford University Press.

Stychin, C. (1998) *A Nation by Rights*, Philadelphia, PA: Temple University Press.

—— (2003) *Governing Sexuality: The Changing Politics of Citizenship and Law Reform*, Oxford: Hart Publishing.

Te Awekotuku, N. (2001) 'Hinemoa: Retelling a famous romance', in A. Laurie (ed.) *Lesbian Studies in Aotearoa/New Zealand*, Binghamton, NY: Harrington Park Press.

—— (February 2003) 'He Reka Ano: Same Sex Lust and Loving in the Ancient Maori World', paper presented at Wellington Conference, Outlines: Lesbian and Gay History in Aotearoa.

Tuiwai Smith, L. (1992) 'Maori Women, Discourses, Projects and Mana Wahine', in S. Middleton and A. Jones (eds.) *Women and Education in Aotearoa 2*, Wellington: Bridget Williams Books.

Wiesner-Hanks, M. E. (2001) *Gender in History*, Malden, MA: Blackwell.

Young, C. L. and Boyd, S. B. (2006) 'Losing the Feminist Voice? Debates on the Legal Recognition of Same Sex Partnerships in Canada', *Feminist Legal Studies* 14(2): 213–40.

Yue, A. (2008) 'Same-Sex Migration in Australia', *GLQ: A Journal of Gay and Lesbian Studies*, 14(2/3): 239–62.

Chapter 12

UnSettled

Ruthann Robson

It is geography – not sexuality – that is identity.

Ask anyone in my family.

'Sorry, girl, you can do what you want with – you know – but you'll always belong to the land.' For the umpteenth time, my grandfather tells me he was born on this land and will die on it. Like his own grandfather.

His timeline is generations; he does not like numbers or dates. I, however, have become an academic; I adore numbers and dates.

When I bring a girlfriend, no matter what she looks like, my family will ask her where she is from; they will ask her where she is from 'originally'.

They believe they are 'originally' from 'here'. They do not consider themselves accidental Americans. They do not imagine they are linked to the slag-scattered ground at the northernmost cusp of the Appalachians, by coincidence, by the vagaries of history, by the actions of unknown others, by chance rather than fate.

They have no language evoking a distant homeland. They do not utter words like *settler* or *pioneer*; these terms are reserved for people who journeyed westward across the North American continent. They do not say *immigrant* or *exile* for anyone in our family; these labels evoke darker-skinned people wearing darker-colored clothes.

When the word *colonial* is mentioned in my aunt's house, it refers to a plaid couch purchased from Sears & Roebuck.

When the word *colonial* is assigned in Mrs. Keller's fourth grade class, it refers to a mostly black outfit worn at Thanksgiving.

It is not in my aunt's house, but in Mrs. Keller's classroom that I learn how to lust: I fall in love with the map on the wall. It is not Mrs. Keller or my first girlfriend Patty who seduces me; it is the blue oceans flat against the beige wall.

When I leave home, I travel to regions my family cannot imagine. I go to the places we could have been from.

I send postcards back home, even as I know they are destined for the burning can in the yard. I keep postcards for myself, jotting a different message.

DEAR FOLKS: The Golden Gate Bridge in California is really golden.	*Ah, those golden girls in Golden Gate Park; and those nights on Valencia Street.*
G'day, as they say here. Australia really is a big country. Though everyone seems crowded at the edges.	*I can't wait for the Sydney Gay and Lesbian Mardis Gras.*
HEY EVERYONE: In Toronto, they say YOUNG street – it's really long! Inside the Eaton Centre there are golden loonies.	*And in the twilight, when the stores are closed, Canadians like to be close . . .*
Dear PA & MA: It is very beautiful here in New Zealand, but a bit old-fashioned. Though not as old-fashioned as this postcard.	*And the women in their sweaters are not so old-fashioned, really. No, not at all.*
Greetings to ALL: Found this old-timey postcard of Zulu girls in a little store in Hillbrow in Johannesburg. May go to see some mines and goldfields next week!	*Zulu girls? Well, all types of girls here. Though mingling can be difficult.*

I am far from home, but home follows me.

Near Half Moon Bay on the coast of California, I see the precise shade and shape of my grandmother's eyes.

At Bondi Beach, I spot my great grandfather's aquiline nose.

I order Arctic Char in a posh Toronto restaurant from a waitress sporting my aunt's horsy face.

That determined smile of my great uncle tightens across a bicyclist climbing a hill in New Zealand.

In the Apartheid Museum in Johannesburg, I view an identity card laminated with a photo of my cousin's lost twin.

When I am traveling, before I speak and reveal my accent, I am often mistaken for a native.

Or if not a native-native, then a non-native-native.

> A disruption of the concept of 'native' is one of the legacies of the white settler colonies as consolidated into the nation-states of the United States, Australia, Canada, New Zealand (Aotearoa), and South Africa from their beginnings as the offspring of British imperialism.

I read this, or something like this, in a scholarly treatise.

As you may have guessed, reading scholarly treatises, like journeying far from home, is not common in my family.

You may also know whether or not a family eschews or celebrates words like settler or pioneer or immigrant, they avoid words like indigenous. Words like theft or appropriation. Or like genocide.

This could be my tale:

> *My sister, when she frequented Haight-Ashbury addicted to amphetamines, fixed her hair into two long braids the way my mother had for all those years my sister and I were 'Indians' for Hallowe'en. We wore fringe skirts my mother sewed from beige remnants, the skirts getting shorter as we got taller, my mother piecing in vertical panels that she tried to disguise with fringe. My sister and I called each other 'paleface' and laughed as we used what my father called my mother's 'war paint' to draw chevrons and stripes on our skin. When my sister died of an overdose, I cut my hair nubby and went into the Santa Cruz mountains to a woman's commune where Moonflower was the most popular name. I fell in love with one of the Moonflowers, who later had breast augmentation surgery and became a croupier in one of the better Native American gaming casinos, north of San Francisco.*

History, even if it is manifest destiny, has its little plot twists. The original treaties between the United States government and Native Americans promised Native American tribes 7.5 million acres of land in California; but the government 'misplaced' these treaties in one of its offices. Thus, only 0.5 million acres was transferred. If I can still correctly apply what I learned from Mrs. Keller's advanced math lessons, this is approximately seven percent.

In Australia, there were no treaties. The doctrine is terra nullius, but it does not mean that the land was uninhabited; the British colonizers documented their encounters Aboriginal peoples, language itself being a propriety act. What terra nullius did come to mean is that the Aborigines did not own the land – they were nomadic peoples who had not cultivated, not improved, not asserted dominion over the ground.

Massacres, when the Aboriginal people refused to leave the land, were merely the results of misunderstandings.

This could be my story:

> My mum liked to trace her ancestors to the original criminals what landed at Botany Bay, though this was a lie, like most things my mother said, including anything about my larrikin father. She was keen on the pubs, my mum. She said growing up in Rooty Hill as she did had made her thirsty; her ma a cleaning lady at the Native Institution in Blacktown, her pa some long-gone bushranger, and she had to take care of the scrawny chooks in the daggy yard. No life for me, I reckoned, and took the train thirty kilometers east to Sydney soon as I could, coming for the Mardis Gras, staying for some chook of my own.

The Stolen Generations are features of both Australian and Canadian responses to indigenous peoples. The legal strategy, as codified and uncodified, removed children from their parents and put them in residential schools to 'civilize' them, to assimilate them, to whiten them.

There were, one imagines, some good intentions, some notions of charity, some religious fervor.

In 2000, the Australian Federal Court held that the part-Aboriginal plaintiffs did not have a claim for damages against the government for their physical assault and sexual assault at the hands of white missionaries in charge of the schools. We must not reevaluate the past – the judges proclaimed – 'by reference to contemporary standards, attitudes, opinions, and beliefs'.

In 1999 a Canadian court upheld damages against the Anglican Church on behalf of Floyd Mowatt, a Status Indian who had been legally required to attend a residential school and who had been illegally sexually assaulted for several years by his dormitory supervisor.

My grandmother took care of me for a while, after my mother left, long after my father left, and I lived with her in snowy flatlands of Southern Ontario until she left too, dying one brilliant morning under the coverlet she said her own granny had quilted. She was old, I thought, but later I realized she wasn't that old, only worn out. The farm belonged to her, free and clear, she said, another thing that didn't seem to be true, though I'm not always certain about that. My uncle tried to put me in a home for girls, but after a male pastor tried to get into my panties, I fled north to the city, Toronto. I slept in Queen's Park, near the university full of American draft dodgers and their fairy-tale girlfriends with long blonde braids.

In both Canada and New Zealand, unlike in Australia and the United States, the Crown – meaning, of course, the monarch of Great Britain – assumed a personal duty to the native peoples of the colonies through the treaty process.

The Treaty of Waitangi was entered into by Queen Victoria through her Lieutenant-Governor, William Hobson, in 1840. On the Māori side, there were approximately 540 iwi and hapu chiefs and representatives who signed after the document had circulated throughout the North and South Islands.

The Māori call these islands Aotearoa, land of the long white cloud. The Queen called these islands New Zealand, accepting the name the Dutch had imposed, although the land had for some time been part of Her colony of New South Wales in Australia, a colony of a colony.

Having a treaty is an improvement over not having a treaty, but there is still the tricky question of language. In the case of the Treaty of Waitangi, written in both the language of English and of Māori, the troublesome words are *sovereignty* and *kawanatanga*. The English version cedes to Her Majesty the Queen of England all powers of sovereignty that the Māori possessed. The Māori version allowed the Queen kawantangtanga, a right of governance, while retaining rangatiratanga, chieftainship.

My mother ran a small shop on Victoria Street, selling coloured woolen yarns, and my father ran sheep. The highlight of their lives – they admitted one evening as we ate yet another disgusting dinner of hogget and mush-rooms on toast – was when my brother won the Rural Bachelor of the Year at Fieldays, the 'largest agricultural event in the Southern Hemisphere'. The highlight of their lives was not – they did not need to add – what they called the 'renaming' of Hamilton Lake to Lake Rotora, or their only daughter leaving university to work in a woman's bookstore, or Parliament passing the Civil Unions Act.

Colonization is more successful in some places than others.

In New Zealand/Aotearoa, a nation of 4 million people, 80 percent are Pakeha, the white descendants of the Queen's settlers. The Māori are 15 percent.

In South Africa, a nation of 47 million people, the white descendants of the English and their rivals the Dutch, now comprise 9 percent of the population. The black Africans comprise almost 80 percent, although they are divided amongst various linguistic and cultural groups, often called tribes.

The white minority of South Africa once ruled the nation

with brutality;

with words: Apartheid, township, homelands, Soweto, Bantu, Coloured, sanctions, Krugerrand;

with laws: Prohibition of Mixed Marriages Act of 1947, Population Registration Act of 1950, Group Areas Act of 1950, Natives Act of 1952 (the pass laws); Reservation of Separate Amenities Act of 1953 (requiring separate but not equal), Terrorism Act of 1967 (establishing the secret police and indefinite detention), Bantu Homeland Citizens Act of 1970 (stripping citizenship from blacks).

But now things are different.

After my brother manned the government casspir, patrolling the townships, he was never the same. For one thing, he wouldn't talk, only drink. I imagined learning explosives to smash the Apartheid state, but I was never dexterous and when I heard it was akin to embroidery, I decided I'd write poetry instead. My father called the Nationalist Party the 'Nazis', but I knew he voted for them. He was English, to be sure, but he had that Afrikaner love of order and guns. He was a miner in the Witwatersrand gold reefs, but it did not make him rich at all. He supported the colour bar – it meant his job, or as he explained, 'food for you all'. By the time of the Constitution, the rainbow nation, the presidency of Mandiba (Nelson Mandela), my father was long retired, of an injury and disability. He did not live to see the Constitutional Court declare same-sex marriage consistent with our new democratic ideals of equality and dignity. 'Now that', my mother said, 'would have killed him'.

Don't you wish I had a more pleasant imagination?

But I cannot imagine how a simple boat ride across those seductive blue seas, however treacherous, can so transform a people. These settlers, these pioneers, these migrants, these emigrants becoming immigrants did not set out to be conquerors, imperialists, plunderers, or murderers. They only wanted the finer things in life: a plaid couch, a mostly black outfit.

They were the victims!

The women were orphaned girls, unwed mothers, spinster witches, or prostitutes rounded up and put on boats and sometimes not even told their destination.

The men were not heroes, bearded and ruddy as Odysseus, off for adventures, but debtors and drunkards and third sons in a regime of primogeniture or prisoners or gamblers or troublemakers or just plain hungry.

They were queer, certainly, some of them were queer.

Somewhere I learn the original meaning of the term diaspora, from the Greek, διασπορά, a sowing of seeds. I thought it meant simply dispersal; scattering. But it meant migration to a conquered land to enforce the claim of empire.

Whether they knew it or not, whatever they intended, the women and men of the 'Anglo-Celtic diaspora' were the warriors of white settler society.

Perhaps after centuries, perhaps after empire had been forced and its claims harvested, perhaps there can be some remorse?

Or perhaps not.

Co-sponsored by California Senator Barbara Boxer, Senate Joint Resolution 4, in the 110th Congress, 'apologizes on behalf of the people of the United States to all Native Peoples for the many instances of violence, maltreatment, and neglect inflicted on Native Peoples by citizens of the United States' and 'expresses its regret for the ramifications of former

wrongs'. The Bill is stalled. A predecessor Bill died in the 109th Congress.
And a predecessor to the predecessor died in the 108th Congress.

It is thought by some that the Resolution tarnishes 'our' ancestors. They
were not violent wrongdoers! They were heroes.

If anyone was bereft, oppressed, dispossessed, they were. They were the
ones who traveled unimaginable distances to reach their homes.

And what did they – what did we – do?

> *It was we who did the dispossessing. We took the traditional lands and
> smashed the traditional way of life. We brought the disasters. The alcohol.
> We committed the murders. We took the children from their mothers. We
> practised discrimination and exclusion.*
>
> *It was our ignorance and our prejudice. And our failure to imagine these
> things being done to us. With some noble exceptions, we failed to make the
> most basic human response and enter into their hearts and minds. We failed
> to ask – how would I feel if this were done to me?*

This is from Paul Keating's famous Redfern speech in 1992, his apology to
the Aborigines when he was Prime Minister of Australia. Some say this
speech cost him the next election and gave Australia a conservative government for over a decade under John Howard.

Howard denounced what he called the black armband perspective: the
belief, as he phrased it, 'that most Australian history since 1788 has been little
more than a disgraceful story of imperialism, exploitation, racism, sexism
and other forms of discrimination'. Although on the eve of another election,
Howard became a bit more conciliatory; maybe it was time to allow a referendum on recognizing Aboriginal people in the Constitution's preamble.
John Howard lost the election.

On 13 February 2008, as one of his first acts the new Prime Minister of
Australia, Kevin Rudd, stood in Parliament and delivered his Apology to
Australia's Indigenous People. In a three-minute speech, he uttered the word
sorry nine times.

A few months later, on 11 June 2008, Steven Harper, the Prime Minister of
Canada, stood in the House of Commons in the Canadian Parliament and in
a speech a bit over ten minutes apologized for the Indian Residential Schools
in Canada on behalf of the Government of Canada and all Canadians. In

English, he said sorry twice and some form of apologize nine times. He also said: *Nous le regrettons*; *Mamiattugut*; *Nimitatynan*; *Niminchinowesamin*, apologizing in French, Ojibwa, Cree, and Inuktitut. Only one of these is an official language of the nation of Canada.

He said the 'government of Canada' apologizes to the 'approximately 80,000 living former students' of the residential schools.

He did not give a number of living former teachers or administrators or missionaries of the residential schools.

He did not mention any Queen, only the churches.

The Queen – Her Majesty Queen Elizabeth II of England – had appeared in New Zealand 13 years earlier to apologize. In November 1995, visiting the former colony of a former colony, she said:

> The Crown acknowledges that its representatives and advisers acted unjustly and in breach of the Treaty of Waitangi.

And the:

> Crown expresses its profound regret and apologises unreservedly for the loss of lives because of the hostilities arising from its invasion, and at the devastation of property and social life which resulted.

I was incorrect, I suppose, to say that the Queen apologized. The Crown, however, apologized and was sorry.

Theorists of apology – and it would surprise my family to know such people exist – posit that sincerity is one of the necessary hallmarks of apology. Metonymy – a word unfamiliar to my family – seems incompatible with sincerity.

The Crown is an object.

Except when it is not.

Theorists note that apology is an expression of responsibility. The Crown, as an object, is accountable for its past deeds. But the Queen, this Queen, Elizabeth and not Victoria – born in 1926 and ascending the throne in 1952 – how can she be answerable for events that occurred in 1863?

Perhaps it is easy to apologize for something you have not done.

Perhaps it is more difficult to apologize for your own acts. In South Africa, some people sought amnesty for the crime of killing someone. Most of them were people who were once in power, but some of them were resisting violence with more violence.

Other people sought apologies. They recounted the horrors of the years of repression, including watching members of their families be killed.

After apartheid, there could have been a war crimes tribunal. Instead, there was the Truth and Reconciliation Commission, the TRC.

Words tumbled; tears surged; pain swirled between stories and incoherence. One theorist criticized the hearings as more 'church service' than 'judicial proceeding'.

Which is not to say that everyone said sorry.

'If you are able to say, I am sorry that policies of my government caused you pain. Just that. It would be a tremendous benefit to all of South Africa.'

Bishop Desmond Tutu addressed P. W. Botha directly. Tutu was the chair of the TRC, responsible, some said, for its Christian cast. Botha was the former Prime Minister of South Africa, responsible, many said, for the worst brutalities of apartheid.

Botha remained silent, astonished, he later said, that he should be asked to apologize.

Unlike Botha, the judges and lawyers of apartheid were not subpoenaed to appear before the TRC. But the judges regretted that they were asked to respond at all. Their written statements were more apologia than apology.

Rare was this: 'It is difficult, if not impossible, for me, as a white South African, to draw a clear and steady line between my personal and professional failures ... I acknowledge and regret these failures. I am deeply saddened by the consequences of these failures on the lives of black people and I wish to apologize for my role in denying them their full and equal humanity.'

More typical was this: 'The courts had no power to question the validity of the laws Parliament made.' Or as the 90,000-word submission from the

General Council of the Bar of South Africa phrased it: 'Regrettably, by adopting an approach to judicial review which was derived from England . . .'

The Queen of England herself, appearing in South Africa in November 1999 for the 'Commonwealth Summit', but not for the TRC, did not apologize.

She did not apologize to the Afrikaners for the Boer War on the hundred year anniversary of its beginning, although she had been expected to apologize, and although she said the war should be remembered 'with sadness' of the 'loss of life and suffering' by everyone, caught up in the war.

She did not apologize to the Xhosa, although she was called upon to meet 'royal-to-royal' and begin by apologizing, as well as making efforts to return the skull of Hinsta, believed by some to have been taken back to Great Britain by soldiers as a trophy.

She did not apologize to Robert Mugabe – she denied reports that she had – for the actions of one her 'gay subjects' outside of a London hotel. The gay subject had staged a 'citizen's arrest' of Mugabe for his treatment of sexual minorities in Zimbabwe. Mugabe accused the government of Great Britain, although not the queen specifically, for setting the 'gay gangsters' upon him in retaliation for plans to seize white-owned farm land.

Section 52 of the Magna Carta, signed by King John of England and 25 Surety Barons at Runnymede, England, on 15 June 1215, provides:

If any one shall have been disseized by us, or removed, without a legal sentence of his peers, from his lands, castles, liberties or lawful right, we shall straightway restore them to him.

Restoration after a wrongful taking, it seems, is an English legal principle.

One of the three committees of South Africa's TRC was the Reparations Committee. In addition to individual apologies and expungement of criminal records, there was a government grant of US$85 million to the 22,000 officially recognized victims of apartheid – a one-time payment of US$3,900 for each victim.

The unofficially recognized victims of apartheid receive no payments, but do have a new Constitution, a new democracy, an Apartheid Museum and affirmative action. Lawsuits against the mining industry for financing apartheid have been discouraged.

Land redistribution is not on the South African Parliament's agenda.

Unlike in New Zealand/Aotearoa. When the symbol of the Crown delivered her symbolic apology, she added:

> The Crown acknowledges that the subsequent confiscations of land and resources under the New Zealand Settlements Act 1863 of the New Zealand Parliament were wrongful.

And have caused Māori to:

> suffer feelings in relation to their lost lands akin to those of orphans.

'The Crown appreciates', she said, the Māori sense of grievance and 'the principle *i riro whenua atu, me hoki whenua mai*', meaning as land was taken, land should be returned.

One well-known theorist – well-known amongst other theorists if not amongst people like my family – does not appreciate the principle of *i riro whenua atu, me hoki whenua mai*. He imagines the problem is one of 'meta-ethics' and argues the usual 'illocutionary force' of 'moral judgments' cannot be applied to the past. He agrees the confiscation of land from the Māori was wrong; he contends this injustice has been superseded by a change in circumstance.

Consider the possible circumstances: the Māori could have sold the land in 1911 for a fair price or an iwi chieftain could have lost a parcel, fair and square, in a game of chance. But there is no need to descend into the counter-factual. Since 1863, the date of vast seizures of Māori land, and 1992, the date of his article, in New Zealand/Aotearoa:

> The population has increased manifold and most descendants of the colonists, unlike their ancestors, have nowhere else to go.

It would not surprise you, I'm sure, to know he is Pakeha, one of the white descendants of the Queen's settlers. But would it surprise you to learn that he has found somewhere else to go, albeit another white settler nation?

I imagine that when he is not theorizing, he looks up and sometimes sees a person who looks like a member of his family.

And in his former home, in New Zealand, would it surprise you to know that there are many descendants of many other white settlers, who have decided there is somewhere else to go than their home in South Africa? Although there are those who say New Zealand, that former colony of a former colony, is still second best. It seems that some of these white settlers are planning to resettle in Australia.

And that some – a million? – of white South Africans have relocated to Australia?

In Canada, one theorist – who remains in Canada and who does not seem to believe that injustice can be superseded – criticizes the 3,500-page Report of the Royal Commission on Aboriginal Peoples issued in 1996. He argues the Royal Commission failed to reconcile Aboriginal and non-Aboriginal differences and commonalities. Despite land reform, apologies, reparations, monetary settlements. Despite the rhetoric of 'First Nations' and the theme of nation-to-nation relations.

Perhaps the problem is this: Nationalism as an instrument of colonialism in white settler societies is ineffectual; the imperialist oppressors are not going back home because they are home.

Or perhaps the problem is the hegemony of law and legal analysis, with its paradigm of rights and its parade of wrongs.

Or perhaps the problem is this: roughly half of those identifying as Aboriginal Canadians live in urban communities, sometimes as members of marginalized Aboriginal 'ghettoes' and sometimes as members of an integrated middle class.

In Australia, the problem is the situation in Canada serves as an aspiration.

In its Submission to the Inquiry into the Stolen Generation Compensation Bill 2008, the Sydney Centre for International Law, housed at the University of Sydney Faculty of Law, advocates reparations to indigenous Australians who were affected by the government policies of removing children. The Submission includes 12 footnotes: two cite UN sources; two cite New Zealand sources; and the remaining eight cite Canadian sources.

In the United States, there are no citations to foreign governments. Senate Joint Resolution 4, in the 110th Congress, co-sponsored by California Senator Barbara Boxer, may apologize 'for the many instances of violence, maltreatment, and neglect inflicted on Native Peoples by citizens of the

United States,' but that is Section One. Section Two is a disclaimer: Nothing in the law 'authorizes or supports any claim against the United States'.

The Native Americans – the Indians – have sovereignty. They have reservations, which are like little city-states. They have uranium and precious minerals on that land, though that was not intended. They have tribal court systems. They have tax-free cigarettes and tax-free liquor. They have casinos.

They could have same-sex marriage. On the Agua Caliente Reservation in California – approximately 31,600 acres of the 0.5 million acres awarded of the 7.5 million acres promised – there are 465 same-sex couples according to the 2000 United States Census.

On 15 May 2008, the California Supreme Court declared unconstitutional the California Family Code provision stating that 'only marriage between a man and a woman is valid or recognized in California.' Thus, same-sex marriage must be allowed in California.

On 2 June 2008, the Secretary of State of California certified the eighth ballot measure for the 4 November 2008 general election, amending the California Constitution to provide that 'only marriage between a man and a woman is valid and recognized in California.' Thus, the judges' ruling can be superseded by the change of circumstances of counting votes.

On 4 November 2008, the electorate of California voted to amend the Constitution.

On 5 November 2008, several groups filed suit arguing that the amendment violates the state constitution by undermining a core commitment to protect minorities, including sexual minorities.

On 5 March 2009, the California Supreme Court heard oral argument for several hours.

On 26 May 2009, a decision by the California Supreme Court rejected the constitutional challenge, but ruled that the approximately 18,000 same-sex marriages could not be retroactively annulled.

Back home, my grandfather is dead and my father is angry with dying.

'You are just so unsettled,' he says. 'You're always gone. With some girl and who knows where.'

We are standing not far from where my grandfather is buried. We are standing on what he calls the 'land of our fathers'. We are not talking about his impending cancer surgery. We are talking about acres.

Like my grandfather did, my father checks the boundary markers religiously. He asks me to decipher the deeds, arguing with me about their contents. I never say, 'read them yourself.' Mrs. Keller was a better teacher than my father ever had; I was a better student than my father ever was.

'Never mind a piece of paper,' he yells at me.

I look at the burning can, where he has set fire to the trash day after day. I imagine the postcards I sent him, aflame.

'The corner of this acre is that blood-red rhododendron,' he says. The rhododendron is the most beloved flower of Appalachia. It's on the West Virginia state flag, which, I suppose, is a more pleasant choice than a coal mine.

'How do we know the rhododendron is in the same place?' I ask him.

'Always been there', he says impatiently. 'Plants don't move around, do they?'

The Royal Horticultural Society of the United Kingdom estimates that there are 28,000 cultivars of rhododendrons, which can be an invasive species, as well as poisonous.

The California Chapter of the American Rhododendron Society was founded in 1952 by 'local rhododendron enthusiasts'. The topic for the 22 May 2008 meeting is 'downsizing your garden for smaller spaces'.

The Spring Rhododendron Festival is held the first Saturday in November near Katoomba, in the Blue Mountains, about 90 minutes drive from Sydney.

The Rhododendron Society of Canada, Niagara Region, hosts its annual seed exchange to allow members to experiment with new varieties and to acquire otherwise difficult to obtain species.

The New Zealand Rhododendron Association, incorporated in 1945, was founded to 'create a feeling of unity amongst members' and to secure 'all the advantages of unanimity of action'.

'The Queens Inn, in lovely Hogsback – also known by its Xhosa name *Qabimbola* (meaning Red Clay on the Face) – is a very romantic venue. Weddings are our specialty! Book now for November, when our charming garden will be blooming with exotic rhododendrons in shades of blushing bride!'

'Just remember you promised your grandfather one thing,' my father says. 'When this land is yours –'

'I don't want this land . . .'

'Apologize for even thinking that', he scolds. 'Besides, you don't have a choice. You belong to the land. And it will belong to you, never mind you're . . . you're what you are and you're all over the world like one place ain't good enough for you.'

I sigh.

'Just promise me one thing', he stares at me with the blue eyes of our family; the eyes of a blonde-braided surfer in the California Pacific, of a sunburned Australian-raising chooks, of a Canadian wrapped in a quilt of spring flowers, of a Paheka knitting a fine sweater from New Zealand wool, of a South African miner retired from the Witwatersrand gold reefs.

I sigh again.

'Don't let our land go to some foreigners', he says.

Acknowledgements

This piece is drawn from a variety of sources including cases, statutes, bills, scholarly articles and books, and newspaper accounts. The absence of citations and references is intentional. The essay also includes fictional narrative elements, which are generally italicized and should be apparent from the context.

This piece began as text, then transformed into a visual–oral performance, and now appears here as text. Those interested in the visual component will find it at <www.ruthannrobson.com>.

For prompting and indulging the performance, I am grateful to Kimberly Brooks and the participants at the Queer Empire Workshop at McGill University, and to Drucilla Cornell and the audience at the uBuntu Project lecture at University of Cape Town. For sharing their knowledge and experience of sexualities, cultures, and nations, I am obliged to scholars and friends throughout the globe too numerous to mention; however, Reg Graycar of Sydney and Angelo Pantazis of Johannesburg deserve special acknowledgement for their generosities. For specific suggestions to the piece, I am grateful to Jaco Barnard-Naudé and Jenni Millbank. I am indebted to A. J. Barrow and Emily Reigel, CUNY School of Law, class of 2011, who contributed creative, scholarly, and technical work regarding the images and text, as well as providing critical feedback as did Professor Janet Calvo of CUNY. Finally, the support of Sarah Valentine remains as essential as ever.

Index

A Place of Rage 61
Aboriginals 194, 198, 203
Abraham, J 29
accountability 45–6
activism: neoliberalism 30, 33–4; Poland
    21–2; reproductive outsiders 105–6,
    109; sadomasochism 25–6; same sex
    marriage 122–36; transnational
    activism and solidarity 21–2, 30, 33–4;
    universalism 167–8
Adhikar 57
adoption 117
Advani, Nikhil 63
affluence, stereotype of gay 23–4, 27,
    28–9, 31
African-American Churches 122
Agathangelou, AM 6
AIDs/HIV 21, 40, 62, 147
aimance (lovence) 72–3
Alexander, Jane. *Butcher Boys* 1, 69–71,
    74, 83–4
amnesties 198
Anand 60
apartheid 1, 69–74, 82–3, 195–6, 200–1
apologies to indigenous people 197–200
Arendt, Hannah 73
Aristotle 72
assimilation 2, 24–5, 26–7, 39, 43
Australia: Aboriginals 193–4, 198, 203;
    family values 89–90, 93–4; hate crimes
    26; heteronormativity 89–90, 93;
    judiciary, sexual diversity in the 12,
    86–101; land rights 194; massacres of
    Aboriginals 194; New South Wales,
    swearing in ceremonies of judges in
    86–7, 89–98; reparations 203;
    reproductive outsiders 114–17;
    rhododendrons 205; same sex

marriage 115; silence about sexuality
    86–8; Stolen Generations 194, 203;
    swearing-in ceremonies of judges
    86–7, 89–98

Badgett, Lee 23, 24
Bakhtin, M 56
Bauer, Gary 142
Bedford, Kate 24, 25
Beger, Nico 21
Bell, Virginia 93, 94–6
Bend It Like Beckham 62–3
Benegal, Shyam 61
Berlant, L 87–8
bigamy 137–8
Binnie, Jon 7
Bley, Rudi 174–5, 177
Bollywood cinema 11, 55–68; archive of
    sexuality, cinema as 55–6; culture
    40–1; disability 59–60; erotic and
    phobic 62–5; false appearances and
    mistake identities 61–5; female
    bonding 57–9, 61, 63; Hindu right
    56–7, 58–9, 64; homoerotic imagery
    and sex talk 57–9, 61; looking, the art
    of 65–6; male friendship 59–61;
    realism, lack of 55–6; retrospective
    queering 59–61; song and dance 56;
    television serials 57–8, 62; tolerance
    48; women's sexuality, moral
    framework around 57
BomGay 61
Botha, PW 200
Boxer, Barbara 197
Brown, W 47
Butler, Judith 91, 138–9, 167–8
Butcher Boys. Alexander, Jane 1, 69–74,
    83–4

Calabresi, Steven G 159–60
California, same sex marriage in 9, 10, 122–36, 204
Canada: apologies to indigenous people 197–8; indigenous people 139–40, 194, 197, 202–3; polygamy 137–41; same sex partnerships 173
capitalism 3, 7, 24, 29
Carter, Sarah 140
Catholics 122, 124
celebrity culture 24–5
Central and Eastern Europe, neoliberalism in 29–33
Chaddha, Gurinder 62–3
Chatterjee, Partha 45–6
child welfare, infertility and: best interests 111–14; disclosure regimes 113; genetic relatedness 108, 111–14
Christianity, polygamy and 138–40, 146, 148
Chugtai, Ismat 37–8
Churchill, Winston 181
cinema see Bollywood cinema
cities 28–31
citizenship 6, 25–7, 28
civil partnerships see same sex relationships; same sex marriage
civilization: colonialism 47; marriage 178–9, 181; New Zealand 173, 180; presumption of normative European civilization 140; same sex relationships 173, 180; tolerance 47
class politics 26, 29, 33
collective identity 108
colonialism and imperialism: Central and Eastern Europe, neoliberalism in 30; civilization 47; domestication 175–6, 184; feminization 175–6; India 38–42, 46–7; indigenous people 7, 191–204; law, culture and empire 2–3, 4–9; marriage 177–9; neo-colonialism 7, 30; neoliberalism 30; New Zealand 174, 176–7; polygamy 145–6, 148; post-colonialism 8, 37–41, 48; production of sexuality 174–5; public space 38, 40–1; sexual excess 175–6; sexual subalterns 38–9; South Africa 1; tolerance 38, 42–4, 46–7; United Kingdom 194–203; United States 5–6, 7, 157–8, 160–5, 168–70
coming out 37–8, 185–6

comparative and international law, use in US Supreme Court of 13–14, 157–71; Constitution 158, 160; culture 161–6, 168–9; discrimination 161, 164; European Convention on Human Rights 158, 160; imperialism 157–8, 160–5, 168–70; interpretation and policy-making 159–60; Lawrence v Texas 157–60, 163–4, 170; relativism/ localism 157, 161–70; sodomy, criminalisation of 158–9; traditional values 161–2; universalism 157, 158, 161, 163–4, 167–70
concubinage 178, 181
Connecticut, same sex marriage in 125, 126–7, 129–30
conservatism 23, 24
constructionism 165–6
consumption 24–30, 33–4, 48
Cossman, Brenda 26–8
Cott, Nancy 140
counter-heteronormative movements 39
covenant marriages 128–9
culture: coming out 185–6; discrimination 161; export of Western gay culture 7–8; India 40–1, 44–8; law, culture and empire 2–9; polygamy 138–42, 145–6; relative/localism 161–9; reproductive outsiders 107; sexuality, as matter of 87–8; tolerance 44–8; United States, use of comparative and international law in 161–6, 168–9; universalism 161, 163–9

Das, Chidananada 55–6
De Vos, Pierre 75–7
Defense of Marriage Act (United States) 142, 143–4
degeneration 176–82
democracy 69, 71–83
Derrida, Jacques 71–4
diaspora 197
Diduck, Alison 108
dignity 125–31
disability 59–60
disclosure regimes, infertility treatment and 113
discrimination and inequalities see also gender; race; same sex marriage: capitalism 24; culture 161; economic inequalities 22–5, 27, 32–4; equality

and tolerance marches in Poland 22;
Poland 22, 32–3; polygamy 140, 144–5,
147–8; reproductive outsiders 105–8;
separate but equal 78, 81–2, 123,
125–7; tolerance in India 47; United
States Supreme Court 161, 164
disease or abnormality, homosexuality
and infertility as 108–9
domestication 175–85
domination 42–3, 91–2, 175, 180
Dostana 40, 48, 64–5
Dosti 59–60
Double the Trouble Twice the Fun 61
Duggan, Lisa 25–6
Dworkin, Ronald 163, 164

Eastern Europe 10, 21–2, 29–33
economic inequalities 22–5, 27, 32–4
efficacy 165–6, 170
egg donation 110–14
Elizabeth II 199–202
empire *see* colonialism and imperialism
end of queer theory 2–3
England *see* United Kingdom
Epstein, Steven 166
equality *see* discrimination and
inequalities
erotic and phobic 62–5
Ertman, Martha 140, 146
Eskridge, William 144, 158–9, 161
essentialism 107, 109, 115–17, 165–6
Europe *see also* United Kingdom:
Central and Eastern Europe,
neoliberalism in 29–33; civilization,
presumption of normative 140;
Eastern Europe 10, 21–2, 29–33;
European Union 29–32; left politics
21; Moldova 30; Netherlands 30, 33–4;
Poland 31–4; Romania 30
European Convention on Human Rights
158, 160
European Union: anti–EU discourse,
homophobia and 32; Central and
Eastern Europe, neoliberalism in
29–33; neoliberalism 29–32; Poland
31–3
Evans, David 24
evolution and degeneration 176–7
exclusion and foreignness 9–10
exclusivity and commitment in
relationships 182, 183–4
export of Western gay culture 7–8

family *see also* reproductive outsiders:
genetic essentialism 107, 109, 115–17;
genetic relatedness 108, 111–14;
judiciary, sexual diversity in the 89–91,
93–6; metaphors 90–1; professional-
biological family nexus 90–1, 95–6;
professional kinship relations of
reproductions 92–3; reunification
107–8; values 89–90, 93–4
female bonding 57–9, 61, 63
feminist theory 4, 110, 167
feminization 175–6
fertility treatment *see* reproductive
outsiders
Fire 40, 49, 58–9
Flesh and Paper 61
foreignness, exclusion and 9–10
Foucault, Michel 3, 4, 39, 45, 174, 177,
185
Fourie judgment (South Africa) 79–82
Franke, Katherine 175, 178–9
fraternity 71–4, 79–80, 82–3
fraternocracy 73–4, 82–3
friendship 71–3
Fullerton, Elizabeth 95–7
Fuss, Diana 165

Gellner, Ernest 162–3
gender *see also* women: Bollywood
cinema 57–61, 63; colonialism and
imperialism 175–6; dominance 91–2,
180; feminization 175–6; masculinity
178–9; patriarchal religion 144, 146;
polygamy 140, 144–5, 148; relativism/
localism 167–8; reproductive outsiders
110–11, 115–16; stereotypes 44;
universalism 167–8
genetic essentialism 107, 109, 115–17
genetic relatedness 108, 111–14
genuine and stable relationships 183
geographies of queer theory, contested
21–3
Gher, Jaime 144–5
Girlfriend 63–4
globalization of gay identity 8
Gluckman, A 24
Graff, EJ 143

Hansen, Ellis 66
Hardisty, J 24
Harper, Steven 198–9
hate crimes 26, 184–5

Hegel, GWF 143
Helms, Jesse 142
heteronormativity: Australia, judiciary in
    89–90, 93; counter-heteronormative
    movements 39; domesticity 184, 185;
    India 48, 49, 57; judiciary 88–90, 93;
    polygamy 147; post-colonialism 39;
    reproductive outsiders 111; same sex
    marriage 76–9; South Africa 76–9;
    tolerance 48, 49; welfare state 30
Hindu right 40, 43–5, 49, 56–7, 58–9, 64
histories of queer theory, contested 21–3
HIV/AIDs 21, 40, 62, 147
Hoad, N 7
Hoggart, Lesley 27–8
homoerotic imagery and sex talk 38,
    40–2, 49, 57–9, 61
homonationalism 6, 138, 148
homonormativity 6, 138, 143, 148
homosociality 59, 92
Howard, John 198
Hubbard, Phil 28

identity: anti-identitarianism
    7; *Bollywood* 61–5; Central and Eastern
    Europe 31–2; collective identity 108;
    definition of queer 2; false
    appearances and mistake identities
    61–5; globalization of gay identity 8;
    India, sexuality and 38; politics 7–8;
    reproductive outsiders 108;
    self-identification 8
immigration law reform and same sex
    relationships in New Zealand 14,
    179–86; Civil Union Act 2004 179–83;
    civilization 173, 180; degeneration
    179–82; domesticity 179–82, 183–6;
    exclusivity and commitment 182,
    183–4; gender dominance 180; genuine
    and stable relationships 183; marriage
    as apex of civilisation 181
imperialism *see* colonialism and
    imperialism
India: accountability 45–6; anxiety over
    sexual agency and desire 40;
    assimilation 43; Bollywood cinema 11,
    40–1, 48, 55–68; colonialism 46–7;
    coming out 37–8; culture 44–8; female
    sexual conduct in public 40; identity of
    nation, sexuality and 38;
    heteronormativity 48, 49, 57; Hindu
    right 40, 43–5, 49, 56–7, 58–9, 64;

homoerotic imagery and sex talk 38,
    40–2, 49, 57–9, 61; human rights 41;
    Indian Penal Code 41–2, 44–5, 49,
    163–4; majoritarianism 43–7, 49;
    'Other' 37, 39, 48; personal law
    systems 129; post-colonialism 38–42,
    48; public displays of affection 40, 41,
    49; public space 38; relativism/localism
    163–4; religion 40, 43–7, 49, 56–7,
    58–9, 64, 129; secularism 43–4; sexual
    subalterns 10–11, 38–9, 41–4, 49–51;
    sodomy, criminalization of 40, 41, 49;
    stereotypes, sexuality and gender 44;
    tolerance 38, 42–50
indigenous people: apologies 197–200;
    Australia 194, 198, 203; Canada
    139–40, 194, 198, 200–3; colonization
    176–7, 193–9; land rights 194–5,
    200–2; Native Americans 194, 197,
    204; New Zealand 176–7, 195–6,
    197–8, 202–3; polygamy 139–40;
    sexual assault 194; South Africa
    195–7, 200–2; sovereignty 195; Stolen
    Generations 194, 201; Treaty of
    Waitangi 195, 199; United Kingdom
    200–3; United States 193, 197,
    203–4
individualism 28
inequality *see* discrimination and
    inequalities
infertility *see* reproductive outsiders
international law *see* comparative and
    international law, use in US Supreme
    Court of

Jakobsen, Janet 24, 25
Jodie 61
Johnson, C 75–6
judiciary, sexual diversity in the
    Australian 12, 86–101; family
    metaphors 90–1; family values 89–90,
    93–4; heteronormativity 88–90, 93;
    homosociality 92; institutional virtues
    of hetero-families 93–4; kinship 91–3,
    95–6; life-writing 89; male domination
    91–2; marriage metaphor 90–1;
    professional-biological family nexus
    90–1, 95–6; professional kinship
    relations of reproductions 92–3;
    public, sexuality as 87–8; reproduction
    91–2; silence about sexuality 86–8;
    swearing-in ceremonies 86–7, 89–98

Kakkar, Sudhir 56
Kal Ho Na Ho 63
Keating, Paul 198
Kennedy, Anthony 158–9, 161, 170
Kent, James 142
Khalsa, Ruth 144
Khush 61
kinship 91–3, 95–6
Kirby, Michael 94–6
Klein, Naomi 31, 33
Klesse, Christian 21
Krakow, Poland: March for Tolerance
    22; stag and hen parties 31; tourism
    31–4

Lambevski, Alexander 31–2
land reform 193–4, 201–2
Larsen, Joan L 160
law, culture and empire 2–9
law schools, queer theory in 4
Lawrence v *Texas* 6–7, 143, 147, 157–60,
    163–4, 170
left politics in Europe 21
libertarianism 28
Lieber, Francis 142
life-writing 89
Liverpool's gay village 29
Lloyd, Moya 167
localism/relativism 157, 161–70
lovence 72–3

Magna Carta 199
mainstreaming of gay and lesbian
    movement 23
majoritarianism 43–7, 49, 123, 124, 129
male friendship 59–61
Malmgren, A 22
Manchester's gay village 29, 30
Mandi 61
Maori 176–7, 194–5, 197, 202
March for Tolerance, Krakow, Poland 22
marriage *see also* polygamy; same sex
    marriage: citizenship production 6;
    civilization 178–9, 181; colonialism
    and imperialism 178–9; covenant
    marriages 128–9; Defense of Marriage
    Act (United States) 142, 143–4;
    degeneration 177–9; intrusion,
    protection from 78–9; judiciary, sexual
    diversity in the 90–1; kinship 91;
    majoritarianism 123, 124, 128, 129;
    Marriage Act 1961 (South Africa),

unconstitutionality of 79–82;
    metaphors 90–1; regulation 177–8;
    reproduction 26, 91; sexual excess
    177–9; slaves, marriage of former
    178–9; South Africa 71–82; United
    Kingdom 177–8; United States 142,
    143–4, 178–9
masculinity 178–9
Masti 63
McClintock, A 175
McGranahan, C 5
Mehta, Deepa 58
Men Not Allowed 64
Mere Mehboob 65–6
Milios, John 29
militarized empire 6–7
Mizielinska, Joanna 22
modernity 176–7
Mohr, Richard 163
Moldova 30
moral relativism 157, 161–70
Mormons 122, 123–4, 137–91, 146
Mosley, Erin 69
Mugabe, Robert 162, 170, 201
Mujhe Chand Chahiye 57
murders 82–3
My Brother Nikhil 40, 62

Namak Haram 59–60
Nancy, Jean-Luc 72, 79
Nandy, Ashish 43–4, 46
nationalism 6, 8, 33, 56, 74, 138, 148
Native Americans 194, 197, 204
nature, defying 111–14
Negri, A 6
neo-colonialism 7, 30
neoliberalism 25–32; affluence,
    stereotype of 28–9, 31; anti–EU
    discourse, homophobia and 32;
    Central and Eastern Europe 29–33;
    citizenship 25; class politics 33;
    consumption 28–30, 33–4; economic
    inequality 22–5, 27, 32–4; European
    Union 29–32; homophobic politics
    27–8; individualism and libertarianism
    28; material inequalities 32–3;
    Moldova 30; neocolonialism 30;
    Netherlands 30, 33–4; normalization
    27–8; opposition to neoliberalism 30;
    Poland, tourism in Krakow in 31–4;
    privacy 25–6; privatization 26–7;
    public-private divide 25; Romania 30;

same sex marriage 26; self-governance 26–7; sex workers 28; sexual citizenship 26–7, 28; sexual politics 25; solidarity activism 30, 33–4; space 29; stag and hen parties in Krakow 31; Tinky Winky 33–4; tolerance 48; tourism, promotion of 29–30, 31, 33–4; urban governance 28–31; villages, promotion of gay 28–30; West 29–31

Netherlands 30, 33–4

New York, same sex marriage in 130

New Zealand: Civil Union Act 2004 179–83; civilization 180–1; colonialism and imperialism 174, 177; degeneration 176–82; domestication 176, 179–82, 183–5; exclusivity and commitment 182, 183–4; gender dominance 180; genuine and stable relationships 183; immigration law reform 14, 173, 179–86; land eights 200–2; Maori 176–7, 194–5, 196, 202; marriage as civilizing 179, 180–1; rhododendrons 205; same sex partnerships 14, 173, 179–86; sexual excess and licentiousness 176, 177; Treaty of Waitangi 195, 199

Nichols, Joel 129

Nicol, Mike 69

Nina's Heavenly Delights 62

Osterlund, Katherine 26

'Other' 37, 39, 48, 75–6

Parmar, Pratibha 61–2

parochialism 21

patriarchal religion 144, 146

Peck, Jamie 28–9

personal law systems 129

phobic and erotic 62–5

place, space and 3, 28–9

Poland: activists 21–2; equality or tolerance marches 22; European Union 31–3; queer, use of term 21–2; Tinky Winky 33–4; tourism in Krakow 31–4

politics and economics 23–5

polygamy 137–53; bigamy, convictions for 137–8; Canada 137–41; Christianity 138–40, 146, 148; colonialism 145–6, 148; culture 138–42, 145–6; discrimination 147; European civilisation, presumption of normative 140; fear-mongering 138, 145; gender equality 140, 144–5, 148; heteronormativity 147; homonationalism 138, 148; homonormativity 138, 143, 148; immigrants 140; indigenous people 139–40; Mormons 137–9, 146; orientalism 146; polygyny 137–40; patriarchal religion 144, 146; racial context 140, 141, 143–6, 148; regulation 9; religion 137–40, 144, 146, 148; reproductive outlaws 9; same sex marriage, legalisation of 137–8, 140–8; slippery slope arguments 138, 140–3, 145, 147–8; stereotyping 139; United Kingdom 178; United States 137–8, 140–7; xenophobia 138, 140, 148

polygyny 137–40

Posner, Richard 144

post-colonialism 37–43; India 38–42, 48; public space 38, 40–1; sexual subalterns 38–9; tolerance 38, 42–3, 48; West 8, 37–8

power, tolerance as 47–8

privacy 25–6

privatization 26–7

privilege of gay men 23–4

professional-biological family nexus 90–1, 95–6

professional kinship relations of reproductions 92–3

professionalization of gay and lesbian movement 23

protests against same-sex marriage 122–4

Puar, Jasbir 147–8

public displays of affection 40, 41, 49

public–private dichotomy 25, 185

queer, definition of 2, 21–2

queer disciplines 3–4

queer theory, definition of 1–2

queer, use of term 21–2

Quilt 37–8

race: apartheid 1, 69–74, 82–3, 196–7, 198–200; polygamy 140, 141, 143–6, 148; West 8

rainbow nation 74

regime or culture, sexuality as 88–9

regulation 9, 112–13

relativism/localism 157, 161–70

religion: African-American Churches
122; Catholics 122, 124; Christianity
138–40, 146, 148; covenant marriages
128–9; Hindu right 40, 49, 56–7, 58–9,
64; India 40, 43–7, 49, 56–7, 58–9, 64,
129; majoritarianism 46, 47; mocking
religious belief 123–4; Mormons 122,
123–4, 137–9, 146; patriarchal religion
144, 146; personal law systems 129;
polygamy 9, 137–40, 144, 146, 148;
reproductive outlaws 9, 111–12; same
sex marriage 122–36; secularism 43–4;
tolerance 42–7; United States 122–36
reparations 201, 203
repression 9, 74
reproductive outsiders 105–21; activism
106; adoption 117; Australia 114–17;
child welfare [best interests 111–14;
disclosure regimes 113; genetic
relatedness 108, 111–14];coalitions,
formation of 9, 106, 109; collective
identity 108; commercialisation
113–14; commonalities 106–11;
culture 107; dead partners, having
children of 111; differences and
difficulties 114–17; disclosure regimes
113; disease or abnormality,
homosexuality and infertility as 108–9;
discrimination 105–8; egg donation
110–14; family formation 105–13;
family reunification 107–8;
fatherhood, devaluing or abolishing
115–16; gender 110–11, 115–16;
genetic essentialism 107, 109, 115–17;
government regulation 112–13;
heteronormativity 111; heterosexual
couples 9, 105–14; inclusion,
assistance and approval 111;
knowledge of genetic background,
right to 107; lesbian co-mothers, rights
for 115–16; meaning 106–11; nature,
defying 111–14; polygamy 9; payments
113–14; regulation 9; religion 9,
111–12; same sex couples 9, 105–14;
same sex marriage 115; sperm
donation 107–16; surrogacy 109–14,
116, 117; 'truth' of genetic origins 107;
United States 106
retrospective queering 59–61
rhododendrons 205–6
Richardson, Diane 23, 25–6
Robinson, Andrew 55–6

Robson, Ruthann 75, 145, 175
Romania 30
Rorty, Richard 165, 170
Rudd, Kevin 198

Sachs, A 77
sado-masochist case 25–6
same sex marriage *see also* same sex
relationships: advocacy 125–8;
African-American Churches 122;
agency 128–31; Australia 115; ballot
10, 122–36, 204; California 10,
122–36, 201–4; Canada 26, 173;
Catholics 122, 124; civil unions 78,
81–2, 123, 125–7, 131; Connecticut
125, 126–7, 129–30; covenant
marriages 128–9; Defense of Marriage
Act 142, 143–4; democracy 74, 76–7,
81–3; dignity 125–31; equality, right to
125, 129–30;*Fourie* judgment (South
Africa) 79–82; fraternity, politics of
79–80, 82; fraternocracy 82;
heteronormativity 76–9; intrusion,
protection of marriage from 78–9;
legal protection of gay people 75–81;
love, relationships of reproduction
reconfigured to relationships of 26;
majoritarianism 123, 124, 128–9;
Marriage Act 1961 (South Africa),
unconstitutionality of 79–82;
Mormons 122, 123–4; National
Coalition cases (South Africa) 75–81;
neoliberalism 26; New Hampshire 147;
New York 130; opposition 10, 141,
173; personal law systems 129;
polygamy 9, 137–8, 140–8; protests
122–4; regulation 9; religion 122–36;
reproductive outlaws 9, 115; right to
marry 125; separate but equal 78,
81–2, 123, 125–7; slippery slope
argument 140–3, 145, 147–8; sodomy,
criminalization of 75, 76; South Africa
71–82; strict scrutiny standard 125–6;
superiority, claims for marriage 115;
uniformity 121–2; United States 8, 10,
27, 122–36, 140–4, 147, 201–4
same sex relationships *see also* same sex
marriage: California 123; Canada 26,
173; civil rights 4; civil unions 78, 81–2,
123, 125–7, 131, 179–83; civilisation
180–1; degeneration 179–82;
domesticity 179–85; exclusivity and

commitment 182, 183–4; gender dominance 180; genuine and stable relationships 18; immigration 14, 173, 179–86; migration law 10; New Zealand 14, 173, 179–86; normalization, politics of 26; private welfare, as form of 26; recognition of relationships 8, 26; reproductive outsiders 105–14; South Africa 173; United Kingdom 173; United States 123, 125

Saran, Nishit 59
Sari Red 61
Scalia, Antonin 142, 157–62, 164
secularism 43–4
Sedgwick, Eve 92
Sedley, Stephen 168–70
self-governance 26–7
separate but equal 78, 81–2, 123, 125–7
Seuffert, Nan 140
sex workers 28
sexual excess and licentiousness 175–7
sexual subalterns 10–11, 38–9, 41–7, 49–51
Shabnam Mausi 62
Sholay 60–1
Sikora, T 22, 33
silence about sexuality 86–8
Simpson, Carolyn Chalmers 92–3
slaves, marriage of former 178–9
slippery slope arguments 138, 140–3, 145, 147–8
sodomy, criminalisation of 40, 41, 49, 75, 76, 158–9
solidarity 21–2, 30, 33–4
Somerville, Siobhan 145–6
South Africa 1, 69–85; amnesties 200; apartheid 71–4, 82–3, 196–7, 200; Australian immigrants 202–3;*Butcher Boys* 1, 69–71, 74, 83–4; colonialism 1; Constitution 74–82; democracy 69, 71–83;*Fourie* judgment 79–82; fraternity, politics of 79–80, 82; fraternocracy 82; gay rights litigation 10; heteronormativity 76–9; indigenous people 195–6, 199–200; intrusion, protection of marriage from 78–9; legal protection of gay people 75–81; Marriage Act 1961, unconstitutionality of 79–82; murders 82–3; National Coalition cases 75–81; otherness as sameness 75–6; post-

apartheid 1, 69–71, 74–82; rainbow nation 74; Reparations Committee 201; rhododendrons 205–6; same sex marriage, legalisation of 71–2, 74–82; same sex partnerships 173; separate but equal 78, 81–2; sodomy, criminalization of 75, 76; traditional values 162; Truth and Reconciliation Commission 200–1

sovereignty 5, 195
space 3, 28–9, 38, 40–1, 123, 128
sperm donation 107–16
stag and hen parties 31
stereotypes 23–4, 27, 28–9, 31, 44, 129
Stolen Generations 194, 203
Stoler, AL 5, 15
Storrow, Richard 110, 114
Strassberg, Maura 143–4
Stychin, Carl 25, 30, 184
subalterns 10–11, 38–9, 41–7, 49–51
Summer in My Veins 59
Sunstein, Cass 160
surrogacy 109–14, 116, 117
swearing-in ceremonies of judges in Australia 86–7, 89–98

temporality 3
Thomas, Clarence 159–60
Thompson, Alex 72–3
Tickell, Adam 28–9
Tinkcom, Matthew 24
Tinky Winky 33–4
tolerance 42–50; accountability 45–6; assimilation 43;*Bollywood* 48; civilization 47; colonialism 38, 42–4, 46–7; culture 44–8; equality 47; heteronormativity 48, 49; Hindu right 43–5; homosexuality, as synonymous with 22; India 38, 42–50; Indian Penal Code 44–5; justice 48; majoritarianism 43–6, 49; March for Tolerance, Krakow, Poland 22; neoliberalism 48; 'Other' 48; Poland 22; political conception 45–7; post–colonialism 38, 42–3, 48; power, tolerance as 47–8; religion 42–7; secularism 43–4; sexual subalterns 44–7, 49–50; social and political control 42; stereotypes 44; universalism 48
Tomsen, Stephen 26
Toporowki, Jan 29–30

Tornquist-Plewa, B 22
totalitarianism 73–4
tourism 29–30, 31–4
transnational activism and solidarity
    21–2, 30, 33–4
transgression 24–5, 26–7
Treaty of Waitangi 195, 199
Truth and Reconciliation Commission
    (South Africa) 200–1
Tutu, Desmond 74, 200

United Kingdom: apologies for
    colonialism 197–200; colonialism
    194–200; concubinage 178;
    domesticity 175; indigenous people
    194–200; Magna Carta 201; marriage,
    regulation of 177–8; parochialism
    21–2; rhododendrons 205–6;
    sado-masochist case 25–6; same sex
    partnerships 173; Treaty of Waitangi
    195, 199; villages, promotion of gay
    28–30
United States: affluence, myth of 24;
    African-American Churches 122;
    ballot 10, 122–36, 204; California,
    same sex marriage in 10, 122–36,
    204; capitalism 7; Catholics 122,
    124; civil unions 123, 125–7, 131;
    colonialism 5–6, 7, 157–8, 160–5,
    168–70; comparative and international
    law 13–14, 157–71; Connecticut 125,
    126–7, 129–30; covenant marriages
    128–9; culture and imperialism 157–8,
    160–6, 168–70; Defense of Marriage
    Act 142, 143–4; dignity 125–31;
    discrimination 161, 164; equality, right
    to 125–6; European Convention on
    Human Rights 158, 160; foreign policy
    5–6; indigenous people 194, 197, 204;
    land reform 193;Lawrence v Texas 6–7,
    154, 147, 157–60, 163–4, 170; marriage
    8, 10, 137–8, 122–36, 140–7, 178–9,
    204; masculinity 178–9; militarized
    empire 6–7; Mormons 122, 123–4, 139;
    Native Americans 194, 197, 204;
    neocolonialism 7; New Hampshire,
    same sex marriage in 147; New York,
    same sex marriage in 130;
    parochialism 21–2; polygamy 137–8,
    140–4, 147, 178; protests against same-
    sex marriage 122–4; relativism/
    localism 157, 161–70; religion 122–36;
    reproductive outsiders 106;
    rhododendrons 202; same sex
    marriage 8, 10, 27, 122–36, 140–7,
    201–2; separate but equal 123, 125–7;
    slaves, marriage of former 178–9;
    sodomy, criminalisation of 6, 143,
    158–9; Supreme Court 13–14, 157–71;
    traditional values 161–2; universalism
    157, 158, 161, 163–4, 167–70; white
    gay men, prevalence of 7
universalism 41, 48, 157–8, 161, 163–4,
    167–70
urban governance 28–31

villages, promotion of gay 28–9, 30

Wadia, Riyad 61
Walzer, Michael 162, 166
Warner, Michael 10, 87–8
Wesling, M 8
West see also particular countries;
    Central and Eastern Europe,
    neoliberalism in 31; coming out 37–8,
    185–6; domesticity 185–6; export of
    gay culture 7–8; foreign policy 5–6;
    identity, models of gay 31; law, culture
    and empire 5–6; neoliberalism 29–31;
    parochialism 21–2; post-colonialism 8,
    37–8; race 8; welfare state 30
white gay men, prevalence of 7, 8
Williams, Bernard 166–7
Wilson, Angelia 24, 26
Woltersdorff, Volker 26, 27, 30, 32–3
Woolf, Leonard 157, 161
women see also gender; Bollywood
    cinema 57–9, 61, 63; domestication
    175–6; female bonding 57–8, 61, 63;
    feminist theory 4, 110, 167; India 40,
    57–9, 61, 63; Maori women, sexual
    licentiousness of 177; moral
    framework around sexuality 57;
    patriarchal religion 144, 146;
    polygamy 140, 144–5, 148; public
    sexual conduct 40; surrogacy 110–11

xenophobia 138, 140, 148

Zimbabwe 162, 201